Seek Glory, Now Keep Glory

*The Story of the 1st Battalion,
Royal Warwickshire Regiment,
1914–18*

JOHN ASHBY

Helion and Company

Helion and Company
26 Willow Road
Solihull
West Midlands
B91 1UE
England
Tel. 0121 705 3393
Fax 0121 711 1315

Email: publishing@helion.co.uk
Website: http://www.helion.co.uk

Published by Helion and Company, 2000

Designed and typeset by Bookcraft Ltd, Stroud, Gloucestershire
Printed by Antony Rowe Ltd., Chippenham, Wiltshire

© Helion and Company 2000

ISBN 1 874622 45 0

British Library Cataloguing-in-Publication Data.
A catalogue record for this book is available from the British Library.

For details of other military history titles published by Helion and Company
contact the above address, or visit our website: http://www.helion.co.uk.
We always welcome receiving book proposals from prospective authors
working in military history.

Contents

Acknowledgements

In any lengthy research authors often become involved with individuals who take some part in their work. I am profoundly grateful to the following people who played a major role in producing this book.

In the early stages Pete Briggs was especially generous with his time in helping me sketch my "plan of campaign" and throughout he has always been on hand to give advice and assistance. Mr and Mrs Robert Elkington made everything possible by allowing me to use an unpublished statement written by Lieutenant-Colonel John Ford Elkington and I thank them for allowing me to visit their home, take photographs and for diligently answering my many written questions. Similarly, I am indebted to Jonathon Maguire for not only supplying me with a complete copy of A.E. Mainwaring's statement but also for producing relevant material and photographs.

Shortly after beginning the work I met David Vaux, who seems to have an unlimited knowledge of the history of the Royal Warwickshire Regiment. I thank his family for tolerating my innumerable visits to their home, and David especially for allowing me to use photographs from his collection, besides giving me information and guidance on the story of the Royal Warwickshire Regiment.

I spent much of the winter of 1999 in the Royal Warwickshire Regiment Museum, based at St John's House in Warwick. Major Richard Mills, Vanessa Harbar and Gordon Hutchings were most helpful during a time when the museum was officially closed for refurbishment. They never failed to find me a corner and provide access to the library and archives. The kind assistance extended by the staff at the Imperial War Museum, especially Mr A. Richards, and the staff at the British Library and Public Records Office is also much appreciated. Similar thanks are also extended to the staff of the Coventry Library Service, notably the Coundon branch.

There are many individuals and publishing houses to whom I give sincere thanks for allowing me to quote from private papers, books and other information under copyright. I thank David and Carolann Smith-Dorrien for permission to use text from the papers of Sir Horace Smith-Dorrien; Mrs Barbara Horwill for the use of text from the papers of Artillery Sergeant Albert George; the Rt. Rev. Lord Habgood for permission to quote from the papers of Captain A.H. Habgood R.A.M.C.; Richard Van Emden for allowing me to use material from his work on Ben Clouting; Peter Scott for discussion on his research and allowing me to quote from *Dishonoured*; Mr and Mrs Tony Holt in obtaining permission to quote and use illustrations from Bruce Bairnsfather's books. Thanks also to Little Brown and Company for permission to quote from E.J. Needham's work; HarperCollins for permission to use quotations from the *Memoirs of Field Marshal Montgomery*; Longman Group for permission to quote from the work of Brigadier-General Sir Tom Bridges; IPC Magazines for the use of photographs and references from *The Great War Illustrated* and text from C.L. Kingsford's *The Story of the Royal Warwickshire Regiment*; Cassell Publishing for the use of material from *The History of the Great War*; the London Illustrated News Group for permission to use photographs and copy from *Illustrated War News*. Finally I thank the editor of the *Newbury Weekly News* for permission to quote from that newspaper. I apologise for any inadvertent breach of copyright; I have exhausted all possible sources in an attempt to secure permission to quote from work which may still be under copyright.

I thank Le Général de Corps d'Armée Christian Piquemal of the French Foreign Legion, and the editor of *Képi Blanc*, for allowing me to use photographs from the library at Aubagne. None of this would have been possible without the assistance of Bob Caldwell, who generously gave his time to translate my correspondence with the Foreign Legion and other organisations in France. Historian M. Michel Dutoit, and Monique Sevrin of the Société Académique de Saint-Quentin, were very helpful in providing photographs and details of Council meetings in 1914. Tony Warwick has made a valuable contribution to the photographs appearing in this book. He has been immensely helpful in ensuring that all the artwork, however old and damaged, is up to the highest possible standard. Thanks also to Rob Williams for allowing me to quote from his unpublished postgraduate work relating to court martials in the Royal Warwickshire Regiment.

After the writing was finished there still remained the daunting task of reading the book for errors typographic, or otherwise, and ensuring that continuity was maintained throughout. This burden was undertaken by Lieutenant-Colonel A. Chalmers, to whom I owe an enormous debt of gratitude.

Helpful suggestions and advice were provided by my friend of old, Peter Bailey, Professor of History at the University of Manitoba, who also kindly wrote the Foreword.

Professor Richard Holmes very kindly agreed to read through the text prior to publication. This book has undoubtedly benefited from his valuable comments and welcome advice.

Finally, the following have also played a part in making this work possible: David McGrory; Lieutenant-Colonel Harry Mainwaring; David Bartholomew, Vicar of the Church of the Ascension, Burghclere; Dr. J.M. Bourne; Dr. Carl Chinn; Nigel Dorrington; Lee Lindon; Mrs Carter; James Clarke; Mark Relf. If there are any omissions I trust those concerned will accept my apology, and I thank you all.

Author's Note

The title of the book is taken from inscriptions on the "Seek Gloryy" snuffbox originally displayed in the Royal Warwickshire Regiment Museum; it was stolen a few years ago. In 1785 Lieutenant-Colonel Hedges of the 48th Foot presented it to the 6th Foot. At the time of its presentation the words "Seek Gloryy" were scratched on the box. After the battle of Orthez in 1814, the words "Huzza for the 6th Regiment Now Keep Glory" were added.

Foreword

As a number of significant recent books amply demonstrate, historians continue to refight the First World War. The great political and strategic questions – what were its causes? who was primarily responsible? what were its historical consequences? – continue to generate debate and reinterpretation. Of more absorbing general interest has been the attention to the experience of mass soldiery who submitted themselves to the unprecedented bloody and traumatic ordeal of the Great War. How, we still ask in near disbelief, could they have endured it, and for so long? "Because it was expected of them" is one answer, emphasising the profound hold of the pre–1914 values and the potent fusion of ideals of true manliness and patriotic duty. "Because men enjoy war and killing" is a more disturbing and contentious recent argument. What remains well-evidenced is the compelling loyalty of the men to their immediate comrades – this, rather than any identification with the great causes of king and country, seems the stronger factor in keeping them at their post.

It was the regiment or the battalion that was most likely to extend and reinforce these small-scale loyalties and secure the enduring commitment and tenacity of which we still stand in awe. John Ashby's admirable study of the 1st Battalion Royal Warwickshire Regiment not only makes good a deficiency in the regimental history, especially in the matter of the "two colonels", but takes us into the inner life of a battalion on the Western Front. This meticulously researched and engrossing account of the chums and pals of the Warwicks gives us fresh evidence of how the vital force of *espirit de corps* was relentlessly tested and redeemed in battle, making a valuable contribution to the history of the war as well as the Regiment.

Peter Bailey
University of Manitoba, 1999

Introduction

I t was during a research exercise, related to two brothers who had served with the Royal Warwickshire Regiment in World War I, that I first came across an account of the "two colonels" who were cashiered from the B.E.F. in France during 1914. Although the detail given in C.L. Kingsford's book *The Story of the Royal Warwickshire Regiment* only covered a few lines it was enough to whet my appetite to find out more.

A most useful reference is Peter J. Scott's detailed book *Dishonoured,* which has as its main theme an eight-page privately published "Statement", written shortly after the incident by Lieutenant-Colonel Arthur Edward Mainwaring, one of the officers involved. At the time *Dishonoured* was published in 1994 only one copy of Mainwaring's document had come to light.

I decided to start from scratch, and after considerable spade work discovered a second copy of the "Statement" in the possession of a military historian in Northern Ireland. It was even more surprising to find that a statement written by the other officer involved – Lieutenant-Colonel John Ford Elkington – also existed; it is published for the first time in this book. This pencil-written document had been in Elkington's private papers since it was prepared, probably in 1914, as an *aide-mémoire* for his court-martial.

However, there were some disappointments along the way. Nowhere could I locate the full details of the court-martial or any "official" papers relevant to the affair. Although a thorough search has been undertaken, and despite the fact that these may still be tucked away in the Public Records Office or some such establishment, it appears that they, along with masses of other WWI records, were destroyed by enemy bombing in 1940. Neither have I been able to contact any descendants of Lt.-Col. Mainwaring. Apart from obtaining copies of his will and an obituary in a local paper of 1930, together with a few references from the records of his regiment, I could discover little about the man after he left the army. During my search for information on Mainwaring I contacted over forty people who I thought might be able to help me – besides travelling to various parts of the country – but met with no success. What surprised me about this part of my research was the lengths to which complete strangers were prepared to go in trying to be of assistance. Irrespective of the disappointments, this book presents the facts from both sides for the first time.

In the preparation of the text I tried to make the information both interesting and easy to read. Bearing in mind the accuracy of Scott's work, and that so much of my work is common to his, I had to find another way of covering the story. As there is no full account of the involvement of the 1st Battalion Royal Warwickshire Regiment in World War I, other than that which appears in Kingsford's general history of the Royal Warwickshire Regiment, I decided to concentrate on this battalion during the whole period of the War. The story of the "surrender" fell conveniently into my planned narrative as Lt.-Col. Elkington was the commanding officer of the 1st Battalion. This study is not meant to be of an academic or authoritative nature, and is certainly not comprehensive in its coverage of the activities of the British Expeditionary Force in France during August 1914, but as much material as possible has been recorded concerning the experiences of the men of the 1st Battalion.

I have been as accurate as the numerous references will allow and where ambiguities do exist I have tried to present a fair cross-section of the facts. It is somewhat pointless, unfair, and in any case not possible, to attempt to re-write history, with clear judgements on an incident which happened nearly one hundred years ago, but further evidence can be added. I have left readers to come to their own conclusions. What I have done on some occasions is to comment on facts presented by other writers in respect of both the story and its characters. I wish to make one passing comment: there is no doubt that in diligently following their family traditions and experience Elkington and Mainwaring showed that they were dedicated and brave soldiers, and most importantly, always had at heart the interests of the men under their command.

The major event in this book took place early in the war during a period of unexpected movement. The whole of the B.E.F. was retreating, and along with the French army, was fragmented across northern France as the overwhelming masses of German troops surged towards Paris and an eagerly awaited surrender by the allies; that, of course, never happened.

What really prompted me to write about the "two colonels" was the fact that the whole story and its characters could have been a piece of schoolboy adventure appearing in the now defunct *Boys' Own Paper,* which I read avidly as a boy. However, in this case the story is one of fact, not fiction.

PROLOGUE

A Brief History of the Royal Warwickshire Regiment 1675–1914[1]

D uring the reign of Elizabeth I it became practice for English troops to be based in the Netherlands in the service of the States General. Such men enjoyed the reputation of being great fighters, consequently Dutch monarchs and others were keen to employ them. In 1674 a British force of some ten companies was reformed into four regiments at Bois-le-Duc.

Two of the new regiments were English, and one of those, commanded by Colonel Henry Lillingston, eventually became the 6th Foot, later the Royal Warwickshire Regiment. The second English regiment became the 5th Foot, later the Royal Northumberland Fusiliers. One theory put forward as to how these numbers were designated is that they represented the order of disembarkation upon the regiments' return to England in 1685. This was primarily to assist in suppressing the rebellion, started by the Duke of Monmouth, which sought to secure the Protestant succession to the English throne. By the time the 5th and 6th foot arrived the rebellion had been crushed. They returned to the Netherlands but in 1688 were back in England with William of Orange, at the request of English Protestants.

In April 1690 the regiment sailed to Carrickfergus in Ireland, and engaged the troops of James II and his allies at the Siege of Charlemont, under the command of Lt.-Col. Philip Babington. Three months later the joint Dutch and English armies, under the overall command of William of Orange, met and defeated James' army in combat at the Battle of the Boyne, an action noted for the number of nationalities involved. In August of the same year the men were involved in an unsuccessful attack on Athlone. By September, a much-depleted regiment had taken up winter quarters at Roscrea, but by April 1691 its strength had been increased by 300 recruits from England. Athlone was finally taken in June and the regiment then moved on to Limerick, whose siege finally ended on 3 October 1691; James fled to France.

Between December 1691 and January 1692 the 6th Foot was in barracks in England. Thereafter William III concentrated on the war with France, and once again the regiment was in action, this time participating in William's unsuccessful attempts to relieve Namur. On 3 August he was no more successful against the French at Steenkirk, north of Mons, where he commanded ten battalions of English, Dutch and Danish troops. This engagement was not without heavy losses, especially to the 6th Foot. In November they were forced to return to England for rest and further recruitment. There they remained throughout 1693.

In August 1694 the 6th Foot returned to Flanders and garrisoned Bruges. The next action was part of a further campaign to recover Namur in July 1695, but final capitulation and formal surrender was not achieved until 6 September. As a result of its distinguished performance, displaying "conspicuous bravery", the regiment received its first battle honour – "Namur". For the next four months the 6th was based at Bruges, during which time further recruits from home were drafted into the regiment.

By March 1696 the threat of Jacobite plots and a possible invasion by the French were causing serious problems in England. The 6th Foot and several other regiments were recalled, the former being based at Windsor, where it remained until June 1697. The regiment then returned to the Continent, taking part in King William's review of his army at Brussels during September. It returned home in November and was based near Huntingdon. By August 1698 the regiment had begun a four year posting to Ireland.

On 15 May 1702 war was declared between England and France, but the 6th Foot did not, as expected, see action under Marlborough in the Netherlands; instead it was destined to join the armies on the Spanish Peninsula. The regiment sailed to Cadiz in August, but remained in Spain for only a short and relatively uneventful period before returning home, landing in Portsmouth on 18 November. Service in the West Indies and Newfoundland followed in 1703, but by March 1704 the 6th was back in Plymouth, where it undertook garrison duties until the following year.

In 1705 the regiment participated in the Earl of Peterborough's expedition to Spain, reaching its destination north-east of Barcelona on 22 August. It was during this campaign that the 6th excelled, with – as Kingsford puts it – "extraordinary marches, brilliant engagements and gallant exploits."[2] Barcelona was captured by a brilliant feat of arms. The regiment's commander, Colonel Southwell, proved to be a model soldier and capable tactician. The regiment particularly distinguished itself at the Battle of Almanza on 26 April 1706. The 6th and 33rd Foot were on the left of the Third Brigade. Moving forward gallantly after the sudden retreat of the British cavalry, the regiment poured such a steady and destructive fire upon the enemy's flank and rear that the cavalry was encouraged to renew the attack on the front, thus driving the enemy back with great loss of life to their former position. It was upon this occasion that a standard bearing a white antelope upon it was taken from the enemy and carried off the field.

In August 1710 the Battle of Saragossa was fought, and in December of the same year a detachment of the 6th Foot fought at the Battle of Brihuega, Catalonia, where the British captured thirty standards and colours. However, losses were high, including some 300 officers and men taken prisoner. In October 1712 the regiment moved to Ireland and remained in garrison there until 1740. The fighting in Spain ended in 1712, from which – at a high cost in manpower – Britain gained Newfoundland and Nova Scotia from the French, and Gibraltar and Minorca from the Spanish.

After a brief visit to Aberdeen, the regiment sailed for Jamaica on 8 November 1741 with a contingent of nearly eight hundred men. This particular expedition did not achieve a great deal. Indeed, by the time the regiment sailed for home in October 1742 sickness and disease had accounted for the deaths of some 350 officers and men.

During the Jacobite '45 Rebellion the regiment served in Scotland. During the march north, in the summer of the previous year, regimental history was made when a woman, Hannah Snell, enlisted in Coventry under the pseudonym "James Grey". According to some accounts the undetected recruit deserted when the march reached Carlisle as, at that time, "he" was under the sentence of 600 lashes. Other commentators record that "he" received a commuted punishment of 500 lashes and then deserted. Perhaps it was not only the injustice of the punishment that prompted the desertion, but rather the fact that Snell recognised someone, also in the ranks, who may have betrayed her. The rest of her days were just as eventful as her service in the 6th Foot; still hiding her gender she joined the marines and enjoyed an adventurous life, only becoming "female" again in 1750 after leaving the military.

Upon its arrival in Scotland the regiment was dispersed among the Highland forts between Inverness and Fort William. An interesting story from this period concerns an "old sweat" named Molloy and twelve other men, who were left in charge of the small fort at Ruthven, which they defended with distinguished bravery. The following letter from Molloy to Sir John Cope explains all:

> This goes to acquaint you that yesterday there appeared in the little town of Ruthven about three hundred of the enemy, and (they) sent proposals to me to surrender this redoubt upon condition that I

should have liberty to carry off bag and baggage. My answer was that I was too old a soldier to surrender a garrison of such strength without bloody noses. They threatened hanging me and my men for refusal. I told them I would take my chance. This morning they attacked me about twelve o'clock (by my information) with about one hundred and fifty men. They attacked fore-gate and sally-port and attempted to set the sally-port on fire with some old barrels and other combustibles which took place immediately, but the attempter lost his life by it. They drew off about half an hour after three. About two hours after, they sent word to me that two of their Chiefs wanted to talk to me, I admitted and spoke to them from the parapet, they offered conditions, I refused, they desired liberty to carry off their dead men, I granted. There are two men since dead of their wounds in the town and three more they took with them, as I am informed. They went off westward about eight o'clock this morning, they did the like march yesterday in the afternoon, but came back at nightfall. They took all the provisions the poor inhabitants had in the town, and Mrs M'Pherson the barrack-wife, and a merchant of the town, who spoke to me this moment and advised me to write to your honour, and told me there were above three thousand men all lodged in the cornfields west of the town last night, and their camp is called Dalwhinnie. They have Cluny M'Pherson with them prisoner as I have by the same information. I lost one man, shot through the head by foolishly holding his head too high over the parapet. I expect another visit this night, I am informed, with their petardoes, but I shall give them the warmest reception my weak party can afford. I shall hold out as long as possible. I conclude, honourable General with respect,

Your most humble servant, J. Moloy, Sergt. 6th[3]

Although the above letter was written in August it was not until February 1746 that the fort finally surrendered to the Jacobites. Cope later recommended Molloy for a commission.

On 21 September 1745 two companies of the regiment took part in the ill-fated Battle of Prestonpans. They received serious losses, every man being either killed, wounded or captured. The oldest exhibit in the Royal Warwickshire Regimental Musuem is a drum reputed to have been captured from the 6th at Prestonpans. Until its discovery in 1905 it remained in a Highland crofter's hut. By the time the fate of Charles Edward, the Young Pretender, was decided at the Battle of Culloden on 16 April 1746, those losses had become much higher. The aftermath of the rebellion kept the regiment in Scotland until August 1751.

In 1752 new colours were presented to the regiment by Royal Assent of George III. The regiment's association with Warwickshire began in 1778, by which time it comprised twelve companies. Men were stationed at various locations throughout the county. In 1782, after Warwickshire had been officially confirmed as the regiment's designated county, it became known as the 6th or 1st Warwickshire Regiment of Foot. In the same year the regiment adopted its march *The Warwickshire Lads.* New colours were presented in 1768, 1778 and 1785. Compared with the intense activity of the '45 Rebellion, the period until the early 1790's was relatively quiet, with garrison duty being undertaken in Jersey, Ireland, Nova Scotia and New Brunswick.

The declaration of war with revolutionary France in February 1793 resulted in the 6th being transferred from New Brunswick to the West Indies. In August 1793 the regiment landed in Barbados, but on disembarkation could only muster 340 men as sickness had once again taken its toll. Six months later, despite having received reinforcements from England, the number of fit men was still below 500. The regiment displayed great courage when fighting at the victorious Battle of Martinique, where it received its second battle honour. It was not involved in the taking of St. Lucia. Only a small number of its men were present at the taking of Guadaloupe, which again fell into French hands only two months later. The net result of Britain's five-year West Indian campaign was the capture of Martinique and St. Lucia. Apart from battle casualties the regiment had seen disease gradually whittle away its manpower – so much so that all fit men were drafted into the Norfolk Regiment, the remainder sailing for England.

After spending three years in Ireland the 6th undertook an uneventful posting to North America and Canada. It returned to England in September, 1806. After rest and being brought up to a strength of 1,000 men, the 1st Battalion was posted to Gibraltar in May 1807.

The period spent in North America coincided with Napoleon's rise to power. In 1807 the Emperor attacked and annexed Portugal, and the following year bestowed the Spanish throne upon his brother Joseph. These actions were to cause his downfall and enabled Britain to take its opportunity. Portugal was Britain's oldest ally, therefore an army under Sir Arthur Wellesley was despatched to Portugal to fight the French. The 6th left Gibraltar, landing in Portugal 1 August 1808. During the following months it was to earn more battle honours. The first of these was won at Roliça on 17 August, followed four days later by another in the victorious Battle of Vimiero.

Following the surrender of 18,000 French soldiers to the Spanish, Napoleon raised a large army and marched to Madrid with the intention of then proceeding to Lisbon. By this date Wellesley had been replaced by Sir John Moore, who took over the relatively small army of 14,000 troops. Even so, this army would be sufficient to cut Napoleon off from France. Realising this danger, the Emperor decided to cut off and attack the British. He first had to position himself between Moore and the coast, where the British fleet was laying at anchor ready to evacuate the outnumbered and retreating army. The race to reach Corunna was won by Moore. The main body of the army managed to board ship and move away as Moore fought a rear-guard action in what is considered to be one of the greatest feats of the British Army. The 6th lost half its men in the Battle of Corunna in January 1809, but received a further battle honour. A short time later the pitiful remains of the British army landed in England.

The regiment's next assignment was to take part in the ill-fated Walcheren expedition of 1809. Napoleon had developed Walcheren Island as a major naval base, thereby threatening military force against Britain as well as being in a position to jeopardise her commerce. Britain decided to attempt to negate this threat. Tactically things went wrong from the outset, and to worsen the situation ague and typhoid fever broke out, large numbers of men from all regiments being stricken down. The campaign was aborted and, by the time the regiment returned to England in December 1809 only 10% of its complement were fit for duty. It took many months to rebuild the regiment's strength.

During the period following the Battle of Corunna an army under Wellington had been making progress on the Iberian Peninsula. The 1st Battalion 6th Foot sailed for Portugal in October 1812 and arrived in Lisbon in mid-November. Wellington's plan was to drive the French away from Salamanca towards the Pyrenees. The French army had been reduced in numbers by Napoleon, in order to support his army in Germany. On 21 June 1813 Wellington defeated Joseph's army at the Battle of Vittoria, the 6th being awarded honours for its part in that victory. This was followed by heavy involvement in the Battle of the Heights of Echalar. In this engagement the 6th, part of a force facing odds of four to one, took a strategic position from the enemy. Wellington considered this action to be the most gallant and finest he had seen. As the French moved north over the Pyrenees and back into France, the regiment remained at the forefront throughout and gained further honours – "Pyrenees", "Nivelle", "Orthes" and finally the overall honour "Peninsular".

In May 1814 the 6th Foot's participation in the Peninsular War ended with orders to sail for Canada. Two year earlier war had broken out between Britain and the United States, and the enemy was now threatening to invade Canada. An earlier invasion in 1812 had been thwarted, but the British garrison required reinforcement. The Americans crossed the Niagara river and captured Fort Erie. An attempt to retake it failed so the British laid siege. The 6th came up the St. Lawrence river and joined the army outside Fort Erie on 2 September 1814. Three days later the Americans took the initiative and attacked the British; for a short period they were successful. However, the British mounted a memorable bayonet charge which forced the enemy back into the fort. For its part in the action the 6th received the honour "Niagara". As the year came to a close both sides were being hindered by atrocious weather and on 5 November the Americans vacated Fort Erie and returned home. A peace treaty was signed between the two countries before the end of the year. The regiment remained garrisoned in Chippawa until July 1815, when it was recalled once again to fight against Napoleon. It joined Wellington's army in mid-August – too late to take part in the Battle of Waterloo.

From September 1815 until January 1816 the regiment formed part of the Army of Occupation and was based in Paris. In February it moved north to Pas-de-Calais, returning home in October 1818. The regiment remained in England until November 1821, when it sailed for the Cape.

After its arrival in Cape Town in November 1821, the 6th was posted to Grahamstown on the Kaffir frontier. In March 1825 orders arrived for the regiment, now up to a strength of ten companies, to sail for its first tour of India. It arrived in Bombay two months later. Once again, sickness dogged the regiment's period in a testing climate. This time the main curse was cholera, which broke out throughout the tour of duty. There was no action during the regiment's seventeen year stay in India, during which time the 6th was stationed at Mandvi, Colaba, Poona, Dasa and Bombay. In 1832 King William IV decreed that the word "Royal" should be added to the regiment's title: in future it would be known as the 6th, or Royal (1st) Warwickshire Regiment. On 9 October 1841 the regiment left Bombay, arriving home in January 1842.

In 1846 a second battalion was raised, and was stationed for a short while in Ireland before moving to Canada. It then sailed to the Cape, joining the 1st Battalion which had arrived towards the end of November. Both battalions served with distinction in the Kaffir War and excelled themselves in defending Fort Cox. The regiment was awarded a medal, and the honours "South Africa, 1846–7, 1851–2–3" were added to the colours. On 26 February 1852 a sad event occurred off the South African coast when a troopship, *Birkenhead*, foundered in the dark and began to sink. Among the troops on board was a draft of the Royal Warwickshire Regiment. As the women and children filled the lifeboats the troops, marshalled on deck, stood quietly in rank. There were insufficient boats to save the men and as the ship broke up Ensign Metford and 47 men of the regiment perished. On the cessation of the Kaffir War the 6th was stationed for two years in the Keiskama Hoek area, followed by postings to Grahamstown, Fort Beaufort and Fort Peddie.

In 1857 mutiny broke out in India. One of several reasons was the firm belief that cartridges, the end of which had to be bitten off before use in the new Enfield rifle, were smeared with either cow grease or pig fat. It was necessary to grease the cartridges to afford easy entry into the rifle's barrel. The fat of the cow was sacred to the Hindus and that of pigs untouchable to Mohammedans, thus consternation spread through the ranks of the sepoys. In addition, there was general discontent in several parts of the country, and the stubborn resistance of the Sikh princes indicated to the Indians that British troops could be engaged in a fair fight, especially in a climate which was hostile to them. The seriousness of the Indian Mutiny required a large British military presence, and the Royal Warwickshires were sent from the Cape to India in December 1857. By this time the regiment had been reduced once more to a single battalion, although this lasted for only a brief period of time before the regiment gained a second battalion permanently.

Whilst still consisting of a single battalion the 6th sailed for India, being firmly established there by February 1858. By this time the decisive fighting in the Indian Mutiny was over, however the regiment was involved in minor operations such as the Oude campaign, and also endured a spell in the Jugdespore Jungle. Although only 2 men were wounded during this episode, 6 died from sunstroke. Again, tropical illnesses such as boils, smallpox, dysentery and outbreaks of cholera were rife. The doctors were of the opinion that lighter cotton clothing would have made all the difference but their suggestions went unheeded. There were instances amongst some troops, such as the Dragoon Guards who wore heavy helmets, of their headgear being so hot that it seared the flesh.

The final event of this tour took place in the latter months of 1860, whilst part of the regiment was on an expedition to the Tibetan mountains, an area where the Rajah of Sikkim was causing trouble. The regiment had postings in Azimghur, Benares and finally Barrackpore. Late in 1861 orders were received to return to England – by the time of departure, as was common practice with troops serving abroad, more than 300 men had transferred to other regiments. So, it seems life in India wasn't all that bad! The remainder arrived back home on 24 May 1862.

Not long after being raised the 2nd Battalion went to the Ionian Islands in Jamaica, and thence to Trinidad. In 1879 it was transferred to India, followed by a tour of duty in Ceylon, before returning home in 1896.

In 1867 the 1st Battalion returned to India once again, its first base being Rawalpindi. In August 1868 trouble broke out amongst the Hazaras

Sergeant S. Girling, one of the Battalion's earliest recipients of the Distinguished Conduct Medal, awarded for service during Kitchener's 1898 Sudan Campaign. (David Vaux Collection)

and the battalion participated in the subsequent expedition. All participants in the campaign were awarded the Indian General Service Medal plus clasp. The men remained in India for another 12 years, eventually leaving for Aden in February 1880. Their stay in the Middle East was short and by the end of the year the men were back in England. They remained there for the next 15 years.

In 1873 the regimental depot was established in Warwick. In 1881 the title The Royal Warwickshire Regiment was adopted, and two battalions of Warwickshire Militia and two volunteer battalions became part of the regiment.

The 1st Battalion's next notable posting was to the Sudan, in 1897. After the Arab rebellion of 1882 had been crushed Britain decided on maintaining a "provisional occupation" of Egypt. Although on the surface it appeared that the Sultan of Turkey retained suzerainty, with the Khedive responsible for local affairs, in reality Britain maintained control. The Egyptian army had been reorganised and officered with British soldiers.

Officers of the 1st Battalion, 1906. Rear row (l. to r.): Lt. R.F. Woodward; Lt. G.F. Waterworth; Capt. G.B. Marriott; Capt. D. Day; Capt. C.R. Macdonald; Lt. E.G. Sydenham; Lt. H.C. Sinnott; Capt. A. Boxwell; Lt. and Qmr. J. Harwood; Lt. E.J. de P.O. Kelly; Lt. J.F.T. Halliday. Middle row(l. to r.): Capt. A.S. Toogood; Capt. R.H.W. Brewis; Major H.R. Vaughan; Lt. Col. F.G.F. Browne; Capt. and Adj. L.W. Johnson; Major P.T. Westmorland; Major St. J.A. Cox. Front row (l. to r.): 2nd Lt. C.L.N. Newall; 2nd Lt. K.F. Franks; Lt. G.W. Bond; Lt. G.D. Martin; Lt. B.G.R. Gordon; 2nd Lt. F.A. Macartney. (Fred Bremner)

The Royal Warwickshire Regiment made several tours of India. Here the 1st Battalion is shown on parade at Quetta in 1906. (Fred Bremner)

"G" Company, 1st Battalion, on manoeuvres in India, c.1906. (Fred Bremner)

Workshops of the 1st Battalion in India, c.1906. The four trades shown are those of armourers, typesetters/printers, carpenters and cobblers. (Fred Bremner)

Meanwhile the *Sirdar*, Lord Kitchener, was making plans for the reconquest of the Sudan from the Mahdists.

The 1st Battalion formed part of Kitchener's army of reconquest. Its first major action was the Battle of The Atbara on 8 April 1898. Four months later the regiment participated in the advance on Omdurman. On 2 September the Mahdists again suffered a severe defeat at the Battle of Omdurman. Khartoum was taken, and, after twenty years the Khalifa's reign of tyranny had come to an end. The double honours of "Atbara" and "Omdurman" were added to the regiment's colours. The regiment's first Distinguished Conduct Medals were also awarded for services in the Sudan campaign, to Sergeant S. Girling, Corporal R. Danley and Lance-Corporal G. Marsden. In late September the battalion departed for another tour of India.

Following its arrival in Bombay towards the end of 1898 the 1st Battalion spent the next fourteen years in India. It participated in two important expeditions, Bazar Valley and Mohmand, for which its men were awarded the Indian General Service Medal plus '1908' clasp. The 1st sailed for home on 11 December 1912.

The 2nd Battalion Royal Warwickshire Regiment was involved in the Boer War 1899–1902, its 1,100 men arriving in Cape Town on 15

Lieutenant W.E.W. Elkington (standing at far left in peaked cap), Royal Warwickshire Regiment, with shooting team, Meerut, 1902. (David Vaux Collection)

December, 1899, as part of General Kelly-Kenny's 6th Division. The battalion was divided into two contingents. The first lived up to the regiment's tradition of being hard marchers and fighters and was involved in the British success at Paardeberg. The second contingent was posted to the Orange River Colony before moving to Bloemfontein. The regiment was involved in actions at Diamond Hill, Belfast and Komati Poort. After arriving at Komati Poort in January 1901 the 2nd experienced serious outbreaks of sickness and by April there were only just over 30 men fit for duty. Nevertheless, another honour was added to the colours, "South Africa 1899–1902". Four months later the regiment sailed from Cape Town to Bermuda, its main duty being to guard Boer prisoners of war. Arriving in England in November 1902 the 2nd was then posted to Malta, remaining there until the outbreak of war in 1914.

Before ending this account of the Royal Warwickshire Regiment in South Africa it is worth noting that an important event in British military history was made during the war. In 1899 the regiment comprised the four regular battalions (1st, 2nd, 3rd and 4th), two militia battalions (5th and 6th) and finally the 1st and 2nd volunteer battalions. Elements from all eight served in South Africa, the first occasion in British military history that volunteers and militia had accompanied regular forces on active service abroad.

By the beginning of the twentieth century the Royal Warwickshire Regiment had earned an abundance of honours which had been awarded for exemplary service throughout the world, often under conditions that required great physical endurance; even greater glory was at hand. On 4 August 1914 Britain declared war on Germany. The rest of this narrative is chiefly devoted to the build-up and service of the 1st Battalion only, in what was to become known as the Great War.

Part I – Euphoria?

CHAPTER 1

On The Brink:
The Outbreak of War,
July–August 1914

During the nineteenth century the power of Prussia had continued to increase. Under the guidance of that great statesman, Otto von Bismarck, the German states became an imperial empire. Bismarck declared openly that Germany had no plans for further territorial expansion. Following victory in the Franco-Prussian War of 1870/71 Germany had annexed Alsace-Lorraine, thereby humiliating France, but Bismarck insisted that his overall intention was to promote European peace through an alliance between Germany, Russia and Austria-Hungary. That may have been his plan, but events turned out rather differently.

In 1888 Kaiser Wilhelm II succeeded his father. Within two years he had forced Bismarck to resign. The Kaiser's policies did little to strengthen peace. He disagreed with Russia and showed considerable hostility towards France. The result was unexpected. Those old enemies, France and Russia, became allies, and in 1893 formed a Dual Alliance, whereby they would stand together in the event of any interference from Germany or Austria-Hungary. In a reciprocal move the Triple Alliance between Germany, Austria-Hungary and Italy was formed.

Britain purposely distanced herself from these arrangements, stressing her intention to remain in "splendid isolation", but if anything, she tended to favour the German bloc, having always been suspicious of the Tsar and Russia. In addition, Britain's policies towards France generated acrimony. Prime Minister Salisbury (1895–1902) certainly supported a pro-German policy and the British Royal family's relationship with the Hohenzollern dynasty had to be taken into consideration. After all, the mother of the Kaiser was Queen Victoria's daughter, and this helped to forge a stronger bond between the two countries.

During the first few years of the new century Germany began to build an impressive navy. Whilst a strong naval force would be of no advantage against either France or Russia, its formation was certainly of concern to

The German Kaiser with von Moltke, Chief of Staff, during pre-war manoeuvres. (London Illustrated News Group)

Britain. As far as conflict with France or Russia was concerned, Germany already possessed a considerable military advantage thanks to its massive army. Britain became deeply concerned about its isolation, and made three unsuccessful attempts – the last in 1912 – to forge an alliance with Germany.

The next stage of events in Eastern Europe also alarmed Britain. Germany cemented another alliance, this time with Turkey, and was granted a concession to construct a railway to Baghdad. The Germans, who were in such a formidable position, had little inclination towards a strong friendship with Britain which, by now, was having second thoughts about her "splendid isolation". Whilst not being particularly favoured by any of the Continental countries, Britain felt it would be advantageous to have allies. In 1904 the decision was made to establish the *Entente Cordiale* with France, but this was no alliance in the usual sense of the word, being more an informal arrangement.

In 1905 the Russo-Japanese War had ended in the total defeat of Russia. Although Britain had a pro-Japanese policy, having signed a treaty with Japan in 1902, the Russian defeat provided a favourable opportunity for it to foster a new relationship with Russia, thereby gaining an ally rather than a possible aggressor. As a safety measure Britain renewed its treaty with Japan.

By 1906 Europe was divided into two camps. The subdued undertones of potential conflict became stronger, leading to an arms race. To counter-balance Germany's vast investment in its fleet, Britain injected massive sums of money into developing its own navy. According to some this was to the detriment of the army.

Indications of Germany's serious hostility, especially towards France, were witnessed by two significant incidents. The first occurred in 1906 when Germany and France disagreed over Morocco. The outcome was Germany's insistence upon the dismissal of the French Foreign Secretary. Then five years later, a German warship, on the directions of the Kaiser, entered the Moroccan port of Agadir. Under no circumstances did France want war. To alleviate the threat of serious conflict, the joint negotiations were favourable to Germany, with France relinquishing part of the Congo on the understanding that Germany recognised a Morocco that remained under French control.

However, Germany was still determined to implement an expansionist policy, seeking to form a colonial empire similar to that of Britain. There was very little evidence that large numbers of the growing German population had elected to emigrate to its colonies, such as Cameroon, German East Africa, German South West Africa and Kaiser Wilhelm Land (later New Guinea). Whether serious or not, Germany also made known its concern that because of the "entente" between Russia, France and Britain, Germany considered itself threatened by two potential enemies, due to the geographic position of France and Russia. The overriding motive for a possible war was that Germany also wished to expand in an easterly direction.

Both Austria-Hungary and Germany were wary of the possibility of Russia expanding its territory into the Balkans, an area which had been ruled by Turkey for centuries. Austria-Hungary finally gained complete control following the Balkan Wars of 1911–13. The southern area of the Austro-Hungarian Empire was populated by large numbers of Slavs, upon whom Austria-Hungary kept a close watch, especially in Bosnia and Herzegovina. The Austrians feared that in times of trouble their Slavic population would appeal to Russia for help, thus giving the Russians an opportunity to manipulate the Balkan League.

In 1914, the assassination of the heir to the Austro-Hungarian throne at Sarajevo rapidly brought the situation to a head. Spoiling for a fight, Austria-Hungary accused the Serbs of planning the assassination, and put forward a series of demands for compensation which Serbia could not have met without losing its independence. Despite the fact that Serbia was prepared to comply with all save one of the demands, Austria-Hungary still considered it had no alternative but to declare war. This declaration of war was soon to claim millions of lives, both military and civilian, throughout Europe. The equilibrium of Europe was shattered at a stroke.

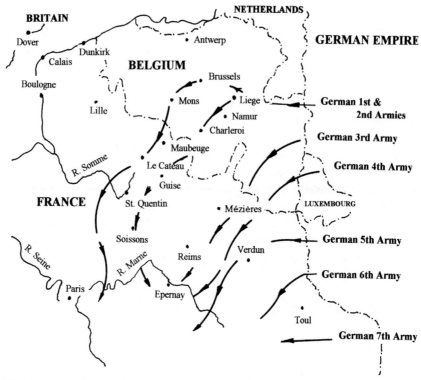

The German advance, August 1914.

Russia initially attempted to mediate, but eventually saw no other solution than to come to Serbia's aid. In turn, Russia's ally France joined them. This was followed by the implementation of the treaty between Germany and Austria thus drawing the former country into the conflict. Britain, on the other hand, had previously maintained a position of neutrality. Therefore it came as a surprise to Germany and Austria-Hungary when Britain became involved. Along with France and Britain, Germany had signed an earlier treaty that guaranteed Belgium neutrality. Germany also declared that its troops would not enter Belgium in the event of war. However in 1914 Germany insisted that its troops be granted free passage through Belgium in order to gain access to Northern France, thus breaking the treaty. Britain stood by its commitment, and German troop movements into Belgium automatically brought Britain into the conflict. The subsequent invasion of France also threatened Britain directly – it would be only a short trip across the Channel for Germany to invade Britain.

The three main contentious issues which had been simmering away for a quarter of a century came to the boil – the bitterness between Germany

German infantry cross the border into Belgium near Aachen, 9 August 1914. (Private collection)

Wounded German cavalrymen receiving treatment during their advance into Belgium, August 1914. (London Illustrated News Group)

and Russia, France's indignation in respect of Alsace-Lorraine and Germany's determination to match Great Britain as a sea-power.

In the period preceding the conflict both Germany and France had formulated detailed plans of attack, the chief ones being the Schlieffen Plan and Plan XVII respectively. Each felt confident that when implemented, theirs would result in a swift and decisive victory. Plan XVII was a failure from the day the French commander, General Joffre, implemented it in August 1914. The French plan – as assessed by the German high-command – concentrated all Joffre's efforts on taking Alsace-Lorraine. Using Joffre's major forces in this way meant that northern France was left poorly defended. It was this area in which the Germans, under General Alexander von Kluck, planned their major offensive, via Belgium, as laid down in the Schlieffen Plan. The overall intention was a rapid conquest of France within six weeks.

Initially the Schlieffen Plan enjoyed a measure of success, but the advance soon became one of careless confidence. The movement of hundreds of thousands of troops together with their supplies, in some 500 trains up to the Belgian border, was carried out with precision. After this, the planned advance was to be on foot. Many units were expected to advance up to twenty-five miles per day.

When they invaded on 4 August the Germans did not expect to encounter strong resistance from the Belgians. It came as a shock to them when they met considerable resistance which caused a slowing-down of their own carefully-timed programme. The Germans suffered an unexpectedly high number of casualties at the hands of the Belgians. They were shattered by the Belgian stand at Liège, where the seriously outnumbered, yet intrepid, forces of General Leman held the enemy at bay. The Belgians only gave way on 16 August following the German introduction of powerful siege guns which destroyed the "invincible" fortresses around Liège. General von Kluck's First Army of 320,000 men advanced towards Brussels, intending to destroy the depleted and retreating Belgian Army during their advance. The Belgians retired to Antwerp from where they continued to mount small attacks on the German First Army. On 20 August Brussels fell to the Germans, who had soon occupied all of Belgium except for the Antwerp area and the Channel coast.

The popular British Press gave full coverage to the alleged atrocities and vandalism committed by the advancing Germans, who were said to have shown no respect for the rules of war as dictated by the 1906 Hague Convention. This specifically laid down that fighting be confined, as far as possible, to troops, thus ensuring the protection of unarmed civilians. Whilst advancing through Belgium the German armies gave ample evidence of their total ruthlessness as large numbers of civilians lay dead in

Belgian infantry at Namur, where they made such a magnificent stand. (London Illustrated News Group)

One of the huge Krupp siege mortars used to such good effect against the Belgian fortifications in August 1914. (London Illustrated News Group)

their wake. The British newspapers had no hesitation in claiming that Germany had brought barbarism into the strategy of modern warfare with their acts of murder, pillage, mutilation, torture and arson.

How much of this was simply propaganda? There is no doubt that German behaviour was certainly a contentious topic. Reports of mass execution were a different issue, and all too often true. For instance, there were frequent instances in which the slightest hint that a particular building or district was being used by Belgian soldiers to hold up the German advance brought about a swift and brutal response from the invaders. It was not uncommon for the buildings to be fired and civilian occupants shot as a reprisal. Hostages were sometimes marched in front of the occupying army as a form of protection, and on several occasions it was German policy to force civilian submission by heavy-handed and unwarranted means. Although "vandalism" was a propaganda issue, it was one in which there was frequently more than a grain of truth. One of the most devastating events occurred at Louvain in August 1914, where executions, pillage and wanton wholesale destruction of buildings and their contents occurred. However taken as a whole, serious as many of the reported incidents were, some were greatly exaggerated by what can only be described as a capricious British press.

During the previous century Britain's newspapers had reported events such as the Crimean War, Indian Mutiny and Boer War in great detail. Artists were employed to provide illustrations. Initially, there was no censorship, and letters home from officers and men were reproduced verbatim. Such correspondence often contained serious criticism of superiors or told of poor performances shown by certain regiments whilst on the battlefield.

During the Indian Mutiny, for instance, the *Illustrated London News* published reports which were readily and eagerly absorbed by an often gullible reader. No holds were barred – the more gruesome the text or illustration of "our lads" dealing with the enemy the better. Artists made great play of alleged atrocities inflicted upon British women and children, illustrating these events in lurid detail. If a Bible or religious icon could be included in the picture, together with a few villainous faces of Sepoys at the window, or breaking down a door, all well and good. This was Victorian melodrama at its best: dramatic scenes playing upon the imagination.

During the First World War things were different. Censorship and secrecy were of prime importance. The camera replaced the artist, although not completely; indeed, war artists are still used today. Even during the first months of the war several artists were still producing superb examples of Victorian-style artwork, the graphic detail, especially on the faces of the subjects, as expressive as ever.

Belgium was beaten and the Germans swept onward. However, by this time some of the troops, especially conscripts, were reaching a point of exhaustion and stragglers began dropping out of the advance. Because of the wide dispersal of the troops, the supply system became overstretched and could not keep pace with demand. Finally, there was virtually a complete breakdown of German communications. Nevertheless, following the German invasion of Belgium on 4 August, the First and Second Armies had occupied Belgium within three weeks, and were now very close to northern France.

Britain had become involved in the conflict when Belgium was invaded, declaring war on Germany at 11 a.m. on Tuesday 4 August 1914.

At the time war was declared the military establishments of each of the major European powers were convinced of their own invincibility. It had only been the wholesale procrastination of their statesmen which had delayed their generals in taking action. It took Britain a few days to make a decision regarding the best way in which to deploy its troops.

Germany had every confidence in its well-equipped troops. There had been considerable progress in the development of armaments during the half-century preceding the war. Germany had realised that success in future wars would depend heavily upon the expertise of the engineer and the chemist. For instance, Krupps had exhibited an all-steel breechloading cannon at the 1851 Great Exhibition. Germany had also developed a chemical industry. Britain had been the workshop of the world, but had lost its competitive edge by the 1870s. In the field of technical development, German competition was showing itself to be more than a match for the nation that had given birth to the Industrial Revolution. Germany certainly gained an advantage in the way in which its armaments industry was prepared for the mass-production of weapons of all kinds. It was confident that its 5.9-inch shell, which had a devastating explosive capacity, would stop the French in their tracks. The German siege guns were capable of smashing the most powerful fortifications quickly and effectively. Overall, the German army was amongst the foremost in Europe.

Experiences in the Boer War and the Indian Mutiny had highlighted many weaknesses in the organisational and tactical capabilities of the British Army. In the ten years between the Boer War and 1912, the complete structure of the army changed. Using new equipment and vastly different methods of training, Britain developed what it considered to be an elite force of six infantry divisions and one cavalry division which, if necessary, could be assembled and transported to the most likely location of war – Western Europe. It was an open secret for years, that when the time was right, Germany would force war upon its European rivals.

Accordingly, the War Office and Defence Committee had made all the necessary plans and arrangements for a quick and efficient mobilisation and embarkation of the army at very short notice.

The reforms of the British Army were initiated by Sir John Broderick, Secretary of State for War, and continued by his successor Lord Haldane. By 1888 the army had been issued with the .303 Lee-Metford bolt-action magazine rifle. This was developed further, and in 1895 was reintroduced as the Lee-Enfield, which became the standard rifle for over half of the twentieth century. There were other new weapons. The machine-gun had undergone further development and, by the turn of the century, the army was issued with the fully automatic Maxim gun firing at the rate of 600 rounds per minute. Breech-loading guns had been in service with the British army for some time prior to the outbreak of war. Due to the use of smokeless powder guns no longer gave away their position when fired.

The reorganised section of the army of nearly 160,000 men, referred to as the British Expeditionary Force (B.E.F.), was made up of volunteer regulars who were still serving or were on the list of reserves. At that time a regular soldier initially enlisted for twelve years, which entailed service with the colours followed by a period on the reserve, during which time he could be recalled at a moment's notice should the need arise. Finally, an option of serving a total of twenty-one years could be taken up. In 1914 about two-thirds of the B.E.F. were reservists. This meant that on the outbreak of war, despite the fact that at some time all the men comprising this force had undergone essential training, much of its manpower was "civilian". Reservists did undergo a short period of annual training which covered many facets of warfare, including musketry, arms drill, bayonet practice, large-scale manoeuvres and living under canvas. One note-worthy fact was the imbalance of physical fitness between reservists and serving men, and this soon manifested itself on the Western Front. Ben Clouting, who has a significant part to play in this narrative, makes specific reference to fitness:

> The reservists in particular found the going unbearable. Many had been called up after five years on the reserve and had not marched in all that time. Their feet weren't up to the stone-set roads, in stiff, unbroken boots. Blood oozed through shoe soles, or from bits of rag tied round blistered feet. Boots, jackets, caps everything was dumped, except rifles and ammunition.[1]

According to figures issued in 1903, nearly 30% of applicants were consid-ered physically unfit for service. The main reasons for rejection were inad-equate chest measurement, defective vision and being underweight. There is little reason to expect that this figure was very different eleven years later.

While this army, under its commander-in-chief Field Marshal Sir John French, was the finest Britain had ever produced, and its preparation for war had never been more thorough, there were flaws which the authorities had overlooked. Compared with other European nations, Britain was sadly lacking in manpower However, there was one very strong point in the B.E.F.'s favour – the accuracy of its marksmanship, which was second to none. This would prove to be a very important advantage. Cavalry regiments were also trained in the use of the Lee-Enfield .303. The British were still somewhat lacking in understanding the strategic requirements of modern warfare compared with their Continental counterparts. However, all the combatants anticipated being involved in a fast- moving war, where mobility of troops was all important. Recent wars in which Britain had been involved were typically fought in a rural environment – they were wars of the machine-gun and rifle. The Boer War, for instance, was fought in large open spaces, where actions such as Spion Kop proved that the accuracy of the concealed rifleman was all-important when firing on infantry advancing uphill and over open spaces. There were certainly a number of Boer War veterans in the B.E.F., but they had fought against troops who were largely irregulars. The Germans were a different story.

In the coming war troops were expected to carry heavy packs on their backs, averaging 60lbs. but often weighing up to 90lbs. The extra weight was made up of further rounds of ammunition and personal items. Britain's troops had no experience of fighting in a European built-up area. Germany, on the other hand, had fought fewer wars, but these had been fought in Europe, where valuable experience was gained in manoeuvring over European roads, using European transport systems, railways and rivers.

Despite the size of her army, and its weaknesses, Britain still displayed that confidence of old, whereby it would give its best and apply its well-known determination to fight to the end. Battles would be lost, but the war would be won.

Both in Britain and on the Continent, towns and cities still had very concentrated populations. Towns had expanded in population but not always in size. Such large concentrations seemed to offer inviting targets. As we have seen, Germany showed what she was prepared to do, irrespective of the terms of the Hague Convention. Because of each nation's determination to win, they showed little anxiety about what could happen in their large towns and cities during the period leading up to the war. However, whilst there was some devastation at the outset of hostilities, the great devastation on the scale predicted never happened.

Britain was looking forward to going to war. Many thought it would be "over by Christmas", Easter at the latest. War veteran Harry Maskill told of the firm belief that one British soldier was worth two, or even three, of any other nation. Britain's morale was tremendously high; it was confident of its great naval tradition and had beaten Bonaparte. Britain had waged successful wars against Chinese, Maoris, Africans, Red Indians, Egyptians, to name but a few. The victor had also acquired territory at the expense of the vanquished – Gibraltar from Spain, Canada from the French, New Amsterdam from the Dutch. Often Britain had suffered more than a bloody nose, but had always been victorious. Many will remember part of a poem *What Can a Little Chap Do?* written by John Oxenham, which was widely read at school during the 1940s. It appeared in *Princess Mary's Gift Book*, which was still being used in schools in 1940 even though it had been produced during WWI to boost the Queen's "Work for Women Fund". It summed up the common attitude at that time:

He can march in the queue,
Of the Good and the Great,
Who battled with fate
And won through

The verse was supported by pictures of British heroes such as Scott of the Antarctic, Nelson and Gordon.

The war would change the perception of many people. After 1918 many veterans held strong feelings about the way statesmen and generals had conducted the war. Once hostilities were over and the men were back home, they switched off from the outside world as far as possible. Feelings for many who had witnessed the mass suffering and bloodshed were so strong that they never discussed the war again, or only on occasions, and then only with fellow veterans. Their medals never again saw the light of day. In the case of one anguished and embittered member of this writer's family, the medals were "thrown behind the fire and that was that"!

In 1914 Britain was a great nation; the amount of wealth that was pouring in was staggering. The country was the centre of a thriving and complicated network of worldwide trade which was the envy of the world. As one veteran stated: "At that time we had both the finest railway and sewerage systems in the world. Look at them today, our railways are problematic and the sewerage system is collapsing." Wealth was reflected in the sanatoriums, hospitals and schools. Even today this can be seen by looking at the ornate town halls, theatres, museums, pubs and religious buildings. The country and Empire appeared immensely powerful. As has already been seen, there was tremendous jingoism.

On the news of the Declaration of War, the *Daily News* reported the scenes in London:

The enthusiasm culminated outside Buckingham Palace when it became known that war had been declared. The word was passed round by the police that silence was necessary, inasmuch as the King was holding a Council for the signing of the necessary proclamations. The news that war had been declared was received with tremendous cheering which grew into a deafening roar when King George, Queen Mary and the Prince of Wales appeared on the balcony. Westminster, Charing Cross, and the main thoroughfares round Westminster were thronged all last night with excited crowds who displayed marked tendencies towards mafficking. Both in numbers and in noisiness it far exceeded the crowds of Monday. Union Jacks were everywhere to be seen, and the air was filled with the sound of patriotic songs; Trafalgar Square was almost impassable.

A hostile crowd assembled at the German Embassy, and smashed the windows. A special message was sent out to Cannon Row, and a force of mounted and unmounted police was quickly on the scene, but had considerable difficulty in restoring order.[2]

Final preparations by the Directorate of Mobilisation had been in place since the end of July; the actual decision to mobilise the B.E.F. was not taken until late in the day on which war was declared – 4 August 1914.

CHAPTER 2

Going to War:
The B.E.F., August 1914

It was generally expected that within 24 hours of the general mobilisation order embarkation would begin, but this was not the case. The Government had previously planned a smooth, trouble-free mobilisation thanks to earlier initiatives by Haldane, Secretary of State for War, but the position on 4 August, the first day of mobilisation, was less clear. There were no final details about which units of the B.E.F. were to be embarked, nor their destination. These decisions were finally made on 6 August, the same day that Lord Kitchener was appointed Minister for War.

The Command of the B.E.F. was assigned to Field Marshal Sir John French, an experienced officer of cavalry. At the age of sixty-two his suitability for such a demanding post was questionable. A small, red-faced man, he was known for his hot-headedness, and moods which veered between exciteability and depression. Lieutenant-General Sir Archibald Murray was appointed French's Chief-of-Staff. Major-General Henry Wilson was Sub-Chief of Staff, General Staff Officer Intelligence was Colonel G.M.W. Macdonough, and the post of Adjutant-General went to Major-General Sir C.F.N. Macready. Finally, Major-General W.R. Robertson was Quartermaster-General.

The B.E.F. was divided into the Cavalry Division, I Corps, II Corps and III Corps. Of these, the first troops to go to France were: 5 brigades of the Cavalry Division, commanded by Major-General Edmund Allenby; I Corps (1st and 2nd divisions), under Lieutenant-General Sir Douglas Haig; II Corps (3rd and 5th divisions), under General Horace Smith-Dorrien (a replacement for its original commander, Sir James Grierson, who had died unexpectedly of a heart attack); III Corps (4th and 6th divisions), commanded by Major-General T. d'Oyly Snow, were not initially utilised. The 4th Division included the 10th Brigade, on which this narrative will be mainly concentrated. As only part of III Corps later went to France, Snow joined II Corps under Smith-Dorrien.

Field Marshal Kitchener, who was appointed to the post of War Minister by Prime Minister Asquith on 6 August 1914. (IPC Magazines)

Whilst discussing the command structure of the B.E.F., an assessment of its serving officers repays study, particularly in light of their suitability to the anticipated new style of warfare.

For many years the major source of recruitment into the officer ranks was from the public schools. Therefore it follows that they came either from long established wealth, often with a military background, or from families who had attained their assets through the many entrepreneurial opportunities provided by the expansion of the Empire. Should their sons elect to make the army their career, the family would ensure that they had a private income if necessary. Wherever such people lived, either in town or country, they had always enjoyed a dominant social position which was accepted by the lower classes. It was, of course, more evident in the counties, where the rich owned much of the land, and built their mansions and grand houses. They largely held themselves aloof from the local villagers, and socialised only with their own class. In his diaries, Kilvert highlights the constant socialising in the large country houses as demonstrating the isolation the rich could maintain. They shared similar values and outlook. Their children were sent to the best schools, and two of the most popular vocations for their young sons were the church and the army.

At public school boys were taught the tenets of loyalty amongst one's peers, the importance of strength of character and the acceptance of authority; to obey without question and never "rat" on a colleague. They were never to talk "shop" in the mess; they could talk cricket, pig-sticking, polo or hunting, but never "shop". Couple such an attitude with a "country seat" and connections through money and influence, and the son was well on the way to gaining preferment and promotion in their chosen career. The grade of pass which young candidates achieved in their Sandhurst or Woolwich examinations contributed to their eventual place-ment. "High fliers" could expect to be accepted into the Indian Army or Royal Engineers, whilst average or lower scorers would be posted to lower status regiments:

> Failing to do well enough at Sandhurst to gain a commission in the Indian Army, Bernard Montgomery went to the Royal Warwick-shire, which was unfashionable but sound and inexpensive.[1]

In 1914, 70% of colonels originated from the peerage, gentry, military families or the clergy; 73% of generals were from the same social classes.[2] Nevertheless, it should also be borne in mind that, irrespective of the class divide, these pioneers of the Empire and military men were national heroes, supposedly embodying Christian morals, putting their country first and struggling against odds being considered *de rigeur*.

After retirement from the army it was not unknown for country squires to try to maintain an army-style discipline on their estates and in local villages. In rural Herefordshire there was one old officer who would march his household staff to church each Sunday, and when visiting the local school insisted that the children were made to march round the play-ground and salute "the squire".

In the years leading up to the war there were some developments in the training of the army and the equipment used. Serious efforts were made to "professionalise" it. But what about the men who were responsible for imple-menting these developments? If the B.E.F. was the elite force many claimed, did it also possess an elite set of commanders? As this narrative concerns the 10th Brigade, and especially the 1/Royal Warwickshire Regiment, it is worth-while looking at comments made at the time in respect of training and the quality of officers. We need look no further than the contemporary diary of

Brigadier J.A.L. Haldane, who was commander of 10th Brigade (4th Division, III Corps). The 4th Division commander to whom Haldane was answerable was Major-General Thomas D'Oyly Snow, C.B.

Aylmer Haldane was something of a controversial character, who did not hold back his criticism of both higher and lower levels of authority at division- and brigade-levels, as his Shorncliffe Diary during the period April 1912 to August 1914 shows. The following diary entries contain some of his more enlightening and often amusing comments.[3]

1913

19 February
Capt. Mansfield who is in arrest for money troubles, last night broke his arrest and went out and slew a cock and six hens belonging to Col. Churcher. He is now in close arrest, and I think will have to be placed under observation for madness.

24 February
The drunkenness in all four of my battalions is too high. It is difficult to stop it as drawing attention to it may lead to screening it.

5 March
Capt. Mansfield not having paid his mess bill will now be ordered to resign.

6 March
(Col.) Campbell came to see me about Stewart-Richardson, sick at Osborne. Apparently several dishonoured cheques have turned up. He will have to retire, and he will be no loss, though a gentlemanly fellow.

19 March
Heard from C.O. Royal Dublin Fusiliers, (Mainwaring). He feels the remarks in the Annual Report on his unit as to education not being good, and musketry being below the level of the brigade, also cases of drunkenness being numerous. Irish regiments are certainly less well-educated than others. Gravesend offers temptation to drink, but the musketry has declined for the past 3 years. With the new rifle and musketry exercises done this winter it should improve.

26 March
Referring to Maj. Shewan – he is rather weak, it is unfortunate he is at Gravesend.

31 March

Spoke to Col. Campbell regarding bad behaviour of his regiment at Hythe. If it continues I shall either have larger piquets or put it out of bounds. Capt. Mansfield 1/Royal Irish Fusiliers has been removed from the Army. He was a useless and bad officer. Capt. Stewart-Richardson – 2/Seaforth Highlanders, a weak and dissolute person, has sent in his papers and will be a good riddance.

25 April

The Special Reserve officers are again giving trouble in the 2/R. Dublin Fus. One of them, Hamilton, hired a bicycle and pawned it.

3 May

The G.O.C. 4th Division (Snow) again showed his ignorance of any tactical principles and had we have not been fighting an imaginary enemy (territorial troops) we should certainly have been beaten; as it was the fight was considered drawn whereas by massing against the enemy's nearest flank he could have been routed. General Snow ignored the principles of economy of force, of direction (of) the mass and security. He however, was quite pleased with himself.

15 May

Saw Sinnott's company doing an attack. He did three phases successively which is against my orders, I have not seen such an old fashioned operation for years! I shall have to teach the Warwicks everything as I don't think the C.O., (Vaughan), is capable of doing so. Then saw Day's company of the Royal Warwickshire Regt. He had his company all out in a line on outpost duty and not demonstrating as ordered. There is no doubt that officers do not read my training instructions. Shall have to frighten Lt. Col. Vaughan as I had to do Churcher last year with good results.

19 May

[Haldane went again to see the Warwicks training]. Sinnott was doing nothing of value, he seems to me to be a useless officer.

20 May

Neither Sinnott nor his C.O. seem to have common sense or knowledge.

24 May

(Trooping of the Colour). Warwicks very slow. I dislike their black buck which they have on ceremonial parades. Today, it had to be dragged past. Too much circus about it.

11 July

(On seeing Warks. attacking during exercises). C.O. much improved as teacher.

24 July

(Troop operations). Then on to see Royal Irish Fusiliers who were very leisurely about doing their work. Churcher had not reconnoitred the ground in advance and the attack was spoiled by a hay-field. He blamed the hay-field for being there not himself. I corrected him. There is too much "eye-wash" about this battalion, they do not take interest in anything but sport and the C.O. is a humbug. As long as he is in command much improvement is impossible, but it is not easy to get rid of a C.O. in peacetime. (N.b. I may mention here that on the retreat from Mons Churcher's behaviour – and earlier – was so unsatisfactory that I got him sent home and Major Burrows put in command, when matters in the battalion at once improved).

26 August

Had 2/Royal Dublin Fus. in main attack. Some officers are very stupid at grasping an order, no matter how clearly and carefully given.

4 September

… Bradford and (Maj.) Elkington lead theirs [battalions] well. Mainwaring commanded in defence satisfactorily.

20 September

Their Colonel [Mainwaring], has got colitis and goes back to Gravesend. (N.b. When the 1914 war broke out, knowing that he was not fit for service, I tried to get him "spun". I did not succeed as the doctors did not support me and the result was that he was cashiered after Le Cateau.).

25 October

Five courts-martial – one is Quartermaster Sergeant R.E. fighting in the R.E. mess and trying to get a drink after hours. Two A.S.C. men stealing each a loaf from the bread store, and a boy from the Warwicks attacking another with a bayonet – ordered the last to be dealt with by his C.O.

31 October

Saw Warwicks doing bayonet practice. Major Poole, the commander of the Company is very slack. He was president of a court-martial and allowed his captain at the same time to go out hunting so that he was not with the company.

1914

[Note: Lt. Col. John Ford Elkington was appointed C.O. of the battalion in place of Lt.-Col. Vaughan on 24 February 1914].

7 March
Went through preliminary work of C.O.'s for divisional exercises. Elkington has written best orders.

19 June
Royal Warwicks in good condition.

In his book the *The Killing Ground,* Tim Travers makes a most interesting analysis of the men who made the army their career. Promotion was all- important, but to progress in an army whose traditions were upheld by a handful of men at the top it was necessary to "know a man who knows a man". The promoters also had their preferences. For instance, junior officers who had served in India were more likely to progress if their senior officer was also a man who had seen service in India.

Generally, the important thing was to have someone who would be prepared to put the officer's name forward when the opportunity came. Tim Travers refers to this as the "protector-protégé" relationship. A typical instance of this being the association between Lord Roberts and Sir Henry Rawlinson, present from early in Rawlinson's career. Often such relationships had reciprocal arrangements, whereby protégés were sometimes in a position to put in a good word for their protectors with, for instance, family members who may have been either military men or statesmen.

Several of the staff officers were very protective of their "personal armies". They would openly criticise each other and sometimes displayed a mind set which did not sit well in a military context, a case in point being General Smith-Dorrien's relationship with Sir John French, notably at Le Cateau.

The process of change from a traditional to a professional army caused anxieties among some members of the officer corps. While some were not totally against change they maintained their traditional stance, often due to a lack of understanding or insisting that changes should be made their way. There were two schools of thought, as Travers puts it, "the traditional gentlemanly ideal and the technical, functionally competent, professional ideal."

It initially appears that the army was commanded by people with a traditional "mental set". During the first months of the war a very large number of the senior officers, whose pre-war conceptions prevailed, were

Shorncliffe Camp, from a photograph taken c.1909. (Author's collection)

Upon mobilisation, many private motorists as well as large companies had to surrender their vehicles to the Government for military use. (London Illustrated News Group)

weeded out, to be replaced by men whose ideas were more sympathetic to the new army and a different type of warfare. Perhaps this proves what a "leveller" war can be, with its high mortality rate. The original officer mentality was virtually eliminated within the period of four years. The size of the army rapidly increased with recruiting campaigns and eventual conscription, which brought in tougher and younger men who, in turn, provided fresh minds devoted to the problems of war. These minds were receptive to technological development and new thinking, what John Terraine called "modern industrial warfare". They also provided the necessary bridge to close the traditional gap between staff officers and "Tommy Atkins". Nevertheless, although current thinking towards such men as Haig is gradually changing, this general's hostility towards artillery is one instance of how he was impervious to change. At the other end of the scale, the man in the trenches was also on a learning curve.

Declaration of war had an immediate effect on civilian life. For instance, one serious consideration was what should be done in respect of the large numbers of Germans who were resident in Britain. Some held important posts, such as financiers, importers and exporters, whilst others had established thriving businesses, especially in London's bakery trade. Many had arrived years earlier as refugees and married British women. The British government remained indecisive, whilst in Germany British subjects were harshly treated.

Any known German spies were arrested, and the authorities kept an eye on some 200 suspected spies. A decision was made which gave German subjects six days' grace in which to return to their homeland. There were numbers of young German army reservists resident in Britain at that time.

Espionage became a military offence, and many suspects were banned from owning pigeon lofts, photographic equipment and firearms. Such measures were totally ineffective and did not prevent several incidents of industrial sabotage. On a number of occasions fires were deliberately started in Portsmouth Dockyards. One man, Karl Lody, a lieutenant in the German navy, was tried at the Tower of London, found guilty, and shot for espionage. A British subject of German descent received penal servitude for assisting spies.

When war broke out investments were frozen, bank loans were virtually unobtainable, money owing from several European countries was not forthcoming and much general business was curtailed because of Britain's trade with overseas countries. The man in the street spent his money only on necessities, and luxury goods became unsaleable. Similarly, retailers were not keen to accept large amounts of stock from wholesalers. As soon as the public became aware that war was imminent they began stockpiling food and other essentials, to the extent that many shops would only serve regular customers. One unfortunate result of this supply and demand problem was an increase in prices, to the detriment of the poor.

One thing that war has always done is to regenerate a nation's religious faith. For many non-attendees going to church suddenly became important, sometimes motivated by fear and sometimes by a stirring national pride. Support and guidance from a deity, often common to both sides, was devoutly and diligently sought by some, with the request for the strength to "knock the living daylights" out of the enemy. Others posed the perpetual questions to their Almighty: "Why do you let Christian fight Christian? What sign can we expect to show who you support?" According to many well-documented accounts, heavenly support did manifest itself in assisting the B.E.F., as we shall see at Mons.

Due to government indecision relating to a policy of arms production several factories were on short-time, and many staff and manual workers were unemployed during the first few weeks of hostilities. On 4 August the State took control of the railway network and several lines were shut down, but the private traveller was not much affected by these measures.

Mobilisation involved a great deal of work for the postal system. The exercise was somewhat eased by foresight, with a formal mobilisation letter addressed to each reservist. It contained precise instructions on how the individual was to join his unit. What of the recipients, how did they feel when this letter dropped through their letterbox? Many would have already known that they would be victims of the initial wave of unemployment the war caused, so, in their case, the "invitation to war" may have been welcome. For the self-employed man things would have been different. The business which he had diligently built up during his period on the reserve, never really expecting to be called to the colours again, would disappear overnight. The majority of the thousands of men recalled were sad to leave, but as with all wars, there were many who looked upon the "call-up" as a path, however precarious, to a life of adventure with their mates, away from their wife and the usual complement of children of varying ages:

> Being a reservist, I was naturally called to the colours at the outbreak of the war between England and Germany on August 4 1914, so I downed tools; and although a married man with two children, I was only too pleased to leave a more or less monotonous existence for something more exciting and adventurous. Being an old soldier, war was of course more or less ingrained into my nature; during those few days before the final declaration I was at fever heat and longing to be away.[4]

The Government relied on thousands of citizens who were not directly involved in the mobilisation to play their part. In fact, civilians were obliged to billet territorials and reservists alike wherever it was considered necessary. The authorities were in a position to commandeer whatever they wished – donkeys, horses, carts, and especially motor vehicles and the petrol to power them.

One of the most involved logistical exercises was the large-scale feeding of men and animals in a war which was expected to be mobile – static trench warfare was never envisaged. Fortunately, there had been long-standing arrangements to stockpile such necessities as flour for bread and oats for the horses. Daily rations allocated to a soldier in 1914 were as follows: 1¼ lb. fresh or frozen meat, or 1 lb. preserved or salted meat; 1¼ lb. bread or 1 lb. biscuit or flour; 4 oz. bacon; 3 oz. cheese; ⅝ oz. tea; 4 oz. jam; 3 oz. sugar; ½ oz. salt; ¹/₃₆ oz. pepper; ¹/₂₀ oz. mustard; 8 oz. fresh or 2 oz. dried vegetables; ¹/₁₀ gill lime juice if fresh vegetables not issued; ½ gill rum; not exceeding 2 ozs. tobacco per week. The latter two were at the discretion of the commanding general. Iron Rations consisted of: 1 lb. preserved meat; 12 oz. biscuit; ⅝ oz. tea; 2 oz. sugar; ½ oz. salt; 3 oz. cheese; 1 oz. meat extract (2 cubes).[5] However, a veteran of Mons or St. Quentin would have split his sides laughing at such rations; a glass of fresh water was difficult enough to procure!

In many ports ships were modified to accommodate the massive numbers of troops and the millions of tons of equipment expected to be shipped abroad. Luxury liners were not spared in the haste to prepare the required shipping. It would take time and great space to amass the main components of the B.E.F. at Southampton, the major port of departure. Hundreds of trains from all over the kingdom were converging on this south coast port. As soon as the men detrained they marched to a vast rest camp set up on common land on the outskirts of the city. From there the various divisions were called to embark in a fast and orderly fashion. The men were in fine fettle and the air was filled with the popular music hall songs of the day.

At various bases around the country both regulars and reservists assigned to the B.E.F. began their preparations for departure. For many it was amid an air of euphoria, for others an air of foreboding. Ben Clouting recalled the atmosphere at Tidworth Camp, near Salisbury:

> With the news that war had broken out, Tidworth went crackers. Everyone was very excited at the prospect of a fight, troopers firing off blank cartridges in a show of delight. We were going to war; we were going to do something. No one stopped to think what it actually meant. We were about to wipe the floor with the Germans and anything else was inconceivable.

> Our first instructions, (which must have caused great delight), were to let everything go rusty. Nothing was to be polished – buttons, cap badges, buckles, stirrup irons – anything that could reflect sunlight and so give notice of our presence in France.[6]

During the preparation for departure Clouting and other troopers, along with two veterinary officers, were detailed to go to R. Whites' mineral water factory in Birmingham, to select draught horses which would be assigned to the Army Service Corps or the artillery. When the work was finished the detail went on a tour of the factory where their:

Great care had to be taken when loading anxious horses aboard ship. Altogether, some 20,000 horses were initially transported to France with the B.E.F. (London Illustrated News Group)

The people of Boulogne showed great hospitality towards the newly-arrived British troops. (London Illustrated News Group)

… presence aroused much interest, and some over-excitement among some of the ladies working there. We were soldiers about to go to war and in August '14 this impressed everyone. Flushed with pride, and giddy at the proposal of going to France, I returned to Tidworth.[7]

Ben Clouting was still only sixteen years of age!

On the third day of mobilisation, i.e. 7th August, the whole Battalion, at full war strength, paraded at 5 p.m., complete with mobilised transport. It was a marvellous sight, and a truly wonderful piece of organisation accomplished in three days. Imagine it – between 500 and 600 Reservists collected from all over the country, (though chiefly, of course, from the county of Northamptonshire), clothed, fully equipped, transported from Blackdown Camp, with clothing and equipment properly fitted, the transport brought up to war strength with new vehicles, harness and horses (most of which last named had to be practically rebroken to do their work in a military style); in addition, the peace-time establishment of the Battalion reclothed and served out with their mobilisation kit. And all this had to be carried out in three days.[8]

Departures carried on day and night, and as soon as a ship was loaded it sailed off into the Channel. It was only then that the ship's captain and army staff officer opened their sealed orders to learn the port of destination and the area of troop concentration respectively. As the *Daily Telegraph* optimistically reported:

For ten days the departure of the Expeditionary Force, openly gathered from military centres, concentrated without pretence of concealment at popular south-eastern ports; requiring the willing co-operation of thousands and tens of thousands of civilians, to whom the ultimate destination of the corps could have been no secret; and above all, trusting the clear loyalty of the Press – who, of course, knew the whole thing from end to end – and of the relatives of the men who had gone; the Expeditionary Force went away without a word printed or uttered on this island that could have betrayed the fact.

With the numbers of spies allegedly in the country it is difficult to believe that there was not a fair contingent of "interested" observers at the few major ports on a coast directly opposite France.

Advance parties of the B.E.F. arrived in France from 7 August, the main elements arrived between 12 and 17 August. They then moved to the agreed point of concentration in the Le Cateau/Maubeuge area, a few miles from the border and the Belgian town of Mons.

The landing of troops in France was accomplished with the same efficiency as the departure from Britain. At Boulogne, for instance, once men, horses and equipment had been unloaded, the troops marched to rest camps on the outskirts of the town. Close to the Napoleon Memorial on the Calais road was sited Marlborough Camp. St Martin's Camp was on the road to St Omer, and the third site was St Leonard's Camp on the Pont

Men from the Royal Warwickshire Regiment about to embark for France, August 1914. (David Vaux Collection)

de Briques road. For several days prior to the B.E.F.'s arrival, French Territorials had prepared the sites by clearing the ground and installing a basic water system. As they marched through the town en-route to the camps the smart well-drilled British soldiers were again in high spirits and, as in England on their departure, the air was filled with their singing. They received a magnificent welcome from the Boulonnais, whose women showered the marching men with flowers, running up to them and planting kisses on their cheeks in appreciation of the fact that they had come to support their own sons, husbands and fathers in the hostilities. Soldier and civilian alike could never, amid such scenes of happiness and national pride, have envisaged how short-lived the celebration would be.

There was an even better welcome for troops disembarking at Le Havre. Not only did they receive the "flowers and kisses" reception as their comrades in Boulogne had done, but something more inviting to men and officers alike: that universal constant associated with instant friendship, "the booze", was flowing freely. The men were given beer and the officers were "living in great luxury and drinking enormous quantities of fine wines". Many of the men gave away cap badges and uniform buttons as souvenirs and as a gesture of thanks for the welcome they received.

Prior to the outbreak of war, a composite company belonging to the 1/Royal Warwickshire Regiment was based on the Isle of Sheppey. During its stay the men enthusiastically arrested several suspected spies, most of whom, it turned out, were innocent. It was also intended during this exercise to give the men experience in digging trenches. But since the men had been supplied broom-heads instead of picks, that particular idea had to be abandoned. The outbreak of war saw a rapid return to the regiment's base at Shorncliffe, however without immediate plans to proceed to France.

Whilst the main body of the B.E.F. was arriving in France, the 10th Brigade was moved to north-east England as a defensive measure. This coast was considered to be a possible area for landing spies and saboteurs, as well as a point for invasion. There were several German residents in the north east, some of whom allegedly owned radio equipment. The 1/Royal Warwickshire Regt. and 2/Royal Dublin Fusiliers were based at Strensal Camp near York, whilst the other half of the brigade (2/Seaforth Highlanders and 1/Royal Irish Fusiliers) were stationed at Darlington. It is unknown whether any spies were arrested or any radio equipment confiscated, but this posting did provide an opportunity for more fitness training. As the 1/R. Warks. war diary records, several route marches and exercise sessions took place – a policy which would pay dividends later.

After only a week, orders were given for the whole of the 4th Division to assemble in Southampton. In the early hours of 22 August, the 1/R. Warwicks and 2/R. Dublin Fusiliers embarked on *SS Caledonia* as the 2/Seaforths and 1/R. Irish Fusiliers went aboard *SS Lake Michigan*. After the King's Proclamation had been read to the troops both ships sailed down the Solent before midday, arriving at Boulogne later that evening. As well as the 10th Brigade, the 4th Division comprised 11th, 12th and 19th brigades supported by 'B' Squadron 19th Hussars, four Royal Field Artillery battalions, one Royal Garrison Artillery battery, two field companies of Royal Engineers and, finally, a section of the Royal Flying Corps.

By early morning on 23 August *SS Caledonia* and *SS Lake Michigan* had disembarked their passengers and the 10th Brigade marched to a camp near the Napoleon Monument on the outskirts of Boulogne. At midday orders were received to entrain, and men, equipment and horses were later loaded onto a troop train. Each company was issued with a quantity of maps, which the officers managed to stow either in their haversacks or various pieces of luggage. Robert Gould makes an amusing comment on the entraining: "The last straggler, whose surname had been a boon to N.C.O.'s since his days as a recruit days – Private Daft – was hauled aboard by acting Corporal Green and the Warwicks finally steamed off to war."[9]

Of course, the "old sweats" had seen it all before. Their concerns were such as what would happen if their enlisted service period came to an end during a period of war; could they go home? No doubt they kept quiet about their previous experiences of war – experiences which included sometimes sudden, or sometimes lingering deaths of close colleagues; remaining hungry and unwashed for long periods; infestation with lice and fleas; chronic dysentery for days on end, to name but a few. Among the younger element, many of whom had never experienced "serious fighting", the feelings were no doubt mixed between the excitement of going to war as part of an "elite" army, and coming perhaps to the stern realisation that this would be "a big one". As things turned out, the future could not have been worse. Over the next four years "old sweats" and young recruits alike were going to face a stubborn enemy, in conditions never before experienced by fighting men, with a resultant death rate never imagined possible.

In the comfort of their first-class seats were two gentlemen officers, one in the 1/R. Warwicks, the other in the 2/R. Dublin Fusiliers, who had also seen it all before. They were experienced men with fine military backgrounds, but neither, in their wildest dreams, would have predicted that within a matter of days they would both be dishonourably cashiered from the British Army.

The first of the officers, John Ford Elkington, Lieutenant-Colonel 1/Royal Warwickshire Regiment, was the eldest son of Lt.-General J.H.F. Elkington (1830–1889). Lt.-General Elkington had joined the Royal Warwickshire Regiment in 1846, seeing his first service in the Kaffir War of 1847–51, from which he received campaign medals. After being promoted to captain in 1854 he went to the Crimea, serving throughout the campaign as Assistant Quarter-Master-General to the Ottoman Turkish contingent. He was awarded the Order of the Medijideh, the Turkish Medal and the brevet rank of major. During the Indian Mutiny he served as A.D.C. to Sir John Michael, accompanying him to China in 1857 and being present at the Battle of Peking, 1860. He was promoted to lieutenant-colonel in 1858. Following his return home he married Margaret Jamieson in 1865. That same year Elkington and his wife joined the regiment in the West Indies.

Their first son, John Ford, was born in Newcastle, Jamaica in 1866. The regiment returned to England in 1867, and in November of that year Elkington Snr. was given command of the 2nd Battalion. He was stationed at Aldershot until 1870, and then in South Wales, Ireland and the Channel Islands. C. L. Kingsford states that in 1873 the Duke of Connaught commented on "This excellent Battalion, so well commanded by Colonel Elkington".[8] In 1875 the regiment returned to England, spending a year at Aldershot and then moving to Dover. In 1877 Lieutenant-Colonel Elkington handed over command of the regiment to Colonel Fielden. Between 1880 and 1885 Lt.-Col. Elkington was Deputy Adjutant-General of the Auxiliary Forces. After retiring from active service in 1885 he was appointed Governor of Guernsey, and held that post until his death in 1889. As well as John Ford, he had four other sons and one daughter.

Lieutenant-Colonel John Ford Elkington. (Mr R. Elkington)

The first son, John Ford Elkington, was educated at Elizabeth College, Guernsey and the Royal Military Academy, Sandhurst. As a newly-commissioned officer he joined his father's regiment, the Royal Warwickshires, in 1886, being promoted to captain after six years.

Between 1900 and 1902 he served in the South Africa War, during which he was mentioned in despatches, awarded the Queen's Medal with four clasps and reached the rank of major. Between 1902 and 1906 he was stationed in Britain. April 1906 to February 1907 saw him serving with the 3rd Battalion in South Africa. In 1908 he married Mary, daughter of John Rew Esq. of Liverpool. In 1910 he was promoted to lieutenant-colonel and following the regiment's return from two years' service in Malta he took command at Shorncliffe Camp in February 1914.

To complete this family's history, it is worth making note of the careers of John Ford's four brothers. Robert James Goodall Elkington (1867–1939) enjoyed a distinguished career in the Royal Artillery. In September 1913 he was promoted to lieutenant-colonel whilst serving in Lucknow, India, where he commanded U Battery, R.H.A. He was then ordered home to Bulford, taking command of 40 Brigade R.F.A., part of 3rd Division. By the time he joined the 56th Division in 1916 he had been promoted to brigadier-general and C.R.A.

Charles Jarvie Elkington passed out of Woolwich in 1887 and was commissioned in the Royal Engineers, being promoted to lieutenant in 1890. He served in Egypt from 1889 until his death from typhoid fever in 1893.

After attending the Royal Academy at Woolwich, George Edward Elkington was also commissioned into the Royal Engineers (1890), being promoted to lieutenant in 1893. He served in Egypt in the Dongala Expedition under Sir Herbert, later Lord, Kitchener. Here he saw action at Firket and Hafir, where he was mentioned in despatches and awarded the Order of the Medijideh, the campaign medal and the Egyptian medal with clasps. During this campaign he contracted cholera, and although he recovered, his constitution was weakened. After serving in the South Africa War for six months, he died of enteric fever at Bloemfontein in January 1901.

The youngest of the five boys was William Ernest Walter, born in 1874. Like his father and eldest brother he was commissioned into the Royal Warwickshire Regiment during 1898. Among the appointments he held were A.D.C. to Sir George Wolsey, G.O.C. Madras and Burma; orderly officer to General Campbell, C.O. Border Brigade at Aldershot; Musketry Instructor at the Small Arms School at Hythe. During WWI he served at Gallipoli and in Mesopotamia, where he was wounded. He later served in the Lincolnshire Regiment, before dying in May 1957.

The other officer in 10th Brigade in whom we are interested was Lieutenant-Colonel Arthur Edward Mainwaring, Commanding Officer 2/Royal Dublin Fusiliers, who also hailed from a military background. His father was General William George Mainwaring, C.I.E. Bombay Staff

The five sons of Lieutenant-General J.H. Elkington: standing, l. to r., John Ford; Robert James Goodall; William Ernest Walter; seated, l. to r., George Edward; Charles Jarvie. (Mr R. Elkington)

Corps (1823–1905). Mainwaring Snr. enlisted in 1843, becoming an ensign in the Honourable East India Company's Bombay (European) Regiment, later the 103rd Bombay Fusiliers. He served in the 1848–9 Punjab Campaign, receiving the campaign medal plus two clasps. In 1857 he was awarded the Persia Campaign Medal, again plus two clasps. He served in the Indian Mutiny 1857–8. During 1863 he married Ellen Soulez, daughter of Captain Haines, R.N. A year later, by which time his first son, Arthur Edward, had been born, he was a major, commanding the 30th Native Infantry (Jacob's Rifles) at Jacobabad, Upper Scinde, Bombay Presidency. During the 1879–80 Afghan War he was C.O., Jacob's Rifles, from which he was awarded the campaign medal and mentioned in despatches. 1881 saw the 102nd and 103rd Royal Bombay Fusiliers become the 1st and 2nd battalions Royal Dublin Fusiliers. Mainwaring was promoted to general in 1894.

Officers belonging to the 2nd Battalion, Royal Dublin Fusiliers, 1913. Lieutenant-Colonel Arthur Edward Mainwaring is seated in the centre of the front row. (Private collection)

Another pre-war image of Lt. Col. Mainwaring (seated, second from left), with members of the Royal Dublin Fusiliers Regimental Staff, 1912. (Private collection)

It appears, from the small amount of information available, that Lt.-Col. Arthur Edward Mainwaring spent his early life in India. He left the Royal Military College in 1885, on completion of an Honorary Queen's India Cadetship. That same year he began service in Egypt as a lieutenant in the 2/Royal Dublin Fusiliers. He served in the South African War of 1889–1902, during which he was awarded the Queen's Medal with 3 clasps, and the King's Medal with two clasps. Between 1901 and 1902 he served as a press censor in South Africa. In 1902–03 he was Adjutant of the 3rd Battalion (The Kildare Militia) and later the 2nd Battalion in County Cork. He became C.O. of the 2/Royal Dublin Fusiliers in 1912. That same year he married Clarice Hare, twenty-nine year old widow of Lieutenant Henry Hare, King's Own Yorkshire Light Infantry.

Mainwaring was a prolific writer, the following are some of his works: *Cut Cavendish, or, Whist in a Few Whiffs* (1905); *The ABC of Croquet* (1910); *The Dublin Fusiliers Engagement Book* (1910); *The Whist-Drive Manual* (1912); *Crown and Company* (1912); *A Pocket History of the Royal Dublin Fusiliers* (1912, as editor); *Fishing and Philandering* (1914).

Mainwaring had two brothers, Reginald and Guy, but exhaustive research has discovered nothing about them. It appears they were not military men.

Also on that troop train steaming towards northern France was a senior subaltern who had served in the 1/Royal Warwickshire Regiment since hostilities on the North-West Frontier some six years previously. He was to survive both the First and Second World Wars. Eventually, he was to become Field Marshal Viscount Montgomery of Alamein.

CHAPTER 3

"An Interesting Situation": Le Cateau and the Retreat from Mons, August 1914

It is not necessary for this work to give detailed coverage of all the battles and movements of the various groups forming the B.E.F. Nevertheless, in order to build-up a narrative of events prior to St. Quentin on 27 August, and subsequently the history of the 1/Royal Warwickshire Regiment, it is necessary to highlight certain characters, and the movements and activities in which their regiments were involved. Of course, particularly close attention is given to the elements of the 4th Division/10th Brigade following its arrival at Boulogne.

By 21 August British cavalry patrols were well established in the Mons area. Ben Clouting's 4th Dragoon Guards were east of the town and as they moved further north were informed by locals that there were uhlans (a British term wrongly applied to all German mounted troops) in the vicinity. These were a reconnoitring party from General Alexander von Kluck's First Army, consisting of 320,000 men. An initial attempt to capture four of the enemy as they approached "C" Squadron of the 4th Dragoon Guards failed and the Germans retreated. Another character central to our story, 43-year old Major Tom Bridges, commanding "C" Squadron, was in something of a quandary. His plan to take prisoners was one thing, but was it wise to pursue the retreating Germans, who would soon be passing-on the information about British positions to their approaching comrades? Bridges, who could only guess how close the enemy was, made the decision that 1st Troop, under Captain Hornby, would pursue the Germans. The remaining three troops under Bridges' command followed cautiously some distance behind. After a brief skirmish the enemy received some reinforcements, forcing Hornby and his men to dismount and take cover. Once they had dismounted the Dragoons opened fire, and it was at this point that WWI history was made. Drummer Thomas, not waiting to dismount and seeing the ideal target of a group of Germans, took aim, fired and found his mark, possibly becoming the first member of the B.E.F. to kill one of the enemy. In

A group of French infantry, dressed in their distinctive 1914 uniform of red trousers and blue greatcoat. (London Illustrated News Group)

addition to this the British took three prisoners. Hornby was later awarded the D.S.O. for his part in the action of 21 August.

The British troops arriving on 21 and 22 August in the many villages of the Mons area, and of course in Mons itself, received a warm welcome from the Belgian civilians, who were described by one report as being "wild with joy" at the coming of the soldiers from the "Great Empire. The locals gave the troops so much food that there was hardly any need for the issue of army rations, and the male population, who were predominately miners and industrial workers, helped in digging trenches. There were opportunities for many soldiers to have a bath or wash-down after their long march. Some of the troops made make-shift rods and spent a few hours fishing in the Mons Canal. This surprisingly relaxed air of goodwill offered little evidence of the strained expectation of the rapidly approaching ordeal. Within forty-eight hours the Battle of Mons would begin.

French dragoons, 1914. (London Illustrated News Group)

On 21 August the main elements of the B.E.F. began their advance towards Mons, which lay inside Belgium, close to the border with France. By 23 August the troops were roughly arrayed in a line Binche – Mons – Condé, with the purpose of covering the French Fifth Army along the River Sambre. II Corps, under General Smith-Dorrien, held the line east towards Mons, where it joined the left flank of I Corps under Lieutenant-General Haig. The 5th Cavalry Brigade at Binche had a dual role, to act as a reserve on the British outer flank and to undertake forward reconnaissance.

During mid-morning on Sunday 23 August the Germans began their bombardment of Mons with heavy artillery fire, and by mid-afternoon were enjoying some success. So much so that Haig retired his men to a more advantageous position on higher ground south of Bray. Binche was already occupied by the enemy, forcing the 5th Cavalry Brigade to move south. In close-range encounters the renowned accuracy of the British musketry was enjoying some level of success. Late in the afternoon came the startling news that the Fifth French Army and two reserve divisions were retreating. On this front the Germans had made great progress, marching up to thirty miles a day in hot and oppressive conditions.

In a very short period the overall scenario had changed drastically. As the French retired, pressure on the B.E.F. became considerably heavier. Sir John French had dismissed earlier reports concerning the size and rate of the advance of the German army on all fronts. However, that evening he accepted that a large proportion of the defending troops were, or soon would be, in a very difficult position and gave instructions to make preparations for a withdrawal. Some brigades retired earlier than others, but the general movement of troops began during the early hours of 24 August.

The British press were keen to point out that initially at Mons the Germans employed hardly any more men in the front-line than the B.E.F., and victory had appeared to be within reach of the British. It was claimed that the German riflemen were untrained and considered to be harmless servants of the well-handled machine-guns and effective Krupp artillery. British musketry was superior, but the Germans enjoyed overwhelming odds in terms of manpower.

By the time the retreat began German pressure was severe: around 70,000 British troops with fewer than 300 guns were confronted by an enemy force of some 150,000 men with over 500 pieces of artillery. Withdrawal was the only sensible option.

It was during the events of this day that "the Divine Hand" came to the aid of the B.E.F. It was alleged that some troops had had a vision of the ghosts of St. George and the English bowmen of Agincourt, and that these spectres had helped the B.E.F. in fighting off German attacks. As the story spread, St. George and the archers were replaced by Archangels. Similarly, there were reports that the form was of a white angel, astride a white charger and brandishing a fiery sword. Evidently no one actually came forward as a witness to the event(s), and some commentators accepted that the myth derived from a short story written by Arthur Machen which was not in fact published until September 1914. Perhaps more credibly, others attributed the stories to hallucinations caused by exhaustion and panic. Irrespective of how it began, the legend "proved" to soldier and civilian alike that God was on Britain's side.

Nothing better could have temporarily relieved the pressure and pain of war. Although the B.E.F. had inflicted heavy losses on the enemy, they had suffered heavy casualties themselves. In some units neither officers nor men could not understand the reasoning behind the order to retreat, since they were under the impression that the enemy had suffered a severe defeat.

Sergeant Albert George recalled the scene at St. Ghislain as the 120th Battery, Royal Field Artillery prepared to evacuate on the 23 August:

> We started to retire at 7.00 p.m. with four guns out of six; as we were galloping through villages infantrymen with ammunition and water carts left them and their horses and ran after our wagons so as to get away as soon as possible. The civilians were also shouting and screaming and running in hundreds and little children were crying piteously, it was an awful ending to an awful day. We thought of England and of what our friends were doing and we envied them.[1]

Due to poor communications Smith-Dorrien's retreat was delayed. Pinned down his corps experienced great difficulty in implementing the retirement order without risking annihilation. His troops were under very heavy shelling from the German artillery, and ceaseless fire from the advancing infantry. Haig's retreating troops had an easier withdrawal, and reached a line Bavay – Maubeuge in the early evening. At the end of the Battle of Mons the total British casualties numbered some 1,600 men. Veterans of the war in South Africa admitted that Spion Kop and Modder River were of little significance compared to the punishment taken by the B.E.F. at Mons.

There were scenes of disorder in several areas as 24 August dawned, promising to be another sweltering and tiring day. Many fatigued and hungry men were rapidly loosing contact with their regiments and the main bodies of retiring troops. Communications became worse and staff officers lost touch with the French. Stragglers were everywhere and, amongst the general chaos, retreating gun limbers thundered past at speed. Under such exhausting and stressful conditions it is no wonder that in many cases the reservists discarded clothing, equipment and even boots to make retreat easier. The success of the retreat was ensured by the rearguard role played by several cavalry and infantry regiments, although a high price was paid in casualties. Wherever a semblance of organisation was maintained units experienced an easier time, the Army Service Corps siting food dumps for men and animals along some roadsides.

On the same day – 24 August – the 4th Dragoon Guards and 9th Lancers were involved in a well-documented cavalry action at Audregnies whilst carrying out rearguard duties. Their orders were to cover the retirement of the 5th Division under Sir Charles Fergusson. About midday the order was given to mount up and prepare to face the advancing German 8th Division. As the German infantry advanced, the 9th Lancers and some of the 18th Hussars prepared to charge. Support was provided by the 1st and 2nd troops of "B" Squadron, 4th Dragoon Guards. Soon troops of "C" Squadron, under Major Tom Bridges, were also in action supporting "B"

German cavalry in Belgium, August 1914. (London Illustrated News Group)

Squadron. The basic objective was to attack eleven artillery guns situated on a hillside over a mile away, which were seriously inconveniencing 5th Division. The troops quickly came under heavy shellfire, and were forced to withdraw without being able to "come to grips" with the enemy. On "Shrapnel Monday", as 24 August became known, the 4th Dragoon Guards lost 81 officers and men.

During the action Major Bridges had his horse shot from under him and whilst on the ground he was kicked in the face by another horse. He was found covered in dust, blood streaming down his face. Although injured, Bridges continued to issue orders, at one point stating "They won't hurt me, I'm an officer!" He then passed out.

Bridges was taken to a nearby cottage which was being used as a first-aid post, where his fractured cheek-bone was dressed. As he lay there he became aware of bullets striking the walls of the building. With assistance he was able to look through a fan-light and was faced with the sight of a large group of German infantry advancing towards him. He decided to leave through the back door of the cottage at once, and soon came across a wounded horse which fortunately could stand his weight. With German bullets all around him, he recalled the sensation of being "… sole target, it seemed, for a whole German army corps." Luck was still on his side and he reached cover, by which time his horse was completely exhausted. In an act of mercy, Bridges shot it.

For a brief while Bridges was in the company of a party of retreating lancers, but as he now had no mount he had no alternative but to proceed on foot. Instead of the cavalry coming over the hill in true *Boys' Own* fashion, his day was saved by a cavalryman driving up in a blue and white

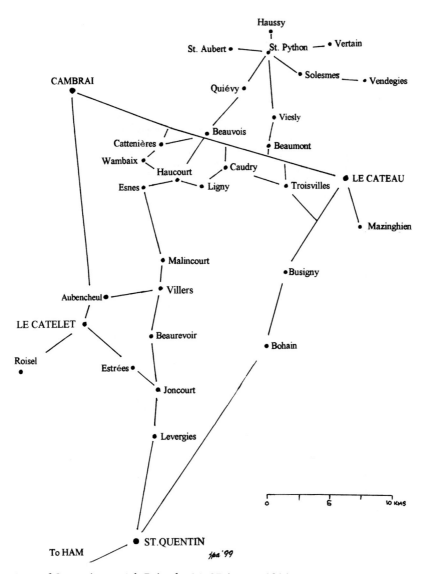

Area of Operations, 10th Brigade, 24–27 August 1914.

sports car. He was then taken to a dressing-station, where he was diag-
nosed as having suffered a splintered cheek-bone and slight concussion.
Two old women gave him a hot drink and found him a straw bed in a
granary out-house.

During the night Bridges was awakened by the clatter of horses' hooves
and, on investigation, saw that a party of German uhlans had ridden into
the yard. This time he did not "hot-foot" it, but went back to bed and slept

until daylight. Over the next two days he joined up with numerous stragglers, and in the end managed to put together a party of nearly 150 cavalry, largely made up of 5th Lancers and 4th Dragoon Guards. Such were the adventures of a soldier involved in the retreat from Mons.

During the mid-morning of Monday 24 August, the trains carrying the 4th Division, which included the 1/R. Warwicks and 2/R. Dublin Fusiliers, arrived at Le Cateau, where they immediately detrained, to be followed later by the 2/Seaforths and 1/Royal Irish Fusiliers. Their orders were to move north and take rearguard action to cover the retiring 3rd and 5th divisions. That same afternoon 10th Brigade marched a few miles northwest and bivouacked in the Inchy/Beaumont vicinity, where Brigadier-General Haldane's headquarters was conveniently set up in the local brewery. Lieutenant Montgomery records that "C" Company undertook out-post duty.

As the intention was to march further north in the early hours of the following morning, Captain N.P. Clarke of the 2/R. Dublin Fusiliers was instructed to investigate the area ahead. On his return he was informed that orders had been received to quit Beaumont at 2 a.m. (25 August), and march north through Viesly and on towards St. Python. By 6 a.m. 10th Brigade were only a short distance from St. Python, and breakfast was taken. An hour later heavy gunfire was heard coming from the direction of Valenciennes to the north.

Haldane despatched Lieutenant C.W. Wasey of the 1/R. Warwickshire to reconnoitre the forward position and, although there is no diary record of what he discovered, orders were given for the 10th Brigade to fall back at 8 a.m. Trenches were dug and firing positions set up in the area of Fontaine-âu-Terte Farm. The 1/R. Warwickshire was issued with iron rations in addition to their daily rations. Small numbers of retreating French and British troops moved through this position, but there was no sign of the main body of the retreating II Corps.

Throughout the day observers kept watch on the advancing Germans and retreating French and British as they gradually moved towards the waiting 10th Brigade. Late in the afternoon, during two hours of torrential rain, the farm area was subjected to heavy shelling which resulted in a small number of casualties. As withdrawing Allied troops began to filter through the lines, intelligence was gathered concerning the size of the advancing enemy. The outlook was grim. The main elements of the 4th Division were deployed as follows – 11th Brigade had taken a position to the rear of the 10th, at Briastre, and the 12th was to the rear of them at Viesly. The 19th Brigade was to the north of the 10th, at Haussy. The 2/R. Dublin war diary and Mainwaring's statement show that their position was in advance of the main force by some 200 yards, and that at 9 p.m. two

Uhlans were seen in front of the British lines and promptly shot. Orders were given for the 4th Division to retire when all of the 3rd Division and 19th Brigade had moved through. Between 9 p.m. and midnight the 12th, 11th and 10th brigades began to retire, in that order. 4th Division's headquarters was to be set up at Haucourt, and the 10th Brigade set off towards that destination via Beauvois.

The general position of the B.E.F.'s 3rd, 4th and 5th divisions in the early hours of 26 August was as follows. The 2nd and 5th German cavalry corps were rapidly advancing towards Esnes, Haucourt, Ligny and Caudry using the road between Cambrai and Le Cateau as a base line. They were faced by the British 7th, 11th and 12th infantry brigades. The 8th, 9th, 13th and 15th brigades were spread out west to east across a front some six miles wide, almost from Caudry to Le Cateau, facing the German 7th and 8th divisions. The 9th Infantry Brigade was positioned to the rear, between Ligny and Bertry. On the far right flank the 14th Brigade, supported by elements of the 19th, was positioned a little south-west of Le Cateau, some thirty miles south of Mons.

The Germans advanced on Le Cateau from the north-east and the west, the latter movement virtually cutting off a southerly retreat for the 14th Brigade. The engagement, which extended over a wide front, was fought in heavy rain. The potato and turnip fields where the action took place were soon turned into a quagmire.

The 14th Brigade was in an impossible position. Because a rearguard action was still vital in order to protect the rest of the retreating B.E.F., Smith-Dorrien made the decision to turn and fight. With the enemy so close the only way he could withdraw was to make a stopping blow which, if heavy enough, would slow the enemy down, thus enabling the British to withdraw unmolested. There was no hope of summoning help from Haig's I Corps, who were on the opposite side of the River Oise. Fortunately, at this stage only three German infantry divisions with their supporting artillery were in direct contact with II Corps.

The Battle of Le Cateau commenced as soon as it was light, the enemy advance being held for a considerable time. As a consequence of this action the British were able to continue their withdrawal later in the afternoon. Both sides suffered heavy casualties. The British defences were described by some observers as very shallow trenches, in fact these were mere "scrapes", often less than one foot deep. There was no opportunity to entrench the position in the accepted sense of the word. The B.E.F. lost over 7,000 men. However this commendable action did allow large numbers of men to continue the retreat.

The following is one of several observations and comments made concerning Le Cateau:

Old wall at Harcourt, showing loopholes made by men of the 1st Battalion during the Battle of Le Cateau. (Royal Warwickshire Rgt. Museum)

Cottage at Harcourt, where British wounded were taken during the Battle of Le Cateau. (Royal Warwickshire Rgt. Museum)

Lt. Gen. Sir Horace Smith-Dorrien, commander of II Corps and of British forces at the Battle of Le Cateau, 26 August 1914. (Private collection)

I saw last Wednesday something I thought I should never see – British infantry bolting out of their trenches like rabbits![4]

This comment was not intended as a criticism of the men in those miserable little trenches, but as a reflection upon the impossible conditions under which they had been expected to fight.

It is also worthwhile considering the clear-cut comments made by veteran Harry Maskill relating to his first confrontation with the enemy. The men believed that when the Germans advanced and became aware of the "British Khaki" they would turn on their heels and run. The British troops became so confident that they stood up to taunt the Germans. But they got a surprise, as Harry delicately put it: "We got a shock, the buggers still came on and didn't stop." This caused much disquiet amongst the men, many of whom left their posts and began a rapid and scattered withdrawal, before being quickly driven back to their positions by their officers. Nevertheless, the incident must have been a psychological shock to the British.

The action and retreat from Le Cateau placed even more pressure on the strained and fatigued B.E.F. The physical and mental pressure soon began to tell on large numbers of men:

> We could see ammunition wagons trying to replenish getting about half-way to the gun, then a couple of shells would burst blowing the drivers and horses to smithereens, it was a terrible sight, but the last two days made us used to it. About 3.30 p.m. the Germans were advancing upon us so rapidly that the General Staff could see it was useless trying to stop the furious advance, so a General Retirement was ordered and it was every man for himself. The retirement was a scandalous sight in the History of Britain, but it will never be published. In our hurry to get away guns, wagons, horses and wounded men were left to the victorious Germans and even our *British Infantrymen* were throwing away their rifles, ammunition, equipment and running *like hell* for their lives. Mind you, not one of the infantrymen was doing this but the whole of the British Expeditionary Force that took part in the battle on that fatal Wednesday, 26 Aug. at Le Cateau." [italics in original passage][5]

As this part of the retreat was taking place it was also observed by an officer:

> I was dog-tired, half asleep and dreaming at times; the reality of the event became obscured; only the physical discomfort was apparent and uppermost in my mind; I felt that we would soon have to chuck it in and go home to tea. There was a general absence of orders; many officers and detachments asked us the way to their units; we did not know, and the only answer we got from the staff officers we encountered was 'Get On', so we followed the rest."[6]

At the same time as the action at Le Cateau was taking place, there was an interesting incident in the Haucourt/Ligny area involving the 10th Brigade. It should be remembered that unlike others, the 4th Division, of which the 10th Brigade was part, was seriously unsupported. While it did retain its own artillery it was under a considerable disadvantage because there was no facility for observing the movements of the advancing enemy. This was due to the fact that it had no supporting cavalry or signals troops, and communications were seriously lacking. Later, the absence of field ambulances would prove to be another serious omission, as wounded were left to be taken prisoner.

Times vary concerning when the action began, but between 5 a.m. and 6.30 a.m. Lt. Col. Elkington of the 1/Royal Warwicks recorded that:

... heavy artillery fire was heard and wagons were seen rushing down a hill opposite us and to our left, many of them being overturned. I immediately got the Battalion together, two companies I formed up in a ditch by the side of the road just in front of us, the remaining two companies in the rear. I looked at the situation and decided that the best way to relieve the pressure was to make a counter-attack up the hill. This I did with my Battalion, but once having gained the top of the hill we came under heavy Maxim and Shrapnel fire and I considered it necessary to fall back. I fell back slowly to my old position and entrenched.[7]

Lt.-Col. Elkington and his men remained entrenched in that position for the rest of the day.

The war diary of the 1/R. Warwicks records that at 5.15 a.m.:

... heavy Maxim fire opened on the King's Own and Lancashire Fusiliers on a ridge 800 yds to our front N of us. The Regiment rapidly got extended and took up a fore position; enemy occupied the ridge and opened Maxim and 9mm fire. At 7 a.m. the forward line in road under Major W.C. Christie attacked the ridge and reached the top, but were, owing to heavy 9mm and Maxim fire unable to hold the position, and withdrew in good order with a company of the King's Own to the road, with a loss of 7 officers wounded and 40 men killed or missing."[8]

Captain N.P. Clarke, commander of "A" Company, 2/R. Dublin Fusiliers, recalled being told by a staff officer belonging to the 11th Brigade:

'They are very hard pushed on that ridge, and my brigadier wants support. The right of your brigade are going to reinforce. Can't you take up your company?' Telling him I would see if I could, I hurried across to the second-in-command and gave him the message. He gave me leave to take up my company, and said that the other front company would come forward to hold my trenches and give us covering fire in case we needed it.... The enemy got over the ridge before we could reach it, and drove our advanced troops off. So the company was ordered to retire, and came back to its original position with the loss of two wounded.[9]

There are several accounts of this particular skirmish. Mainwaring records it in his statement, as does Lieutenant B.L. Montgomery in his *Memoirs*:

Our battalion was deployed in two lines; my company and one other were forward, with the remaining two companies out of sight some hundred yards to the rear. The C.O. (Lt.-Col. Elkington) galloped up to us forward companies and shouted to us to attack the enemy on the forward hill at once. This was the only order; there was no reconnaissance, no plan, no covering fire.[10]

Peter Scott comments that as Montgomery was in "C" Company he would not have been in the first wave of attack, which was made by "A" and "B" companies. However, 2nd Lieutenant C.E. Dalton of "C" Company recorded in his diary that "We were immediately told off to our places and we commenced to advance in two lines, "A" and half "C" company in the first line and the rest of "C" in the second. I was in the second line."[11] The first line advanced to within 100 yards of the top but quickly retired as casualties became heavy. Dalton and his line got within 200 yards of the top before retiring. Thus, according to this account, Montgomery may indeed have been in the first wave.

In his book *Monty, The Making of a General,* Nigel Hamilton makes Elkington directly responsible for the deaths of the men concerned, claiming that he abandoned the others. Bearing in mind the many differing accounts of this incident it appears to this writer that the latter claim by Nigel Hamilton is not true, and that Elkington's statement explains the situation:

> We stayed in these trenches all day exposed to heavy shrapnel fire during parts of the day. Towards evening we commenced to fall back, each trench being held as long as possible, the battalion falling back in batches, we then got separated. I fell back with the men in a sunken road towards the village of Ligny where a better position could be obtained and from there after dark we followed the road. I did not know in which direction we were supposed to retire. During the retirement in the dark it was impossible to keep the same men together for any length of time, there being so many stragglers and the men were continually falling out from exhaustion.[12]

The features common to all reports are that those of utter chaos, the troops being hungry and exhausted, and the darkness of the night. It was not only this particular group who experienced troop separation; it was happening across the front, from Le Cateau to Cambrai. Although Montgomery did comment on Elkington's behaviour, severe criticism need not be assumed. Indeed, Montgomery's diary, written at the time, makes no such entry regarding Elkington, and comments only appear to have come to light some forty years later in Montgomery's *Memoirs.* As will be seen later, Montgomery and Elkington remained good friends for the rest of the latter's life. Consequently, it is difficult to agree with Nigel Hamilton's direct indictment. One other point worth considering is made by Dalton.

"That incomparable army." British infantry, August 1914. (Private collection)

British troops resting in a village, 1914. During the retreat from Mons the men had to march for days with barely a few hours sleep. (London Illustrated News Group)

"It was a very gallant attempt, and carried out in accordance with the teaching of those days, to reinforce where things had gone wrong."[13] In fact, this particular incident and the action taken were similar to a previous one which had occurred on the North-West Frontier in 1908.

As the war diary records, the 4th Division, especially 10th Brigade, was now breaking up. The Warwicks were split into three parts, and in the chaos it was impossible for many of the groups to receive orders of any sort.

In mid-afternoon on 26 August, "A" Company was withdrawn to escort guns. The artillery was apparently 127 Battery, R.F.A. This assignment was successfully carried out. Although there was heavy enemy fire during the withdrawal, there were few casualties.

Lieutenant-Colonel Elkington stated that without orders of any sort, he decided to withdraw south. No doubt he fully expected to join up with the rest of the division. At about 2 a.m. (27 August), he managed to collect another 60 of his battalion, by which time it was a full day since his men had eaten. His immediate aim was to make for St. Quentin, where he hoped that food would be obtainable and, as the town was a railway junction, there might be the possibility of being able to board a train.

Major A.J. Poole, Elkington's second-in-command, was also in the position of trying to locate someone who could give him orders and apprise him of the overall "picture". Poole led another group of the battalion, which may have included Major W.C. Christie, but which certainly included Lt. B.L. Montgomery, together with two companies of the Royal Irish Fusiliers, and men from both the Dublin Fusiliers and King's Own. To his surprise he discovered that the rest of the 4th Division were nowhere to be seen. By this time the enemy had occupied Haucourt and probably Ligny as well. Poole decided to march to Seligny, but that route was dangerous. As there was an increasing German presence in the area he considered the only feasible alternative was to try to avoid the main roads. So it was agreed that his best chance was to take a bridlepath between Cattenières and Caullery. To add to his problems, this track was not particularly well-marked on the map. As there was no transport to move the wounded many were left behind. However Major Shewan, Dublin Fusiliers, did manage to utilise one of his machine-gun wagons to move some of the wounded.

During its night-time movement along the bridlepath Poole's party was inadvertently broken up. This time Major Shewan and his men became detached from the main party. Shewan's group, which included only a handful of men from the Royal Warwicks, eventually made its way north, unlike the rest of the 10th Brigade. During their march they were involved in a serious confrontation with the enemy which greatly reduced their numbers from almost 400 men to just 30 other ranks led by 2 officers. 1 officer and over 40 men were killed or died from wounds. The vast majority of the remainder were captured.

After the incident on the ridge Lt.-Col. Mainwaring found himself in a similar position to Lt.-Col. Elkington:

> ... since it was evident that there was no one left in front of us, but the disabled battery, I wrote a note to General Snow, explaining the situation, and asking for instructions. The Adjutant, Captain R.M.

Watson, volunteered to carry it. In about 20 minutes he was back, and told me that General Snow and the Divisional Staff had gone, that no one remained to give an order of any sort, and that we were left alone. On this information I decided to retire, and, passing the word to everyone to get ready, we, at about 5.30 p.m. retired through the village."[Caullery][14]

By dusk this party had reached Malincourt, (Mainwaring refers to this as Malencieux), where the men were able to rest:

I then went to try and find somebody to give an order or direction of some sort. I met Major Daniell, Acting-Brigade Major of our Brigade. He expressed great joy at seeing me, asked how many men I had, attached 60 of the Warwicks under a Special Reserve Lieutenant to me and promised to send me orders."[15]

Still without sleep, Mainwaring awaited instructions which never came. After consulting his map he decided to march on Ronssoy. Mainwaring refers to this as Rossay. He woke the men and by midnight they were marching south. Three hours later, having taken the wrong road, they reached Beaurevoir, where Mainwaring oversaw the bedding down of the men in barns, but again stayed up himself. "The strain was cruel, but I could trust no one else."

At 5 a.m. on 27 August, Mainwaring and his men continued their march south towards Estrées, with the new aim of marching to St. Quentin via Joncourt and Levergies. At 8 a.m. he met Lt. Colonel Elkington with, according to Mainwaring, 100 men of his regiment. They combined their forces and, as the senior of the two lieutenant-colonels, Elkington assumed command. Together, they continued their march towards St. Quentin.

Before discussing the major events of 27 August at St. Quentin, it is necessary to clear up the situation of the other two groups of the 1/Royal Warwickshire Regiment.

The party led by Major Poole with "A" Company, seems to have experienced a far easier retreat. By 27 August – along with the main body of the 10th Brigade – "A" Company had retreated through Selvigny, Gouy and Haucourt, during which time their strength was augmented by a group of men from the 2/Royal Dublin Fusiliers. The march south continued, the men crossing the Somme at Voyennes before proceeding to Ham. At about midnight on 28 August they reached Bussy. The next day there was a welcome rest for all concerned, the march continuing at 9 p.m. During the night the party arrived at Pont l'Eveque, via Noyon, and during the following day, 30 August, they crossed the Aisne and arrived at

Genancourt. The following day the men marched to Verberie, the Foret de Compiègne providing welcoming shade.

The men were in very poor condition as the march south continued. It was fortunate that the enemy were never encountered. Nevertheless, the march was not without its worries. On 1 September a diversion was ordered, whereby the composite battalion moved to St. Vaast with orders to lend assistance to the cavalry and guns which had been in action at Nery. By the time the troops arrived the activity was all but over. The 10th Brigade occupied Nery for a while, but as no opposition was experienced it moved on to Baron. The journey continued unhindered, and the brigade crossed the Marne at Lagny, arriving at Brie-Compte-Robert during the evening of 5 September.

It will be recalled that Major Poole, together with a party of around 300 men, had decided to move south from the Haucourt area. Captain C.T. Tomes, who was in Poole's party, describes the march:

> It was obvious that the enemy were close around us, and strict silence was enforced as we moved up the field track by the Iris stream through the pitch black night. The flames of houses on fire in Ligny and Haucourt only seemed to accentuate the darkness. It seemed an interminable march, the men were dead weary, and many, falling asleep as they moved, pitched forward into the man in front and fell with a clatter to the ground. Once a rifle went off and we thought it was the forerunner of a fusillade, but nothing happened.[16]

Tomes recalled how the fatigue and strain manifested itself in curious delusions, on one occasion Tomes himself swore that he saw a group of Germans advancing towards them:

> Others thought they were walking up and down hills and yet others have said they saw squadrons of German cavalry at full gallop around us. In view of our experience that night, the legend of the Angel of Mons is easy to understand.[17]

Under such conditions the march to Selvigny seemed to be a distance of ten miles, when in fact it was only two. The men were past caring on their arrival at about 2 a.m. on 27 August, and quickly fell into deep sleep.

Two hours later Major Poole roused the men, insisting that every effort must be made to rejoin the battalion. Reluctantly, the stiff and weary soldiers resumed their march along France's notorious and never ending pavé roads. Dawn indicated another hot and oppressive day, and the heat soon became insufferable. In order to keep pace under such demanding conditions several of the footsore men discarded their packs. It must have been seen as a god-send when a small hand-cart was found, which was

Capt. C.T. Tomes, from a postwar photograph. (Private collection)

utilised to carry the group's two machine-guns which, up to that time, had been carried by hand.

Amazingly, parties of uhlans were observed nearby – often within 1000 yards – but there was never any confrontation. During the late morning a column of infantry was seen near Gouy, and it was anticipated that they were other comrades from the 10th Brigade. Unfortunately, they turned out to be Germans. Tomes commented:

> We were now in an interesting situation. Enemy cavalry patrols all round us, and German infantry within a mile to our right, and ourselves with but little ammunition, dead weary and in no condition to put up a fight. However, by some extraordinary chance nothing happened. The German battalion moved away and the cavalry vanished and so we stumbled on.[18]

Belgian refugees, who left their ruined homes by the thousand, struggled to find somewhere safe. (London Illustrated News Group)

By early afternoon the men were so exhausted that it was decided not to further exert them by pushing the machine-gun cart. The guns were buried and left behind. Realising that it was of some urgency that the men had food and rest, Major Poole and his party took shelter in a wood near Ronssoy. After posting sentries, what little food that remained was eaten and the men spent two hours taking a welcome sleep. But even in this position danger lurked nearby, and one man who left the wood without orders to search for water was taken prisoner by German cavalry.

27 August ended with further marching in the direction of Jeancourt via Hargicourt, during which time Major Poole was luckily able to purchase a little bread. However, because there were so many Germans in the area, it was impossible to replenish the canteens, although every effort was made to do so.

In retrospect, Captain Tome's impression of that day was of having been in a trance, of:

> ... the look of misery on the faces of the few people about, and near one village a group of women were on their knees by a crucifix; the generosity with which the inhabitants brought out all they had to feed us, although, mind you, we were retreating and leaving them to their fate; pathetic small parties of refugees with all their portable household goods in bundles, hand-carts or perambulators and their children being hurried along in panic and fear. Poor souls, they had not a hope to escape. It was certainly the worse aspect of war.[19]

Although the war had only been underway a very short time, the scenes Tomes describes were common throughout northern France.

By the early hours of 28 August the party had reached the outskirts of Jeancourt, where majors Poole and Christie optimistically went to try to arrange a train, but without success. Distant rifle fire indicated that the enemy was not far behind, and the tedious march was resumed. The men's hunger was partially relieved upon arrival at Bernes, where they obtained a little bread and coffee, and were able to replenish their canteens from the village well. During the break at Bernes a French staff officer arrived and informed them that their best route was to make for Peronne via Hancourt. Poole and his men left at 8 a.m., which must have been in the nick of time because, soon after, a French peasant informed them that the enemy was already in Bernes.

Captain H.C. Hart says of the continuing journey:

We were now moving across great open downs, and very soon saw on our right, at some distance, cavalry scouts, whom we recognised as French, and the word was passed down the column, but unfortunately some men in the rearguard opened fire on one of the patrols, without, however, doing any harm. Presently a single horseman rode into the head of the column, and said that they thought we were the enemy, and wanted to know where we were going.

By this time French scouts had crossed our front, and a little farther on there came into sight columns of cavalry, looking most picturesque in their various coloured uniforms, flowing horse-hair plumes and steel cuirasses, and all moving towards us. I don't know how many thousands there were; a truly grand sight.[20]

General Sordet, the French commander, requested that Poole and his men stayed to offer "moral support", which was ludicrous considering the condition of the men. In any case, the British could afford no delays in trying to catch up with the rest of their division. Hart continues:

Meanwhile the cavalry had been manoeuvring all round us, and as we lay on the roadside three or four enemy shrapnel shells passed over the road and burst just beyond. We were in the curious position of being between two hostile cavalry forces in action, and there can be little doubt that the presence of this French cavalry saved us from being taken prisoners.[21]

The march continued under scorching sun, during which time the men drank most of their water.

It was at this point that an event occurred which must have strengthened any beliefs they had in the Angel of Mons. The troops encountered a peasant pushing a barrow, on which was placed a full hind-quarter of beef. Evidently, a group of withdrawing soldiers had been issued rations at the roadside, leaving behind a quantity of beef and biscuits. It was common practice for troops to leave food at the side of the road for comrades who were known to be behind them, and this particular drop was taken as an indication that Poole and his men were directly following other troops from the B.E.F. However, the men were to be sadly disappointed in their expectations of a tasty and very welcome slice of beef with a few biscuits. Hart explains:

> We did not halt, but as I went along I picked up as many biscuits as I could and handed them to the men, who gladly accepted them, and to their credit be it said not a man broke the ranks to help himself, in spite of the fact that they had been so many hours with so little to eat, and many must have been very hungry.[22]

No doubt the officers were very popular! This rigid discipline was further maintained on the journey, as Hart relates:

> Later we struck across country to the Peronne – Ham main road, and lest the temptation of an orchard through which we passed in single-file might be too great and be conducive to straggling, I remained behind to see everyone got through.[23]

As the blistering day wore on the men received some reward when they achieved their goal. Some time around 2 a.m., in the area of Matigny, they saw the very welcome sight of British infantrymen digging trenches. The marching men responded immediately with a renewed spring in their step. A short break followed, which enabled stragglers to catch up. That afternoon the troops crossed the Somme at Voyennes, luckily just prior to the town's bridges being demolished. As the march continued there then followed an ironic situation – bearing in mind the beef and orchard episodes – which must have revived the men's, but not the officers', faith in human nature. In his efforts to save a wagon some conscientious character, perhaps even with a sense of humour, had discarded its entire contents, namely, the kit of the battalion's officers. To be on the safe side, he then set fire to the lot!

Following a march of over 50 miles in just 44 hours things began to improve. After receiving food and drink at a farm, the men arrived at Nesle during the early evening. Later, Major Poole and his men climbed into a column of lorries and moved off to Noyon and Compiègne. By 30 August they were installed in a rest camp, where over 3,000 men from many regiments – including Lt. Colonel Elkington's party – had gathered.

Part II – Injustice?

CHAPTER 4

A Tale of Two Colonels: St. Quentin, 27 August 1914, and Aftermath

Following his stand at Le Cateau, General Smith-Dorrien moved south to St. Quentin late in the day of 26 August, expecting to meet Sir John French. As the town was a railhead, he anticipated that trains could be procured to carry his men. Smith-Dorrien makes an interesting observation about his journey towards St. Quentin, recalling:

> … a discreditable panic which occurred in an infantry column. At about 9.30 o'clock that evening when motoring from D'Estrées to St. Quentin, I saw for miles, by the light of my head-lamps, boxes of ammunition thrown about on both sides of the road, and I actually found the commander and the column just clearing out of St. Quentin empty. The O.C. told me that shots had been fired as he came along the road, he believed from uhlans, and to save his men and horses he ordered all the ammunition to be thrown away and had galloped away, and seemed very proud of it. From enquiries I made I came to the conclusion that it was extremely doubtful if there had been any enemy patrols there at all. The officer was tried by court-martial and dismissed from the service, but immediately enlisted, and, I heard, proved himself to be one of our bravest soldiers.[1]

This state of affairs also shocked Lt.-Col. Elkington, who noted the fact when he came across the same abandoned ammunition a few hours later:

> Along the road we came across the discarded ammunition of some British artillery which extended for at least a mile, this did not have a cheering effect on our men who were tired and worn out.[2]

This was one of many instances in the first few months of the war when regular officers were considered unsuitable for service and dismissed. In fact, by the end of the year, the numbers of regular officers rapidly declined due to dismissals and a very high casualty rate.

After he arrived at St. Quentin, Smith-Dorrien held a meeting with the Director of Railways, who confirmed that might be able to allocate some trains, but not without the permission of the Quartermaster General, who by this time, along with French and his headquarters, had moved further south to Noyon. Lacking no determination, Smith-Dorrien drove to Noyon, where approval was given for all possible trains to be commandeered in order to move the mass of exhausted men, including many wounded. A number of staff officers were also assigned to return with Smith-Dorrien to St. Quentin to assist in this operation.

When Smith-Dorrien and his party returned St. Quentin they were confronted by a disorganised conglomeration of men from several regiments, including some officers. All were subdued and were, as one staff officer put it "… worn out in mind as well as body and hardly capable of taking in the simplest instruction." The sorting-out began, the wounded entraining first. Other transport besides the trains was utilised to take out as many men as possible. Nevertheless, troops remained, as there was still a steady flow of troops entering the town.

Elkington and Mainwaring arrived on the outskirts of St. Quentin sometime around midday, the former setting up outposts, as two German cavalry patrols had been seen. He commented:

> I sent Col. [Mainwaring] into St. Quentin in order that he might make arrangements for feeding the men and getting train accommodation.[3]

Mainwaring related:

> Colonel Elkington sent me on to see what could be done, and I met General Smith-Dorrien in the town, and told him the men were done. He told me it was a marvel that any of us had got away, that we had been up against four-and-a-half to five German army corps, and that he would give us a train to Noyan [Noyon] if I could get one and that if I could not he advised me to march some five miles further on to Ham, and join the 3rd Division. A member of his Staff reminded him that it had marched from there, when he said, 'There are some details there, you had better try and join them.' I said I doubted if our men could do it, and that I would at all events try for a train first. I sent this information to Colonel Elkington.[4]

Elkington received the note, and as suggested, marched into the town to meet Mainwaring at the railway station; this was at about 2 p.m. According to Mainwaring, on his arrival it was discovered that the station staff had abandoned their posts and fled, with the obvious result that there would now be no trains. Upon meeting the colonels agreed to make a determined effort to persuade the men to march to Ham. At this stage General Hobbs arrived by car and advised them that if they approached the mayor he may be able to procure a train and certainly would be able to find some food for their men.

In the public library at St. Quentin there is a useful book by Elie Fleury, *Les Soixante-quatre Séances du Conseil Municipal, St. Quentin Pendant L'Occupation 1914–1917*. This gives full transcriptions of council meetings, and although there are no specific references to the issue relating to the "two colonels", there are some interesting notes relating to contemporary events. For instance, the man who was mayor on 27 August had been the deputy-mayor less than twenty-four hours previously. At 8 p.m., 26 August, an emergency meeting had been convened, since it appeared that within a few hours St. Quentin would be occupied by the Germans. Of a total of 33 councillors, only 17 were prepared to attend the meeting in order to look after the interests of the local people, the rest, it appears, preferred to ignore the imminent danger.

The mayor, Dr Joseph Muller, his deputy Arthur Gibert, and a second deputy, Charles Dessin, were the senior members of those present. Dr Muller delivered an alarming piece of information to the meeting. He had been told by General French that the Germans were systematically shooting mayors originating from Alsace or Lorraine. This was confirmed by the sub-préfet of the State General, M. Vittini, although he later denied having said this. Muller was from Alsace, and Dessin originated from Lorraine. It was the consensus of the meeting that both men should leave the town immediately. They both offered to remain at their posts, and if necessary sacrifice their lives. However, they eventually complied with the advice of the meeting. It is stated that this advice was given to Muller and Dessin "as personal friends", to which a certain amount of ambiguity was added by the words of a M. Dony, "This is an affair between their consciences and themselves." Another councillor added, "We'll manage without them!"

M.Gibert, the deputy, expressed his concern about the urgency with which the position of mayor had been thrust upon him and asked, "But what am I supposed to do?" Dr Muller declined to answer, and reported that he had already tendered his resignation to Préfet Vittini. Thus, deputy Arthur Gibert was installed as mayor of St. Quentin. Next day the meeting was reconvened, and an official minute recorded the previous night's business, before proceeding to discuss the more pressing matter of the German advance.

Muller and Dessin went to Paris, going to great lengths upon their arrival to ensure that the justification for their departure was kept on an official basis. They met with the Minister for the Interior and Préfet de

L'Aisne, who accepted their resignations without criticism. Considering the turn of events at St. Quentin Town Hall during the morning of 27 August 1914, it is not surprising that events unfolded later in the day the way they did.

Accompanied by an interpreter, Mainwaring visited the "new" mayor, who informed him that there was no chance of boarding a train, but that food would be provided. According to Elkington the food arrived at about 3 p.m.

During Mainwaring's meeting with the mayor he says:

> At this moment a breathless messenger handed a note to the mayor, who, on reading it, became very excited, throwing up his hands, and exclaiming it was the end, all was lost. The room was full of excited Frenchmen, so I told my interpreter to tell me exactly what was in the note. He said that the town was surrounded, all exits blocked, that people in motor-cars were coming back, unable to get through, and that the mayor was waiting to surrender the town. I was leaving the room when the mayor caught sight of me and said, 'Ah! Your troops will spoil all. The Germans will shell the town now, and all the women and children will be killed,' or words to that effect. I said, 'You need not fear; if we cannot get our men away, we will not fight in the town. I must go and see my commanding officer.' We neither of us doubted the authenticity of the mayor's statement, for we had ourselves seen shells bursting only some seven or eight miles north of St. Quentin, more than three hours before.[5]

Mainwaring returned to the station to discuss the matter with Elkington. According to Elkington, the two officers tried to arrange a train, but found all the offices deserted. However, here we find a minor discrepancy. According to Mainwaring he alone tried to do this earlier in the afternoon. After further consultation, Elkington told Mainwaring:

> … to go and pacify the mayor and tell him that I would not fight in the town but our men must have rest and food. There was never the slightest intention in either of our minds to surrender to anyone nor did we do so, we fully intended to leave St. Quentin and continue our march on Noyon directly the men were rested. If surprised by the Germans my intention was to fight at the back of the station and not in the streets so as to save unnecessary slaughter of the women and children of whom the town was full.[6]

At this point reports become confused, but the gist of both accounts is that at some point both colonels told their respective soldiers that they had

The Gare du Nord, St Quentin, from a pre-war photograph. (Private collection)

A view of the interior of the Gare du Nord, taken during the German occupation, 1918. (Private collection)

two effective options – to march to Noyon, or to remain at St. Quentin and be taken prisoner. The soldiers of both officers refused to move.

Mainwaring stated:

> The fact is the men could do no more for the time being. Their limit of endurance was reached. I considered it my duty to protect these men, who so nobly had done theirs. I still consider that it was so, and my conscience is clear. (Their conduct was admitted by the Court, by mouth of the President).[7]

Both officers were now in the same position, their men refusing to move. The accounts now begin to differ.

According to Mainwaring:

> He [Col. Elkington] therefore directed me to sign a surrender, and while I was doing so he disarmed the men, putting their rifles and ammunition in one railway shed, and them in another. As I rode back to the mayor I saw terrified women dragging their children indoors, and everyone putting up their shutters.
>
> Everyone but ourselves and a few stragglers had fled, and as I rode up, my brain became obsessed with the one idea that our duty was to save nameless horrors overtaking these poor defenceless creatures. It was Thursday afternoon; I had not slept since Monday morning. I had seen villages burning and others shelled. I could think of nothing else, and that is the whole truth, to which I have sworn on oath. The consequence was that when I came to sign the paper I felt my duty was to make our purpose quite clear. I wrote the names of the officers and the strength of the party, and I said that as the men were unable to march away we would 'surrender unconditionally.' Even as I wrote the words I paused; but the state of my brain was such that I felt if I argued as to conditions it might leave an opening for the Germans to shell the town and kill the civilian population, and then I felt my duty was to make no attempt at terms.
>
> Prostrated with mental and physical exhaustion, I wrote those words, convinced I was doing my duty and a noble act. This upheld me and was my one feeling throughout, and that as to all else I have written here, I swear on oath.[8]

Colonel Elkington stated that:

> Colonel [Mainwaring] proceeded to the mayor with an interpreter and signed a paper to the mayor. This paper I never saw till the trial and did not know till then how it was worded. I am sure when Col. [Mainwaring] signed it he did so under great mental and physical strain and did not realise the consequences. I thought at the time the mayor was exaggerating the situation.[9]

Mainwaring's statement that he was instructed to sign a surrender document under Elkington's direction, whilst the latter disarmed the men, warrants further consideration. Surely, if both colonels had agreed to surrender it would have been Elkington's responsibility, as senior officer, to negotiate terms. As stated later, Elkington denied all knowledge of a surrender document. Considering the alleged close proximity of the enemy, would a man of Elkington's experience disarm his men and store their weapons and ammunition some distance away from them? Mainwaring implies that by taking this action the indications were that there would be no resistance offered when the enemy arrived in the station-yard. On the other hand, Elkington confirms that he put the men in one shed, to rest and to feed, and their arms and ammunition in another "where they could easily be got in the case of need." Elkington was prepared to stand and fight if necessary. The men's behaviour was not particularly rational, and he may have seen disarming them as more of a safety measure than anything else. As Elkington states, the weapons remained close to hand.

At about 4 p.m. – after Mainwaring had returned to the station – there appears to have been a disturbance in the station yard, both colonels attempting to discover what was happening. A cavalry officer was ordering the men to fall in and follow him; they ignored him. Mainwaring explained the situation, but the officer abused the men and rode off. Consequently, Mainwaring began to suspect that the German advance was being delayed, and he later learned that British cavalry were holding the enemy back outside the town. He wrote:

> Later on a cavalry captain arrived, accompanied by the same subaltern. He told me he could guide us out, when I at once said every man would thankfully come. By now I was in command, as Colonel Elkington had left.[10]

Colonel Elkington wrote:

> Colonel [Mainwaring] at once spoke to the men and said if they remained with him he would see them through. I saw the situation had changed and that all was clear. I urged the men to fall-in and come out with me but they would not. As I saw the danger was passed and they could get out when they chose I left the yard about 5.30 p.m. as I was anxious to get on and collect more stragglers.

> I found a deserted horse on the Square and some discarded British saddlery, I saddled the horse and rode out of St. Quentin exactly at 6 p.m. with Major [?] On the way I collected a large number of stragglers from different battalions and marched towards Noyon.[11]

These events have baffled commentators, the popular impression being one of Elkington deserting his men and going off "into the wilderness". However, this was not the case.

A mystery still remains. Which major accompanied Elkington when he left St. Quentin? According to the 28 August war diary entry, Col. Elkington and Major W.C. Christie later rejoined the 10th Brigade with

280 men. Could the major have been Christie? According to Captain H.C. Hart and Captain C.T. Tomes, both of whom were members of Major Poole's party, Major Christie accompanied them. Tomes records that in the early hours of 28 August Poole and company were "… near Jeancourt, and halted whilst Major Poole and Major Christie went off in the forlorn hope of finding a train." Tomes also makes other references to Christie. However, Lieutenant B. L. Montgomery, who was also in Poole's party, does not mention Christie in his brief diary written at the time. If it was not Christie who accompanied Elkington, then it is also certain that it was not one of the other majors of the 1/Royal Warwickshire Regiment. Poole's whereabouts are known; Day had suffered a broken leg; Meiklejohn was wounded, by then, a prisoner of war. Although Elkington was accompanied by an officer it is difficult to establish their identity with any certainty.

The cavalry captain and subaltern both belonged to the mixed party of lancers and dragoons which Major Tom Bridges had assembled. By this time the men had rejoined both the brigade, and were by now taking part in various rearguard actions. Bridges was on the outskirts of the town and recalls:

> Our interpreter officer, Harrison, went into St. Quentin to find out if the infantry were clear, as barring an occasional lame duck, they seemed to have ceased coming down the Le Cateau road, a part of which we could see. On his return, he reported the place swarming with stragglers, he could find no officers and the men were going into the houses and lying down to sleep. I then despatched [Capt.] Sewell with some hefty henchmen, farriers and the like to clear out the houses and get everyone into the market place. He was also to find the mayor and commandeer bread and cheese and beer for our men, who were now on short commons, and have it put down ready by portions on the pavement outside the *Mairie* [town hall], so that if we were pressed, as seemed quite possible, we should not have to waste time issuing rations.
>
> We gradually fell back into the town, leaving two troops and machine-guns to hold the bridge over the river. Harrison had now reported that the remains of two battalions had piled arms in the railway station and that their commanding officers had given a written assurance to the mayor that they would surrender and fight no more, in order to save the town from bombardment.[12]

Major Bridges was also determined to retrieve the "surrender document". He sent Harrison back to tell the two colonels that there was now a cavalry rearguard in position, thus giving them time to evacuate the town. After this meeting Bridges was informed that the men refused to march, on the grounds that they had already surrendered, but that they would move if a train was provided. However, this was not possible. Bridges was no doubt incensed at this attitude, and immediately sent an ultimatum to the men, allowing them half an hour's grace during which period some kind of transport would be acquired. He also informed them that, "I would leave no British soldier alive in St. Quentin. Upon this they emerged from the station and gave no more trouble." He continues:

> I quote this unpleasant incident to show to what extremes good troops will be driven by fatigue. I conducted these negotiations through an intermediary, as I knew one of the colonels well, and had met the other, and they were, of course, both senior to me.[13]

Bridges later moved into the square to confront the men, whose situation was becoming a major problem.

Captain Arthur Osburn witnessed some of the events in St. Quentin, and graphically describes what he saw, making the point that many men were without arms and/or equipment, including essential canteens. Some were drunk, and were firing rifles haphazardly into the air. He learned that earlier that afternoon:

> … a mob of disorganised soldiery had collected at the station, and I was told some had booed and cheered ironically these senior staff officers as the staff train steamed out.[14]

Osburn was attracted to where Major Bridges was addressing the men:

> I could not hear what he said but his words of encouragement and exhortation were received with sullen disapproval and murmurs by the bulk of those around him. One man shouted 'Our old man [the soldier's colonel] has surrendered to the Germans, and we'll stick to him. We don't want any bloody cavalry interfering!' and he pointed his rifle at Bridges. I began to wonder whether Bridges would really be shot if he continued his harangue at the railway station.[15]

With the strong possibility that all British troops would vacate the town before the arrival of the Germans, Mainwaring's one thought was to retrieve the document. He wrote:

> I said I must get the paper back from the mayor. The cavalry officers said they meant to have that. I said I did not mind who had it as long as it was recovered. The cavalry subaltern accompanied me to the *Mairie*, and, pushing on in front, demanded the paper. I was too proud to argue with him for possession of it, as I was still upheld with the conviction that I had done my duty. They took it and sent it to their general.[16]

Some commentators make much of the fact that men were drunk and distressing the local inhabitants. Although Bridges makes no mention of this, the Rev. Harold Gibb, chaplain attached to army headquarters, did. Osburn recalled in detail the confrontation with locals, who approached him to tackle the situation:

> Your men are drunk, will you order them out of the house? I have young daughters in my house – the men have entered my kitchen – it is disgraceful! Why is there no order? Why are there no officers? Your troops have been here for hours up to no good; please order them to go away![17]

Osburn replied by blaming the local people for giving the tired troops white wine instead of bread and butter and coffee, stressing that "… French peasants will give wine away, but nobody had ever heard of a shopkeeper giving *butter* away." In any case, Osburn believed that only a handful of soldiers were drunk.

Bridges recalled this remarkable episode:

> The men in the square were a different problem, and so jaded it was pathetic to see them. If one only had a band, I thought! Why not? There was a toy-shop handy, which provided my trumpeter and myself with a tin whistle and a drum, and we marched round and round the fountain where the men were lying like the dead playing the *British Grenadiers* and *Tipperary*, and beating the drum like mad. They sat up and began to laugh and even cheer. I stopped playing and made them a short exhortation and told them I was going to take them back to their regiments.[18]

Captain Osburn commented that he understood the feelings of the officers and men around the station, and especially those of the two colonels. There was no staff directive; in fact, no orders at all. Food was in very short supply, and, apart from Bridges' actions, they were without support. Osburn stated "… what *could* the remnants of broken infantry do before the advance of a victorious army, whose cavalry could have mopped them up in an hour?" In hindsight, Osburn considered the "surrender" was not only the feasible, but also the brave thing to do. The commanders were two middle-aged men who were totally exhausted, and judging from their appearance, suffering from the severe effects of long exposure to the sun. These factors play a large role in explaining their actions.

With the help of Osburn and others, Bridges prepared the men to march out of the town. Some of Bridges' troops toured the town collecting stragglers. As the men were being rounded up Osburn heard shots. "Perhaps a few drunken soldiers were still having an imaginary wrestle with the Angel of Mons or something more repulsive; white wine can raise many images." Osburn poses a further extraordinary question:

> Or did some of Bridges' squadron shoot a few who too truculently scorned their suggestion that there was still time to run and fight another day?[19]

There is no doubt that Bridges had saved the day, over 400 men having marched out of St. Quentin by late evening. Mainwaring marched in front – a pathetic and exhausted figure, whose men, appreciating how hard he had tried for them, supported him with words of sincere encouragement as they left town. Mainwaring deserves a last word:

> At about 10 p.m. we moved on; two or three wagons had been provided for the men who could not walk, and these were immediately filled. We moved very slowly, with a cavalry escort, and about 2 a.m. halted at a farm and village called Roupy. Here the cavalry left us, and after blocking the road by putting the wagons across it, and posting piquets on it, I lay down and slept till dawn, the first sleep I had been able to get since Monday morning.

> Soon after daybreak the cavalry rejoined us, and escorted us some way, till, telling us to make for St. Surplice [Sulpice], they left us. I must say here that before the two officers withdrew both of them shook hands with me, and said I had done everything a man could do.[20]

When the incident at St. Quentin became known it prompted Sir Henry Newbolt to write a poem about it entitled, *The Toy Band: A Song of the Great Retreat.*

Eventually the party caught up with the 3rd Division. On reaching Noyon they entrained and journeyed to Compiègne, where there were over 3,000 men from a number of regiments. On 28 August Lt. Colonel Elkington resumed command of his battalion at Noyon. It then joined the others at Compiègne, before being moved off by train to billets and a short rest. The men arrived at Le Mans on the morning of 31 August.

During the three day stay at Le Mans the men rested and re-equipped, and in Captain Hart's words:

> … it was a different body of men which entrained again early on 4 September for the front. We arrived at Brie-Comte-Robert that afternoon and there found the rest of the battalion. At 2 a.m. next morning we paraded and started on the forward march, which seven days later ended on the farther bank of the Aisne.[21]

It will be recalled that officers of the 4th (Royal Irish) Dragoon Guards had retrieved the surrender document and forwarded it to their commanding officer. Bearing in mind the conditions under which it was signed, it may have been preferable if the document had been destroyed or "lost". However, it was soon decided that the two colonels should be tried on the following charges: a) cowardice, and, b) conspiring to surrender. The observations of Bridges, Osburn, the two colonels and others would lead one to believe that a court-martial would be one of the least likely outcomes from the events at St. Quentin. The General Court Martial took place on 12 September 1914, at Chouy.

Events on the morning of the 12 September appeared sinister. Ben Clouting, of the 4th Dragoon Guards, makes the following interesting comment:

> The Regiment [4th Dragoon Guards] was on the outskirts of a town when I was one of eleven troopers and a corporal called to fall in with our rifles by one of our sergeants. We were given no explanation, and although we asked the sergeant, we were none the wiser. Told to wait on a street corner until further orders, we hung around for a couple of hours before abruptly being stood down. Nothing was said. I was curious, and waited for the first opportunity to ask the sergeant what it was all about. He told me that we were to shoot two lieutenant-colonels had a court-martial passed death sentences on them. Instead, the court-martial adjudged both to have had a mental break-down owing to severe stress, and cashiered them.[22]

It is worth noting that, as the editor of Clouting's biography points out, at the time of the court-martial Clouting also claims to have been hidden in a stable in Moulins with a Lieutenant Harrison! Although Richard Van Emden states that this contradiction remains unexplained, he does agree with this author that it is unlikely Clouting would simply have made the story up.

The charge of cowardice was dropped, both officers being found guilty of...

> ... behaving in a scandalous manner unbecoming the character of an officer and a gentleman, in that they, at St. Quentin, on 27 August 1914, during a retirement following upon an engagement at Ligny, without due cause, agreed together to surrender themselves and the troops under their respective command.[23]

As Peter Scott points out, "... the defence case was simply that, in attempting to surrender, the two colonels had been motivated solely by the desire to prevent unnecessary loss of life."[24] According to the court the evidence was sufficient for both officers to be immediately cashiered.

The final, poignant, paragraph of Lt.-Colonel Elkington's statement reads:

> I had no one to help me in the defence of myself and the other colonel and was not in a fit state to think clearly, as senior officer I took full blame of any mistakes made and asked for Col. [Mainwaring's] acquittal as I was sure he was not in a fit state to be tried. After the trial we were two days under shell fire and unarmed before being sent home.[25]

Lt.-Colonel Mainwaring's final words on the matter were:

> What the men think of the matter may be judged from the following extract from a letter from an officer in my late regiment, who, unsolicited by me, is collecting evidence in the hope that it may be of use when peace is declared. He writes 'There is not a man here that does not believe implicitly in you and what you did to save them. There are several men in other regiments now swear that you alone saved them, so I am collecting as much information as possible which will assist in bringing things to light when this show is over.'[26]

The complete statements made by lieutenant-colonels Mainwaring and Elkington appear as appendices I and II in this book.

Despite the investigation of many sources, no evidence has yet come to light identifying the person or persons who were trying to clear Mainwaring's name. The outcome of the court-martial does, however, beg one question. It was noted earlier that Brigadier-General Haldane had wished to dismiss Mainwaring on the grounds of ill-health, only to be opposed by doctors. Did the events at St. Quentin finally provide that opportunity? Were the officers victims of a "clear-out"? In 1914, Mainwaring was fifty years old and Elkington forty-eight, and it is true that many high-ranking and long-serving officers were replaced, some as a result of court-martial, during the first few months of the war. Whatever motives lay behind the verdict, both men were sent home. Because of his poor health Mainwaring appears to have retired, but Elkington was a tough campaigner who, despite paying a price for his efforts, was destined to have the last word. As we shall see, he elected to follow a far more severe life than that of being an officer in the British army.

CHAPTER 5

Soldiering On: The Fates and Fortunes of Elkington and Mainwaring

"Jack" Elkington, as he was known to family and friends, was not the type of man who would spend weeks pondering upon the decision about where his future lay. The punishment had been given, taken on the chin, and now it was time to move on. One thing is certain – he was made of sterner stuff than many, who, disgraced under similar circumstances, would have considered the best solution was to go into their library, put their affairs in order, and then do "the honourable thing" by despatching themselves with their favourite hand-made Purdey. Neither was he the sort of person who would come home and spend the rest of his days ruing the events of St. Quentin. Soldiering was the only career he had ever known, and it would be difficult, even under normal circumstances, to take up another occupation. Of course, a renewed career in the ranks of the British army was possible; he would not be the first ex-officer to have followed that path. But that was not his way! At the age of forty-eight he made the decision to move in another direction which had been followed by Englishmen before him – to join the ranks of the French Foreign Legion.

The writer of an article which appeared in the *Daily Sketch* of 8 September 1916 had spoken to a friend of Colonel Elkington, only identified as "one who knows", who claimed that as soon as the court-martial decision was known Elkington remarked, "There is still the Foreign Legion."

Life in the Foreign Legion in 1914 did not – and never has – encompassed the romantic side of life portrayed in "penny-dreadfuls", the novels of P.C. Wren or Hollywood films. It was unique both in structure and regimental history, and many individuals left their imprint on its colourful image. Its members came from all over the world and from all walks of life. They included rogues, vagabonds, men seeking a supposed life of adventure, broken-hearted lovers, men doing "the honourable thing" and those who looked upon life in the Legion as the ultimate challenge. As to

General Paul Rollet (centre), French Foreign Legion, c.1918. This eccentric yet brave officer was known as the "Father of the Legion". Between the wars he "recreated" many of the traditions of the Legion of old, taking full advantage of the myths originated by P.C. Wren and Hollywood. (Courtesy of French Foreign Legion, Aubagne)

language, all Legionnaires were expected to understand French. That was the only language the Legion used, so the sooner its basics were learned the better. If he wished, a recruit could adopt a new name and be confident that the Legion would never betray his anonymity. If Legionnaires served their full term of enlistment they became French nationals, but, in the meantime, had to be prepared to accept a lifestyle summed up by the well-known motto *Legio Patria Nostra* meaning *The Legion Is Our Fatherland.*

Foreign Legionnaires in the trenches, c.1916. By this time their traditional uniform had been discarded for something more akin to that worn by the British. (Courtesy of French Foreign Legion, Aubagne)

All Legionnaires unhesitatingly accepted the century-old words of General de Négrier – "You Legionnaires are soldiers in order to die – and I am sending you where you can die." These were the type of words upon which the Legion's reputation had been built.

There are many accounts of Elkington's life in the Foreign Legion, some of which have no credibility whatsoever. One writer claimed:

> He was such a good soldier that the captain commanding his company drafted him into corporal's school. He was promoted… [1]

Nothing in Elkington's service papers show that he was promoted to corporal. The same writer, referring to Elkington's previous service, also claims that at St. Quentin his battalion was captured by the Germans.

Hugh McLeave's book gives a detailed and, as far as can be examined, accurate account of Elkington's days in the Legion, tying in well with other information which is considered reliable.

Within a few weeks of his dismissal Jack Elkington had arrived in Paris and enrolled in the Foreign Legion as legionnaire second-class no. 29274, going initially to the Mailly Camp outside Paris. His unit was the *2e régiment de marche, 1er étranger.* It is likely that basic training took place in the Rhône Valley, after which the legionnaires marched north, being bivouacked near Lyons at one stage of the journey. In Elkington's own words, he recalls his first meeting with a fellow legionnaire named Wheeler, who soon became a good friend:

> There was an American with me called Wheeler, a famous surgeon. He came over and joined the French Red Cross. He had tired of that and joined the Legion. I met him first time marching up to the front. I thought he was a tramp, and I expect he thought I was one. When we got to Lyon *(sic.)* I went down to have a meal in the big hotel. There I saw the American sitting over a big dinner and he saw me. From that time on we were friends. We saw that neither was a tramp. We marched together, ate together and became great pals.[2]

Dr David Wheeler was from Buffalo and had worked, as had his wife, in a French hospital. According to McLeave:

> Wheeler, an outdoor type, began to reproach himself for sitting in the comparative safety of a front-line hospital; the human wreckage filling his operating theatre depressed him. At forty-two he joined the Legion.[3]

There were three major actions in which the *2e régiment de marche* was involved during Elkington's period of service. The first, an incident during the Battle of Artois, took place on 9 May 1915 on "White Works" Hill 140, in the Vimy Ridge area.

The day commenced with French artillery pounding the ground to be taken. Four battalions of the *2e régiment* launched their assault. Progress was slow and losses were heavy as the men made their way towards the crest of the ridge. The plan was for the 156th Infantry Regiment to give support on the right flank but it was held back. This resulted in the legionnaires being subjected to heavy flanking fire. Regardless, the legionnaires pressed on and with great courage reached the summit. Unfortunately, this position could not be maintained. Urgent appeals for reinforcements brought no response, probably through poor liaison, and defensive positions could not be firmly established. By the end of the day the attackers were back at the bottom of the hill.

One serious error which occurred in the first attack was that in their determination to keep the advance moving, the French neglected to "clear out" the German positions as they were taken. This meant that many of the enemy who had either hidden or were wounded in the trenches were able to mount attacks from the rear. At the end of the day little progress had been made. However, because of its show of courage and determination the regiment was awarded the Croix de Guerre.

In this particular battle things went also went tragically wrong when French artillery began mistakenly firing shells on their own troops. In the same action it is recorded that Elkington showed signs of bravery and leadership:

> On the Artois crest, when everything was crumbling around them, Elkington rallied a section and led it forward to salvage the men from French shells falling at their back.[4]

High casualties reflected the inexperience of many of the men, a notable proportion of whom were raw recruits. Edwin Bergot reports that from a strength of 2,900 men, the unit had lost its commanding officer, a battalion commander, commandants Mullet, Gaubert and Noiré, 50 other officers and 1,889 NCOs and men.

After the serious losses at Hill 140 had been replaced by further drafts of men the regiment resumed the offensive in the same sector on 16 June. This time Hill 119 near Souchez was the target. There had been some improvement in strategy and communications, but once again the artillery was disorganised.

The attack began in the early afternoon, the legionnaires following a unit of Zouaves into action. The Zouaves had been created in 1831 in Algiers from the Zouaoua tribe who were well known as a formidable military force. By 1914 they had evolved into an all-French force whose uniform followed the North African style of dress.

As the attackers crossed the Souchez ravine at the foot of Hill 119, they were subjected to heavy German fire and little progress was made. Casualties were high, especially amongst the Zouaves, and retreat became inevitable. Once again, the men came under fire from their own artillery. Elkington was again in the forefront of the action:

> … he stopped a platoon from charging to oblivion until he had cleared out a German machine-gun position. Even African veterans respected this quiet man who seemed to find his voice only in combat.[5]

The regimental records show that while casualties remained high, they were nowhere near the level of those suffered at Vimy Ridge.

On 28 September came the final action for Légionnaire 2nd Class Jack Elkington. This time the Legion faced the enemy at Navarin Farm, in Champagne, east of Berry-au-Bac. Several attacks by other battalions had failed and it was now the turn of Elkington's and Wheeler's battalion. Their orders were to advance on Horseshoe Wood and Navarin Farm. Hugh McLeave quotes the words of Edward Genêt when discussing this action:

We started out to advance in solid columns of four, each section a unit. It was wonderful, that slow advance. Not a waver, not a break. Through the storm of shell the Legion marched forward. One lost his personal feelings. He simply became a unit, a machine.[6]

However, there is a differing version in a reference highlighted by Douglas Porch:

Then we left the cover of the trench, formed in Indian file; fifty metres between sections, and, at the signal, moved forward swiftly … so we crossed the ridge, offering the smallest possible target to the enemy's guns.[7]

This tactic, which had evidently been practised, made sense. But the plan was somewhat spoiled by the fire of the French artillery.

Once again Elkington and Wheeler were in the thick of things, the former taking the initiative. He cleared out one difficult machine-gun position single-handedly and waved his comrades forward. Then came a shock: another German machine-gun nest opened fire and Elkington, with a leg shattered, dropped into a trench. Wheeler came to his aid but in doing so he too suffered severe leg injuries. Elkington's own words paid tribute to Wheeler:

He gave me first aid, and looking at my leg, said, 'I say old man, they will have to take that off.' Then he fainted across my leg and it hurt like the devil. But he saved my life.[8]

Dr Wheeler gave him a dose of laudanum, which had to see him through the following thirteen hours in that trench. The men were rescued by a passing French patrol from a position just 100 yards from the German line.

Legionnaire Elkington spent many months in Grenoble's Hospital Civil. Initially, the doctors had to ensure his survival, before they began dealing with the shattered leg. Major Ternier performed eight operations on Elkington's leg and avoided the need for amputation. Elkington's bravery was recognised by the French authorities and, during his hospitalisation he was awarded both the Médaille Militaire and Croix de Guerre avec Palme. The French *Journal Officiel* published the following citation:

The Médaille Militaire and Croix de Guerre are conferred upon John Ford Elkington, Légionnaire in Company B3 of the First Foreign Regiment: Although fifty years old, has given proof during the campaign of a remarkable courage and ardour, giving to everyone the best example. He was gravely wounded on 28 September 1915,

Lt. Col. Elkington's fine array of medals. From left to right: D.S.O.; Queen's Medal and bars for South African War, Belfast [S.A. War], Orange Free State, Cape Colony; 1914 Star and clasp; British War Medal; Victory Medal and palm; Delhi Durbar medal 1911; Medaille Militaire; Croix de Guerre avec Palme (army despatches). (Author's collection)

rushing forward to the assault of the enemy trenches. He has lost the use of his right leg.[9]

While in hospital Elkington commented on the action at Champagne:

During the first night of the Champagne attack, Wheeler showed his coolness. There was a false cry for us to charge, and the third company, in which we were, started forward with fixed bayonets. The commandant of the battalion, seeing the mistake, jumped in front of the advancing and excited men and tried to check them. One of the sergeants of the third [company] helped him, and Wheeler with more *sang-froid* than the rest, also helped him. The check succeeded, and the commandant took Wheeler's name. The commandant met a soldier's death directly in front of Wheeler during our attack on the 28th.[10]

When the story eventually reached England, Elkington was visited by the Adjutant-General, who promised his strongest endeavours to persuade the authorities that because of his bravery, Elkington should be pardoned from the findings of the 1914 court-martial and his original rank should be reinstated.

A notice appeared in the *London Gazette* a few weeks later which read,

… the King has approved the reinstatement of John Ford Elkington in the rank of Lieutenant-Colonel, with his previous seniority, in consequence of his gallant conduct while serving in the ranks of the Foreign Legion of the French Army.

Whilst discussing the matter with Lt. Col. Elkington, a correspondent wrote in The *Times*:

Colonel Elkington does not understand what he calls the 'fuss' that is being made of him. 'What else could a man do? I was cashiered, and about a fortnight after the notice appeared in the papers I was in the ranks of the Foreign Legion.'

The interviewer asked 'Under your own name?'

'Why of course', he replied. 'It would not have done for me to have taken another man's name. It was hard work, we were nearly always in the thick of it. Many of the men of the Legion wore medals – medals of all the wars of the last twenty years. I cannot wear mine even if I wanted to – I was cashiered, and had no right to them any longer.'

'Were you ever recognised?' the interviewer asked.

'Only once', he said, 'we were marching in the Champagne country, and had just stopped to drink at a stream when a military motor went by. Someone in the car called out, 'Hullo, Elkington,' and I was afraid that I would be given away.' It was the only voice from the past that came to him, and he took it as such. A few minutes afterwards he was stepping it out heel and toe along the dusty road, a private in the Legion.[11]

There was still further recognition to come with a *London Gazette* announcement in late October 1916 that:

His Majesty the King has been graciously pleased to appoint Lieu-tenant-Colonel John Ford Elkington, Royal Warwickshire Regiment, to be a Companion of the Distinguished Service Order.

Following an interview given to the *Daily Sketch* a correspondent wrote:

Colonel Elkington has proved in a splendid and practical way, that his fault was at least not want of courage, and in that degree his rein-statement is more than a personal vindication. It is a satisfaction also to Colonel Elkington's countrymen. He considered that he had now washed out the stain by doing 'nothing of particular note.' He had won two medals and come home.

Elkington was no longer sufficiently fit for service and returned to the family home, Purley House, at Pangbourne, Reading. Shortly after his return the family moved to Adbury Holt, Berkshire. At the time he had two children, John David Rew, known as David, and a daughter named Jean. A second son, Richard, was born in 1918. When Richard was chris-tened in June of that year one of the sponsors was none other than his father's old Legion friend, Lieutenant David Wheeler, who by then was with the American Expeditionary Force. A few months later news came which must have been especially upsetting to Lt.-Col.Elkington – David Wheeler had been killed in action in France.

Like his father, David Elkington reached the rank of lieutenant-colonel, serving with the Rifle Brigade and being awarded an O.B.E.

Jean Elkington married Lt.-Col. Sir William Richard de Bacquencourt des Voeux, a Grenadier Guardsman who was killed at Arnhem in 1944.

In 1943 further bereavement fell upon the family when John Ford's youngest son, Richard, died from wounds received in action whilst serving with the 10/Rifle Brigade in North Africa.

John Ford Elkington, D.S.O., died on 27 June 1944. Two extracts from an obituary published in the *Newbury Weekly Times* state that:

> Though greatly hampered by being very lame as a result of his wounds, Colonel Elkington took a great interest and active part in all local affairs, and particularly those of Burghclere. He regularly took his seat on the Bench at Kingsclere; he started the Men's Club at Burghclere; was a warm supporter of Newbury District Hospital, of which he was Chairman in 1918. He was the first President of the Newbury Air Training Corps, and was not merely an ornamental one, as before he was laid by with illness he was most regular in his attendance at committee meetings, whilst his advice was always the soundest and greatly welcomed by his fellow members.
>
> Colonel Elkington's outlook and views on life were a great asset to the nation and an example to the community in which he lived. He was absolutely the reverse of the type which many people associate with old-time military men, particularly those who have served in India and the outposts of the Empire. There was nothing of the 'Colonel Blimp' about him. He was most progressive minded, friendly and approachable, and if there was one thing he desired above all else it was that people of all shades of opinion, of whatever political views, should pull together for the good of England and its people. He was a gallant soldier and a great gentleman.[12]

In May 1946 a stained-glass window dedicated to John Ford Elkington and his son Richard was unveiled in the Church of the Ascension, Burghclere, Berkshire. The unveiling was carried out by a family friend who had earlier served with the Lieutenant-Colonel in the Royal Warwickshire Regiment: Field Marshal Viscount Montgomery of Alamein. There are also two plaques in the church, one in memory of Lt. Col. John Ford Elkington and the other in memory of his son-in-law, Lt.-Col. Sir William Richard de Bacquencourt des Voeux.

Group at the unveiling of the stained-glass window dedicated to Lt. Col. John Ford and Richard Elkington, May 1946. Top row (l. to r.): Col. R. Colvin, D.S.O.; Mrs Colvin; Mrs H.J. des Voeux; Lt. Col. Brownlow. Front row (l. to r.): Mrs J.F. Elkington; Field Marshal Viscount Montgomery, with Jane and Elizabeth des Voeux; Lady de Voeux with her daughter Susan; Lt. Col. David Elkington. (Courtesy of the *Newbury Weekly News*)

The tablet in memory of Lt. Col. John Ford Elkington. (Author's collection)

The stained-glass window dedicated to John Ford Elkington and his son, Richard.
Church of the Ascension, Burghclere, Berkshire. (Author's collection)

The *Newbury Weekly News* reported:

Field Marshal Montgomery then delivered the address. Speaking from the chancel steps, he said he had come to unveil these memorials and he felt that he would like to say a few words about those whom they commemorated; two of them very well known to him and a third not so well. John Ford Elkington was the commanding officer of the battalion to which he belonged, and under whose command, he – then a very young officer – went to France in the First World War in 1914. Lord Montgomery said we Britishers had a curious habit of never being set when great events happened in the world, and we always started our affairs by having great disasters, which generally resulted in pulling certain people down with them, through no fault of their own. It so happened that John Ford Elkington was pulled down by disasters through no fault of his own and a good many others were too, but alone of them all, he fought back and made good, proving himself to be a great and gallant soldier. It can be said of him that he did his duty; not only did he fight back, but he made good more than he lost.[13]

This chapter concludes with a summary of the last fourteen years of the life of Arthur Edward Mainwaring. The reinstatement which appeared in the *London Gazette* in October 1916 did not extend to Mainwaring. The stigma of his dismissal followed him to the grave. He had been a sick man for some time. Any attempt to re-enlist in the army would very likely have been unsuccessful due to his age, even had he been fit.

Research shows that in 1920 he and his wife were living in a house named "Mencil Warren", in Church Street, Melbourne, Derbyshire. This author was unable to locate any evidence indicating exactly when they moved into the house. Whilst researching this book, the author travelled to Melbourne, only to find no house of that name in Church Street, and no-one local – resident or local historian – who had heard of the family, or the house. Some older properties have been demolished and new houses erected in Church Street. Nevertheless, family documents indicate the Mainwaring's residence there.

The choice of the house name "Mencil Warren", would not have meant anything to most people, but it certainly did to the Mainwarings. The similar "Mencie Warren" – an ancient form of the family name – was a *nom de plume* occasionally adopted by Arthur Mainwaring. However, most of the books he wrote carried his real name. According to family records the surname derived from the title Ranulphus de Mensil Warin, who fought at the Battle of Hastings. The story goes that his horse was injured in the battle, whereupon he mounted an ass, exclaiming "Devant

Si Je Puis" which, with tongue in cheek, can be given as the Mainwaring family motto, and translated means "In Front If Possible."

In May 1927 Mainwaring and his wife were still resident in Melbourne, but at about this time they purchased Pounsley Mill at, Blackboys, Sussex. Arthur Mainwaring died there on 11 October 1930, aged sixty-six.

It appears that during retirement Mainwaring was a gregarious character. His obituary, which appeared in the *Sussex Express* of 17 October 1930 makes very interesting reading:

> Colonel Mainwaring possessed a large circle of friends of all ranks in social life; in fact, his striking personality inevitably attached him to those with whom he worked or played. A fisherman, raconteur, a cricketer, and an acknowledged authority on whist and bridge, he charmed while he instructed. It was noticed that one tribute of flowers at the funeral was addressed, 'To the Ace of Trumps with love and gratitude.' It was particularly pathetic that a man whose cultured and witty conversation was a delight to all his circle should have lost the power of speech. Owing to a collapse of health, his articulation about two years ago became so affected that hardly anyone but his devoted wife understood him. With her as interpreter he was a delight to old and intimate friends.[14]

In his younger days Mainwaring had been a keen cricketer, on several occasions playing for the M.C.C., and he spent much of his leave on summer tours. The England player Major Poore was a regular partner at the crease. Mainwaring also played billiards and croquet, and on one occasion was runner-up in the Amateur Irish Championship. He was Vice-President of Blackboys Cricket Club, and held a similar position with the local football team.

Besides family there were several military men at Mainwaring's funeral. Among them were: Sir Charles Muhs, Colonel John Leslie, Colonel Haywood, Brigadier-General E. O'Brien, Major O. Tatham, Commander Lambert, Lieutenant-Colonel R. McLean and Colonel Mackenzie.

Part III – Death Tomorrow?

CHAPTER 6

"All Ranks Showed Great Gallantry": The 1st Battalion, Royal Warwicks, September 1914–October 1916

On 5 September 1914 Major A. J. Poole took command of the 1/Royal Warwicks, and the following day saw a change of fortune. News came that the battalion, now an established part of III Corps, was about to resume the advance. The men were to form part of the left flank of three advancing columns, which made a welcome change from the recent days of retreat.

Captain Tomes comments in his reminiscences that there was now a noticeable change in the attitude of the men, and that morale was good. This was no doubt due to the rest they had taken, the food they had eaten, and most importantly, the letters received from home. There was a spring in their step, and once again popular music-hall songs – often incorporating the men's own uncomplimentary words on what they thought of the Germans – filled the air.

The change of fortune for the B.E.F. came about because von Kluck, believing that the British were more or less defeated, turned his attention to the French Fifth Army. However, in doing so, he exposed his own right flank to attack by the French Sixth Army, who were now in the Meaux area. Von Kluck's only option was to wheel and counter-attack. This movement opened up a gap some twelve miles wide between himself and his nearest support, the German Second Army, which was covered only by cavalry. The B.E.F. planned to take full advantage of that gap.

At around 2.30 a.m. on a bright moonlit night the 1st Battalion, forming part of the division's advance-guard, began to move through the Forest of Armainvilliers, reaching Jossigny by mid-morning. Later in the day they completed the twelve-mile march to an area one mile south of Serris, where they bivouacked for the night. Throughout the day they had

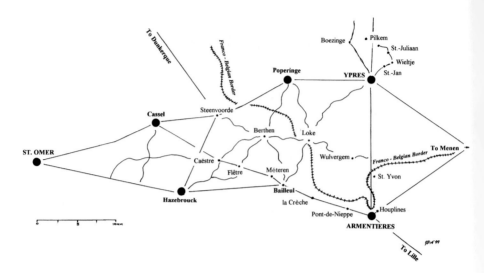

The 1st Battalion, Royal Warwickshire Regiment, Northern France, 1914–15.

been aware of heavy action on both flanks, but experienced no direct contact with the enemy.

Next morning, accompanied by the Royal Irish Fusiliers, the Battalion crossed the Grand Morin at Crecy, and took up a position on high ground north of the town in order to cover the division as it crossed the river just after noon. Resuming the march in hot and tiring conditions, the troops moved a total of eight miles during the day. The night was spent at Giremontiers, and as no supplies had arrived, the men had to resort to iron rations.

The 10th Brigade remained in reserve on 8 September, moving off at 3.45 a.m. There was still no action as the advance continued through Petit Courron. The 11th Brigade was involved in actions with the enemy at La Ferté-sous-Jouarre. The 10th never saw action as the Germans were driven out by the 5th Division.

Despite periods of heavy rainfall the 1st Battalion spent the afternoon in a local orchard eating apples and pears. Early next morning the men marched a further four miles before spending the remainder of the day resting at Les Poupelains.

The River Marne was crossed by railway bridge on 10 September, followed by a fourteen mile march to Hervilliers, where the Battalion bivouacked. The 1st Battalion had no other involvement in the Battle of the Marne. During the march the men witnessed the first evidence of a retreating enemy: the stinking corpses of horses, abandoned transport and guns, a few dead Germans and a landscape torn by artillery fire. From the hundreds of empty wine bottles strewn alongside the road it appeared that the enemy must have made their retreat in good spirits, indeed the British captured some of the enemy who were too drunk to get away.

For the B.E.F. this advance was important, five columns crossing the Marne west of Chateau Thierry, causing the northerly retreat of the First and Second German armies further to the River Aisne. It is recorded that due to general confusion and lack of communications during the retreat it took Colonel Hentsch of German headquarters seven hours to liaise between the headquarters of the two German armies. As the division moved forward on 11 September the 1st Battalion again saw signs of panic from the retreating enemy, and on arriving at Chouy witnessed several buildings on fire. A decision was made to bivouac there and many of the men slept in barns stacked with straw bales. Someone also discovered a healthily-stocked cellar containing wines and liqueurs, and as Tomes puts it "It was an anxious night for us." No doubt it was a very happy one for some!

Continuing their role as advance-guard, the 10th Brigade arrived at Septmonts in the Aisne Valley after a long wet march, from where it was able to observe British artillery bombarding the enemy, who were now about five miles distant. The night of 12/13 September was spent in Septmonts.

After marching through Billy next morning, the Battalion stopped on a railway embankment near Venizel and, after joining up with a party of French Zouaves, covered 11th Brigade, who had crossed the Aisne and were under heavy artillery fire. The men of the 1st saw large German shells, nicknamed "Jack Johnsons", roar over their heads and hit the Septmont ridge behind them. Later that night the 10th Brigade crossed the Aisne at Venizel in single file and bivouacked at Bucy-le-Long. The next two days were spent sheltering on steep slopes north of the Aisne, where the men watched British supply transport running a gauntlet of fire between Venizel and Bucy. Tomes records that the German observers must have been well-trained, because as soon as a vehicle came into open country the area was bombarded with "Jack Johnsons'" and occasionally "there was only a tangled mess of horses and smashed up wagons to tell the tale." At one stage the Irish Fusiliers also came under German fire.

The 1/Royal Warwicks could now "look forward" to a short period in the trenches. During the 17 and 18 September some horses were killed when "A" and "B" companies relieved the Hampshires, who belonged to 11th Brigade. It was at this time that the 1st Battalion lost its first officer to be killed in action, Lieutenant O.A. Knapton. A dozen men were also killed or wounded. Under cover of darkness, "A" and "B" rejoined the Battalion, who were now settled in trenches and caves near Le Moncel. According to the unit's war diary, the 1st Battalion comprised 20 officers and 1,045 other ranks on 30 September. Major Poole also recorded that discipline was "… noticeably worse than in South Africa, probably due to socialistic ideas imbibed by reservists." The Battalion remained near Le Moncel until 6 October, on which date the whole division was withdrawn. After a few long and tiring days on the march the 10th Brigade then entrained at Longueil-ste-Marie and entered Northern France, with its poplar-fringed roads, arriving at St. Omer during the early hours of 12 October. By then, Antwerp had fallen and the Germans were advancing on the Channel ports.

On 8 October Sir John French and the French general responsible for all French troop movements north of Noyan, developed a new plan of operations. General Smith-Dorrien's II Corps was to take up a position on the right flank of the French Tenth Army on 11 October. British cavalry were to move to a position on Smith-Dorrien's north flank and support this attack. After detraining on 12 October, Major-General Pulteney's III Corps was to clear a front and then await Lieutenant-General Haig's I Corps, who were due to arrive at St. Omer on 19 October.

After its early arrival in St. Omer, the 1st Battalion spent part of the day in local barracks before assembling with the entire brigade at the Grand Place at 2 p.m. As this took place a German aircraft dropped a couple of bombs which landed some distance away. A long convoy of lorries and buses then transported the men on a cold, miserable and uncomfortable ride to Cäestre, where they arrived in the early hours of 13 October. Later that morning Haldane received orders to engage the enemy at Meteren.

With casualties now replaced by a draft of reservists, the 1st Battalion was brought up to full strength, and arms and equipment were replaced as necessary. News came of a cavalry action at Mont des Cats the previous day, following which the body of Prince Max of Hesse had been taken into Caëstre. As an important personality, the Germans were keen to retrieve his body. During later negotiations between the Germans and the mayor of the town, an agreement was reached whereby the latter was repaid the burial expenses.

Next day the 10th Brigade moved towards Meteren, again as an advance-guard. Captain Tomes lists the marching order as:

> … advanced guard mounted troops – the divisional squadron 19th Hussars and the divisional cyclist company; vanguard – "A" and "C" companies, 1st Battalion Royal Warwickshire Regiment under captains C.A.C. Bentley and H.P. Williams-Freeman respectively; main body – "D" Company, 1st Battalion R.W.R. under Major W.C. Christie, followed by "B" Company, and then 2nd Seaforth Highlanders and 88 Battery R.F.A.[1]

By mid-morning the 1st Battalion was at Flêtre, where it removed a German barricade from the road, although there was still no sign of the enemy. Intelligence reported that there were Germans west of Meteren, at Berthen and also at Fountaine Houck. Action was imminent for the Warwicks.

New orders were issued for the 1st Battalion to advance and take Meteren, a daunting task as the enemy appeared to be strongly-posted. Besides heavy mist there was now drizzle falling, which drastically reduced visibility. Capt. Tomes reports:

> The ground was very difficult to that we had left; instead of open rolling downs we found ourselves in a slightly undulating country much cut up by hedges, wet ditches, gardens and hop fields, in which the poles and wire made progress difficult. The pavé road ran straight as an arrow from Caëstre to Flêtre and then to Meteren and Bailleul, and was obviously impossible to use if the enemy held these places.[2]

At about 11 a.m. the leading companies crossed the Meteren Becque and immediately came under enemy fire. "A" Company was held up the moment it crossed the stream, although "C" and "D" companies managed to continue their advance, capturing some enemy trenches. This bold move resulted in many casualties, including Lieutenant Montgomery, who had led a successful charge for which he was later awarded the D.S.O. "C" Company became pinned down in a sunken road, where they suffered very heavy casualties. "D" Company fared even worse. One of its casualties was Major W.C. Christie, who was killed as he led his men forward.

Nature was also beginning to act against the advancing troops. They were now moving through mud, which became extremely troublesome as it worked its way into rifle mechanisms with the consistency of cement. Many rifle bolts could only be moved by a heavy blow using a stone. Ammunition began to run low. Despite all this, the positions were held until relief came later in the day.

Major Poole established Battalion headquarters in a small cottage between Flêtre and Meteren. "C" and "D" companies were suffering heavy casualties. From intelligence provided by wounded men such as Sergeant Davis, the progress of the advance could be established. A gap had formed between "A's" right flank and "C's" left, two "B" platoons being despatched to close it. There was one disadvantage common to both sides – due to the poor visibility neither could bring their artillery into action, although machine-guns continued to rattle away. The Warwicks occupied the outskirts of Meteren in the early afternoon, where they remained whilst the rest of the Division made its advance. These included other elements of the 10th Brigade, including the 2/Seaforths and 1/Royal Irish

Meteren – the scene of "C" and "D" companies attack, 13 October 1914. (Royal Warwickshire Rgt. Museum)

The building which served as 1st Battalion headquarters during the action at Meteren, 13 October 1914. (Royal Warwickshire Rgt. Museum)

Estaminet near Meteren, where the 1st Battalion assembled after the action on 13 October 1914. (Royal Warwickshire Rgt. Museum)

The grave of Sgt. Easey, 1st Battalion, among the hop poles near Meteren, 1914. (Royal Warwickshire Rgt. Museum)

Mass grave of the N.C.O.'s and men from the 1st Battalion who fell at Meteren, October 1914. An image taken shortly after the action. (Royal Warwickshire Rgt. Museum)

Fusiliers. During the rest of the day the entire 1st Battalion was withdrawn, which meant it was not directly involved in the occupation of Meteren. This was accomplished by the 12th Brigade's King's Own, who at the time were under the command of Lt.-Col. Creagh-Osbourne, a one-time officer of the Royal Warwicks.

Disappointing as it must have been for the 1st Battalion to have missed the final advance into Meteren, it had nevertheless played an important role in the operation. Casualties were high – 45 killed and 85 wounded. As well as Major Christie, the dead included Lieutenant C.G.A. Gilliat, Sergeant Easey and Colour-Sergeant Thornton, who was never to learn that his promotion to a commissioned rank had been approved. Lieutenant Montgomery's wounds were such that his condition was critical, although he eventually rallied and survived.

For the following few days the 1st Battalion was in reserve. On 14 October it moved to Meteren, occupying billets for one night before

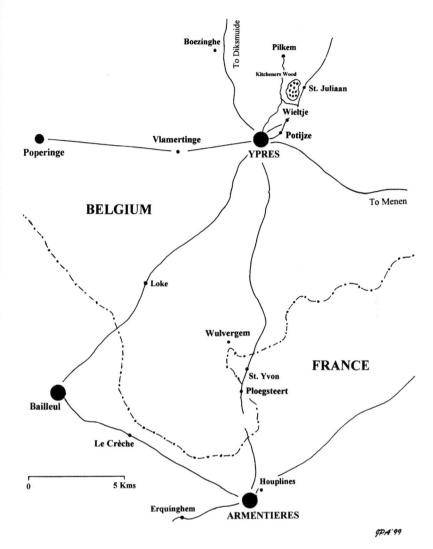

The 1st Battalion, Royal Warwickshire Regiment, Winter 1914 – Spring 1915.

moving on to other accommodation at Bailleul. The next day, 16 October, the Battalion travelled two miles before bivouacking at farm buildings in La Leuthe.

Captain Tomes gives a graphic description of the welcome the Battalion received on arrival at its new billets:

It was a curious experience, the inhabitants were overjoyed at having got rid of the invaders, and received us everywhere with open arms. They went out of their way to make us comfortable and pressed their best upon us; we could have had our fill of old brandy and other delights, and the good people were often quite hurt when we hesitated to sleep in their best beds in our boots. Sometimes there were reports of enemy stragglers hiding in the cellars which we had to search; rather a jumpy business, but we never found any. The behaviour of the Germans had been varied, in some of the houses the contents had been ransacked, wantonly destroyed or indescribably fouled, in others nothing had been touched. One good woman complained bitterly that a Bavarian general had stolen her toilet soap and another that nine chemises belonging to her servant girls had been taken, but we thought they had got off rather lightly.[3]

On the morning of 17 October the 10th Brigade was ordered to cross the River Lys, advance through Erquinghem and occupy Armentières. Progress was slow as hoards of refugees were returning to their homes in the opposite direction. The people were under the impression that the presence of the Allies offered sufficient security for them to consider the enemy had gone once and for all. Unfortunately, that supposition was proved wrong.

Later in the day the 1st Battalion was billeted around the railway station. During the evening some of the officers enjoyed an excellent meal at the Hotel de la Gare. However, before the effects of this dinner had worn off Tomes noted that "… we were turned out at our alarm posts in a hurry." Throughout that morning Armentières came under severe enemy shellfire, and in mid-afternoon the Battalion, along with the Dublin Fusiliers, moved further away. They were now in open country, and as there was no cover the advancing men became an easier target for the Germans. 1 man was killed and 7 wounded, including Captain Tomes. A new position was established in trenches on the outskirts of Houplines, a situation so precarious that all available men were employed in the firing line.

The following day the 2/Seaforths and 1/Royal Irish Fusiliers attacked Frelinghein, a short distance north of Houplines. The Warwicks remained in their positions for the next month, during which they were regularly subjected to heavy shellfire. They also experienced machine-gun fire and constant enemy sniping. Casualties included Captain Bentley, who was mortally wounded. Communications were poor, especially in the trenches, and in his monthly report Major Poole made an interesting comment suggesting that supplies of 1 lb. tins of bully beef, which were too heavy and difficult to carry in an individual soldier's kit, should be replaced by smaller tins, which would also result in less waste.

As winter arrived the earlier war of mobility ground to a halt. It was to be replaced by deadlocked trench warfare. Whereas earlier shallow trenches were generally termed mere fox-holes, these soon gave place to well-constructed and sophisticated systems of passageways, which allowed maximum freedom of movement and communication during their long periods of occupancy. Starting with the frontline trench, on the edge of no man's land, the system moved back via communications trenches – which varied in both depth and direction – to support trenches, and finally to reserve trenches at the far rear. However, even these needed to be regularly maintained, and were liable to collapse in severe weather.

November saw heavy rainfall, frost and snow which caused another serious problem. Mud, besides adding to the already unbearable trench life, further hindered communications. The Battalion's diary comments that the "discomfort was indescribable." In many parts of Flanders the water-table was so close to the surface – sometimes as little as eighteen inches – that deep trenches could not be dug. The common solution was to construct breast-works using wood and sandbags. When completed they stood up to six feet above ground level. Where trenches had been dug, many began to collapse due to the incessant rain, the men from the Battalion and those of the Royal Engineers being constantly employed on repair work. Worst of all there were problems with ammunition because bullets had been manufactured to the wrong size and could not be loaded into rifles!

Some short relief came to the men entrenched at Houplines on 18 November. The 1st Battalion was relieved and moved to billets at Pont de Nieppe. Two days later the men were at last able to wash before occupying clean billets in Armentières. Regular spells were then spent in trenches around Point 63 in the St. Yvon area, although throughout this period the war diary and Kingsford refer to this village as St. Yves. Regular relief was taken at La Crèche. There was a one day truce on Christmas Day giving an opportunity to bury some of the dead. New Year was seen-in by digging new trenches, but again rain hampered the work. Indeed, by February 1915 more rain had fallen in the first weeks of the year than was normal for the entire year itself.

By the start of 1915 the B.E.F. had suffered severe losses – over 50% of the original force were casualties, half of these falling at the First Battle of Ypres. A decision was made to reorganise. Under Commander-in-Chief Sir John French, two armies – First and Second – were formed, commanded by Sir Douglas Haig and Sir Horace Smith-Dorrien respectively. Haig's army comprised I Corps (1st and 2nd divisions), Indian Corps (Meerut and Lahore divisions) and IV Corps (7th and 8th divisions). Smith-Dorrien commanded II Corps (3rd and 5th divisions) and III Corps (4th and 6th divisions). The 10th Brigade, including 1/Royal Warwickshire Regiment, 2/Seaforth Highlanders, 1/Royal Irish Fusiliers and 2/Royal Dublin Fusiliers, remained part of 4th Division. Between 21 January and 28 August 1915 the 1st Battalion was commanded by Lieutenant-Colonel A. J. Poole.

Lieutenant Bruce Bairnsfather, 1st Btn., Royal Warwicks. As on other portraits of him, the cap badge faces in the wrong direction. The original was no doubt lost, and Bairnsfather substituted it with a collar-dog. (Mr and Mrs T. Holt)

Part of the reduction in the B.E.F.'s strength obviously included officers and men from the 1st Battalion, the nominal strength of which was 1,000 men. It is worth taking a brief look at how these losses were replaced. Reservists were initally called up, but their numbers were insufficient to keep pace with the massive casualty rate. After the list of reservists had been exhausted volunteers, and later conscripts, were recruited to maintain the required manpower. The places of regular officers were replaced by professional civilians. Men from the legal and accountancy professions were common among the officers. Those joining the ranks were recruited predominantly from the working classes.

Old Bill, asks the eternal question, "When the 'ell is it goin' to be strawberry?" (Mr and Mrs T. Holt)

A large number of the volunteers and conscripts who joined the Royal Warwickshire Regiment originated from Warwickshire itself. Men from a city such as Coventry hailed mainly from the engineering and motor industries, a female labour force replacing them on the factory floor. Unlike many other towns and cities, Coventry already possessed a well-established female labour force employed in occupations which involved either precision, repetition or intricate assembly work. Thus in some cases, in the absence of such large numbers of men, women who were already working in an industrial environment could be trained to take on further responsibility.

Men from the 1st Battalion in trenches at St. Yvon and Wulvergem, near Messines. Photographs taken between December 1914 and March 1915. (Royal Warwickshire Rgt. Museum)

Upon the outbreak of war there were many mining communities in Warwickshire, the men leaving the pits in their hundreds to join the Regiment. They were especially valuable when constructing and maintaining the networks of tunnels and trenches. The county had a large number of villages and hamlets, where farming and agriculture were the predominant employers. Today, one has only to visit a few such places and read the inscriptions on the war memorials to realise the effect the war had upon even the smallest communities.

The author's family serves as a good example of how the outbreak of war affected Warwickshire people. It had both rural and urban origins. Upon the outbreak of war the maternal side, with the family name of Jackson, had lived for many years in the hamlet of Ratley, near Edgehill, on the border with Oxfordshire. The author's great-grandfather was a seasonal farm worker. Of his seven children, the four girls were in domestic service in local "big houses". Of the three sons, Thomas and Henry gave up seasonal employment and sought better prospects by moving to the city of Coventry. The third son, Jack, also a seasonal worker, initially remained in Ratley before deciding to volunteer for the army, where he felt he would enjoy a more interesting and financially-rewarding life. An important advantage that many agricultural recruits possessed was

Men from the 1st Battalion in trenches at an unknown location, 1914/15. (Royal Warwickshire Rgt. Museum)

that of a skill in handling horses, vital at a time when the army relied upon horses for its basic transport. The paternal side, family name Ashby, had lived in Coventry for well over a century, and all the males were working in industry at the outbreak of war. They were mostly skilled workers, and as would be expected, their wages and conditions at home were more preferable to a life as a volunteer in the services. However one son, John Ashby, did serve, surviving the war only to return an embittered man.

Before describing the 1st Battalion's service during 1915, mention should be made of a particular officer. Bruce Bairnsfather's name was to become popular throughout the trenches, not for bravery or leadership, but for the role he played in sustaining morale during some of the most difficult and disheartening episodes of the war. Although a writer, Bairnsfather was better known as a cartoonist. There were several humorists, especially amongst the officers, who helped to brighten up those dismal, soul-destroying, days in the trenches, but Bairnsfather was a master of the cartoon craft.

The more popular nickname used to describe the rank and file soldier in the trenches was Tommy Atkins, but it was "Old Bill" and his two mates, Alf and Bert, who became cult figures. Bairnsfather created Old Bill as a character with whom a soldier could readily identify and, as

Bairnsfather came from the Midlands, this dialect was usually used in his work. Almost as soon as he reached the front as a machine-gun officer, Bairnsfather began drawing cartoons. They were normally drawn on paper, always contained a dry punch-line, and were sometimes accompanied by a few lines of verse. These items he pinned up wherever the action took him and, when time allowed, he even drew murals in whichever building, or to use a more appropriate word "structure", was being used by the officers. Before long he became an official war artist for the *Bystander Magazine* and many years later his cartoons appeared in the *Illustrated London News* and *Tatler*. His valuable contribution to the men's morale was soon recognised, and because of his fine artwork Bairnsfather was attached to the Intelligence Department in 1916.

For the 1/Royal Warwickshire Regiment the monotonous and miserable life in the trenches continued throughout the winter of 1914/15, with the usual routine of four days in the billets at "The Piggeries" or La Crèche, followed by four at the front. There were occasional outings to Armentières or Bailleul to relieve the troops boredom. According to Bairnsfather, although life was dreary, a shortage of ammunition on both sides meant that casualties were low:

> But if there was not much war there was plenty of discomfort, slimy trenches with no duck-boards, few sand-bags, and no shelter from the incessant rain should have produced sickness, but actually we seemed to flourish on it.[4]

After relaxation, bathing and training at Oultersteen the men were once again back in action during the early days of April. On 22 April the enemy launched a gas attack in an area north of Ypres, directed mainly against French and Algerian troops. Orders were given for the Battalion to prepare to move to a location of which only their colonel was aware. The men marched through Bailleul and had reached Locre by the end of the day. It was soon clear that they were heading for Ypres. The landscape was so bland and uninteresting that Bairnsfather wondered that the Belgians had not given away the area long before, in order to avoid the present situation. The next day's march took the Battalion to within two miles of Ypres, where it soon began to meet stragglers – many affected by shell-shock – returning from the epic action taking place around the town. In the early evening the Battalion moved to a large field close to Ypres, where it was decided to spend the night. Bairnsfather takes up the story as the men sat waiting for the field kitchens to arrive:

> The shelling was getting worse, fires were breaking out in the deserted town, and bright yellow flames shot out here and there against the blackened sky. On arrival of the field kitchens we

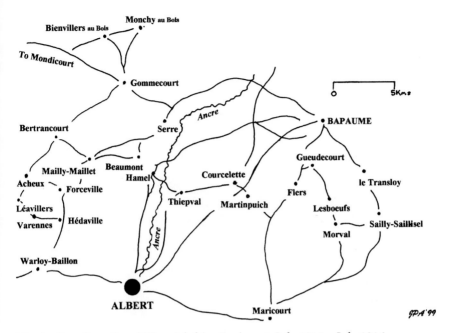

The 1st Battalion, Royal Warwickshire Regiment, July 1915 – July 1916.

managed to get some tea in our mess tins; and the rum ration being issued we were a little more fortified against the cold. We sat for the most part in greatcoats and silence, watching the shelling ... a truly grand and awful spectacle.[5]

Brigadier-General Hull's 10th Brigade, which included the 1st Battalion, was ordered to move out at 4 a.m. next morning, 25 April, and launch a counter-attack with the aim of retaking St. Juliaan and Kitchener's Wood. The orders seem to have been too vague and ill thought-out. Consequently, a suggestion was written in the battalion war diary that more consideration should be given regarding artillery back-up and prior reconnaissance, in future. The 1st Battalion advanced with the rest of the brigade, and was quickly embroiled in a fierce battle as it attempted to support a Canadian unit that had been overwhelmed by enemy gas. At one stage the 1st moved to within 50 yards of the enemy but could proceed no further because of the terrific rate of enemy machine-gun fire. This situation continued for almost two hours. During that period the Battalion's losses are recorded as 7 officers killed, 9 wounded or missing, together with 500 casualties within the ranks:

We could see lines of enemy reinforcements moving up from Kitchener Wood and got them in enfilade, but as more and more

125

Lieutenant A. Jowitt, who was killed during an attack on a German position at St. Juliaan, near Ypres, 25 April 1915. (Royal Warwickshire Rgt. Museum)

men were knocked out so our fire slackened. I did not know what to do. It is a bad business not to know what to do. The enemy made no attempt to follow up their success, they were probably thankful enough to have stopped an attack so nearly successful. The survivors of the Battalion with the rest of the Brigade formed a line in some old trenches north of Weiltje, but none of the wounded could be collected until that evening. They had to lie out in the rain and mud all that day.[6]

The Battalion remained in an exposed position facing St. Juliaan and Kitchener Wood for another five days. It was relieved on 30 April, although in a battered and shaken condition. During the action of 25 April casualties amongst the officers were: Captain Walker, lieutenants Nicolai and Payne, second lieutenants Jowitt, Maclaglan, Crowley, Richard and Cockburn killed; Captain Black and Second Lieutenant Hunt wounded and missing; Lieutenant Lucie-Smith missing, presumed killed; captains Tomes and Bretherton, Lieutenant Tillyer and Second Lieutenant James wounded; Lieutenant Ramsey wounded, missing and presumed killed. Lieutenants Cave and Bairnsfather were hospitalised, suffering from shock.

The next three days were spent in a supporting role, followed by four days of rest. Following the arrival of a new draft of men from England, the Battalion was now ready to go into action once more, and on 8 May moved into trenches at Potijze. Five days rest were taken at Vlamertinge, before a continuous stretch of ten days in the trenches at Wieltje. Close to the Warwicks trenches was a farm known, with typical British humour, as Shell Trap Farm. It was here that a gas attack was launched by the enemy on 24 May, although it caused little trouble. Machine-gun fire, however, was ferocious, and any further advance was extremely difficult. Casualties were low, and only one action of note took place at this time – a Distinguished Conduct Medal was awarded to Lance-Corporal W. W. Milner. The full citation is given in Appendix VIII.

In June the men moved to trenches at "Lancashire Farm", situated on the outskirts of Ypres. A number of men from the Battalion were "loaned" as temporary reinforcements to the 11th Brigade between 5 and 8 July. They were involved in attacks at Pilkem on both 6 and 8 July, Captain Strevens winning an M.C.

An interesting article appeared in the newspapers at this time, entitled *Two Heroic British Soldiers*. Private Swainsford of the 1st Battalion Royal Warwickshire Regiment, writing to a Birmingham contemporary, told of witnessing one of the most courageous acts of the war he had seen so far:

> We had just come out of the trenches for a short rest when we received the information that the Rifle Brigade were to make an attack and that we should be in support. Well, the attack was successful and two lines of trenches were taken. After the attack the Germ-Huns bombarded us terribly, thousands of shells being fired during the three days following. While the bombardment was at its hottest, our C.O. sent an order that a machine-gun was to attempt to get up into the line. This seemed an almost impossible feat, considering the shells that were falling about; but for all that, despite all the advice received on the way up that it was impossible, (I was in the reserve trench and heard the remarks), the officer, a sergeant and a private succeeded in reaching their goal. But no sooner did they get there than the officer was wounded, leaving the sergeant to take charge.[7]

Swainsford then relates information gleaned from men of the Rifle Brigade who witnessed the incident:

> The Warwick machine-gun succeeded in getting up to our position – in itself a most wonderful piece of work. They right away got their gun in action. After 15 minutes continual firing they had the misfortune to be buried, also the gun. They had been in action, as near as I can say, about two and a half hours when the sergeant, looking through his glasses, spotted the place where the German reinforcements, gathered together, were waiting to advance to what was now their firing line; but unfortunately, owing to an advance trench of ours he was unable to fire on them. As soon as he realised this he explained the position to the private who was with him, and then, without the least sign of fear, they both caught up the gun and, despite a terrible fire, ran forward to the right flank, put the gun in position and opened fire. The enemy dropped just as though they had been struck from above, very few escaping. They then picked up their gun and dashed back to their lines without injury: but for all that it was the bravest thing I have seen in this war. The same night I was relieved, and so had to part from them, but in my opinion no praise is too good for those two heroes. Their names were Sergeant J. Cresswell and Private King, Machine Gun Section, 1st Royal Warwickshire Regiment, 4th Division, 10th Brigade, British Expeditionary Force.[8]

Sergeant Cresswell was awarded the D.C.M., the citation for which is given in Appendix VIII.

The overall casualties suffered by the men of the 1st Battalion during this "loan period" were 2 officers and 12 men killed, 54 wounded. So ended the Battalion's time in Flanders. The Brigade left Elverdinge, and on 22 July entrained at Godewaersvelde, arriving in Doullens 10 p.m. the same day. After a short march of two and a half miles, the men spent the night in billets at Freschevillers. Two days later they reached Bertrancourt, after a ten mile march. By 26 July the 1st Battalion was once again settled in trenches, this time at Sucrerie, near Mailly-Maillet.

The Battalion war diary entry for 31 July 1915 gives the following interesting statistics:

> Officers served with the Battalion – 93.
> Of these – 20 killed, 23 wounded, 9 missing or prisoners-of-war.
> Approximate number of N.C.O.s and other ranks – 3,638
> Of these – 324 killed, 1,060 wounded, 381 missing or prisoners.

With regard to casualties, it should also be noted that the Second Lieutenant F. D. Elkington who joined the Battalion on 5 May, and was wounded in the neck by sniper fire on 26 May was no relation to Lt. Col. J. F. Elkington who features elsewhere in this narrative.

Once settled in the Acheux area, the next few months were a period of frustration for both the 1st Battalion in particular, and Britain's war-effort in general. That is not to say there was no action, but very little progress was made. Time followed its usual pattern – a few days in the trenches followed by a similar time spent away bathing, cleaning-up, training, route-marching, trench repairing and church parades. All possible effort was made to give the men some relief and relaxation during these grim and frustrating months and, from all accounts, it was the older men who were better able to cope with the situation. Basic entertainment was provided in the form of theatrical events such as concerts, the "4th Division Follies" and occasional cinematograph shows. Football was popular, and several inter-battalion and regimental matches were played. A league was formed, and on 25 November a tournament was held.

While in the trenches the men were subjected to regular, and sometimes heavy, attack from enemy mortars, artillery and machine-guns. Of course, snipers were ever-present day and night. Some days as many as sixty shells would fall, but at other times nothing would happen for days on end. The Battalion war diaries make several references to tremendous cannonades in the Arras area. As far as the 1st Battalion was concerned the enemy was never far away, often within hailing distance. Indeed, on 3 September the Germans called out, "We are Saxons, you are Anglo-Saxons, what are we fighting for?"

The main area of service was around Mailly-Maillet, whilst rest periods were taken at Acheux. At times the weather was atrocious, and throughout the trench system there was flooding and slippage. On 3 November two men were killed when a dug-out collapsed. Things were so bad that each day every man was put to work clearing mud and doing repair work. Obviously, communication between the massive maze of trenches was severely hampered, and there were a number of instances where communication was totally impossible.

Regular sorties into enemy positions were undertaken by both sides, each attempting to attack troublesome positions, capture prisoners or gather intelligence. The war diary describes one extraordinary event which took place in the early morning of 20 October:

A German approached our left, "D" Company, and after being missed by the sentry a struggle ensued and the German fell into the trench, but shot the sentry in five places with an automatic revolver and ran into "Living Trench" where he shot dead Private Baker and stabbed Private Spittle in the back, making good his escape. Privates Wall and Ball were [also] on duty at the time. Private Wall having to run to the N.C.O. on duty and warn the Company to stand-to. Search was made, no sign of the German. His cap was found in the trench.[9]

Throughout this period the number of casualties was low, but on 7 November five men were tragically and unnecessarily killed by the explosion of a dud aerial torpedo which Private Evans had taken into his dugout.

On 25 September the regiment's 2nd Battalion had participated in the Battle of Loos. The 1st Battalion war diary entry for 21 November 1915 gives the following statement from a wire received: "All comrades send greetings and congratulations on Victoria Cross won by Private Vickers." Under heavy fire he had managed to cut the German defensive wire in two places, thus enabling a successful attack on the enemy trenches. This was the first V.C. won by a soldier from the Royal Warwickshire Regiment.

On 28 August Lt.-Col. G.N.B. Forster succeeded Lt.-Col. Poole as commanding officer of 1st Battalion. Between 26 November 1915 and 14 June 1916 the command was held by Lt.-Col. J.A.M. Bannerman, while Lt.-Col. Forster was on sick leave. Two years later, on 3 August 1917, Lt.-Col. Forster was transferred to 42nd Brigade, being succeeded by Lt.-Col. Sir. G. Lacon.

The New Year of 1916 did nothing to relieve the boring, hum-drum life in and out of the trenches. The unit's war diary notes that aircraft were now a far more common sight on both sides. Days of fairly intense and damaging enemy artillery bombardment were usually followed by a lull, however machine-guns and snipers were as active as ever, and there were regular reports of the use of gas.

On 3 February the King's Own Regiment took over the 1st Battalion's line of trenches. The Battalion marched to billets at Mondicourt. The next few weeks were much easier for the men – fresh clothing was allocated, inoculations were given and training and rifle-range practice were undertaken.

In one sense, February 1916 was an important month for the B.E.F. As we have already seen, artists were at work, helping to introduce humour into often hopeless situations. Trench journalism now came into its own. Hundreds of copies of trench magazines were distributed in the war – the most popular being the *Wipers Times*, which was produced for the first time on 16 February, by men from the Sherwood Foresters. It was printed on a press situated in a building near the Cloth Hall in Ypres (Wipers to the men), at a time when "the air was full of shells." Only one page at a time could be printed, as the men only possessed a limited number of "e's" and "y's". The first *Wipers Times* had a run of 100 copies and was vastly over-subscribed. The circulation for numbers 2, 3 and 4 increased to 200. These displayed a "dud" price because, as the editor put it, "… after the issue of no.1 the barrage became so intense that we were forced to save our paper by elevating the 'alleged' price." The paper ran throughout the rest of the war, although its name and place of publication changed. It appeared as the *Wipers Times or Salient News*, the *New Church Times* incorporating the *Wipers Times*, the *Kemmel Times*, the *Somme Times* and finally the *BEF Times*. The tone and hilarity of the magazine were "often more hysterical than natural."

There is no doubt that such pieces of trench subculture, incorporating undertones of sarcasm and disregard for authority, played an important role in keeping up morale, and were just as popular in the Warwicks as in any other regiment. Taking into consideration the landscape and environment of the front, the correspondence section was a great delight, especially letters concerning hearing the first cuckoo, some of which are reproduced below:[10]

To the Editor, 12 February 1916

Sir, Whilst on my nocturnal rambles along the Menin Road last night, I am prepared to swear that I heard the cuckoo. Surely I am the first to hear it this season. Can any of your readers claim the same distinction?

A Lover of Nature.

To the Editor, 26 February 1916

Sir, As a lifelong reader of your excellent paper, I hereby claim the privilege of a few lines of space to contradict "A Lover of Nature" letter in your last issue. Firstly, I heard the cuckoo myself two days previously; secondly, he doesn't know enough about birds to differentiate between species; and thirdly, in order to prevent his wasting your valuable space, I suggest that what he really heard was a sniper calling to its mate.

Yours etc., "One Who Knows".

To the Editor, 6 March 1916

Sir, I read, with feelings of disgust, a letter in your last week's issue over the *nom-de-plume* of "One Who Knows." Knows what? – I ask. Nothing! – I reply. One who has not the courage to even sign his name. I am surprised that the Editor of a paper with the circulation that you boast should have found room for such a scurrilous, lying effusion. The ignorance of the person is visible in every sentence. Will you please find room for this letter, as otherwise my reputation may suffer in the eyes of those who do not know the true facts.

I am, Sir, Yours faithfully, "A Lover of Nature".

Answers to Correspondents, 17 April 1916

"Lover of Nature" – Nothing doing, that bird's dead.

Answers to Correspondents, 1 May 1916

"Lover of Nature" – We've had just about enough of you and your birds. The mere fact that you've found a cuckoo's nest with three eggs leaves us cold. If it costs us 500 francs just because you heard a gas horn and mistook it for the cuckoo, we shudder to think what might happen if we don't nip your natural history in the bud."

As if that was not enough, correspondence started again in early 1917:

To the Editor, 20 January 1917

Sir, As I was going over the top last week I distinctly heard the call of the cuckoo. I claim to be the first to have heard it this spring, and should like to know if any of your readers can assert that they heard it before me.

I am, Sir, Yours Faithfully, "A Lover of Nature".

The final item on this matter reads:

To the Editor, 5 March 1917

Sir, If you would kindly supply me with the name and address of your correspondent signing himself a "Lover of Nature," I will guarantee that he will not love Nature any more; neither will he hear any more cuckoos. No sir! not this Spring nor next or any other Spring neither. Cuckoo indeed!! I'll learn 'im.

Yours faithfully, "Fed Up".

For the whole of February 1916 the 1st Battalion was away from the frontlines, based at a camp in Mondicourt undergoing regular training exercises, parades and snow-clearing. Football matches played an important part in relaxing the men, and the Battalion played both the Argyll's and 9/Durhams. The Battalion diary records that during route marches the "… older soldiers march very well and end up in great spirits." Besides this break from the trenches, an important and no doubt very welcome occurrence was that the Battalion was kitted-out with new uniforms. The days at the beginning of March followed the same pattern as those of

February, and on 18 March the officers beat their counterparts from the Royal Irish Fusiliers 6 points to 3 in a game of rugby.

On 19 March the Battalion moved into comfortable billets at Bienvillers, but unfortunately soon came under heavy enemy bombardment, the men experiencing some very narrow escapes.

The following is the Roll of Officers serving with the 1/Royal Warwickshire Regiment as of 31 March 1916:

Name and Rank	Remarks
Lieutenant-Col. J.A.M. Bannerman	Commanding Officer
Major Sir G.H.U. Lacon, Bart.	Second-in-Command
Captain G.S. Miller	
Captain S.J. Riley	
Captain A.M. Bramwell	
Captain A.H.K. Jackson	10th Infantry Brigade H.Q.
Captain M.C. Harrison	
Captain G.F. Irvine	
Captain G. F. Hewitt	
Lieutenant A.R. Finlayson	
Lieutenant J.L. Shute	
Lieutenant G.F. Bradley	Hospitalised
Lieutenant C.W. Iggulden	Duty with Entertainment Btn.
Lieutenant R.R. Waters	Duty at Base – Le Havre
Lieutenant D.H. Willis	Acting Adjutant
Second Lieutenant T.D. Dixon	
Second Lieutenant A.P.A.H Kinlock	
Second Lieutenant F.N.H. Beamish	
Second Lieutenant Lord E.B. Seymour	
Second Lieutenant R.W. Gorton	
Second Lieutenant E.J.A. Maunsell	
Second Lieutenant H.T. Elliott	4th Div. School of Instruction
Second Lieutenant T.G. Hancox	
Second Lieutenant W.G.B. Edmonds	Grenade School
Second Lieutenant A.G. Duddell	
Second Lieutenant G.H. Rayner	111th T.M. Battery
Second Lieutenant S.H. Dowson	Transport Officer
Second Lieutenant S.V. Figg	
Second Lieutenant E.G.S. Wagner	
Second Lieutenant F.H. Cox	Town Commandant, Humber Camp

Second Lieutenant C. Partington
Second Lieutenant E. Vevers
Second Lieutenant C.X. Lukey   Machine Gun Officer
Second Lieutenant A.G. Lovelace-Taylor
Captain and Quartermaster T.H. Harwood
Lieutenant R.M. Marshall (R.A.M.C.)   Medical Officer

April began with the Germans celebrating Bismarck's birthday by shelling the Battalion's trenches. On 2 April the Battalion witnessed a British aircraft being shot down and dropping into their lines; by this time aircraft were becoming more common and active overhead.

On 7 April it was decided that it was time to reconnoitre the German trenches. A raiding party of 2 officers and 25 men went into the enemy's trenches with the object of destroying two machine-gun emplacements, killing or capturing any of the enemy in the trench, and gathering as much intelligence as possible. Under cover of heavy artillery fire from 29 R.F.A. Brigade, and 127 Howitzers, Lieutenant J. L. Shute and Second Lieutenant R. W. Gorton led the picked men into the attack at 3.35 p.m. By 4 p.m. they were in the enemy trenches without experiencing any opposition. Lieutenant Shute's group, led by Private W. Hazel "… firstly encountered a shaft sloping down underneath the parapet, which looked somewhat like a mine-shaft." Not being able to see in, and hearing many voices, this was bombed, following which shouts and groans were heard. The party then moved on up the trench and came upon a deep dug-out. Spotting a map-case and Burberry hanging some way down Lieutenant Shute tried to reach for them, but a shot was fired from below and a grenade was thrown up into the trench, so he withdrew behind a traverse. Private Hazel and Lieutenant Shute moved forward again and threw in eight more grenades, which judging from the ensuing noise, appeared to be very effective. The men then received the signal to return.

A similar attack on adjoining trenches was carried out by Second Lieutenant Gorton. Three dug-outs were attacked, using six grenades on each, all appear to have been occupied. Both parties were in the enemy trenches for about six minutes before being recalled. There were no visible signs of the enemy during that time. The German remained well below ground, and there were no rifles or equipment found except for a sniper's periscope which Second Lieutenant Gorton failed to bring back. The diary records that "The raid evidently came as a complete surprise and owing to the intensity of the British artillery's bombardment all sentries had evidently returned to their dug-outs." During the exercise only one man was slightly wounded.

The Intelligence Dept. "Is this 'ere the Warwicks?" "Nao, 'Indenburg's blinkin' Light Infantry." (Mr & Mrs Holt)

The Diary concludes:

> The retaliation was practically nil on our front, about twenty field gun H. E. shells and three heavy trench mortar bombs were fired on the salient. There was no rifle or machine-gun fire from either side during the operation.[11]

For the remainder of April the Battalion followed the usual routine, either in the trenches or back in billets. The time in the trenches varied between quiet days, and days during which there was quite heavy shelling. Snipers were always active, although casualties were minimal. Routine Orders show that 9155 Private T. Attwood, "B" Company, appeared before a Field General Court Martial and was sentenced to three months field punishment for: a) replying insolently to an officer and, b), behaving insolently in the presence of an officer.

Compared with other units, the Royal Warwicks, including the 1st Battalion, seems to have possessed a poor disciplinary record. Recent research concludes that during the entire war there were 1,034 court-martials in the Royal Warwicks, of which 142 (14%) involved the 1st Battalion. Men in the ranks were involved in 29 cases solely for drunkenness, and another 23 involving drunkenness coupled with other crimes. Other main offences included 15 instances of going absent without leave, and 15 desertions. Death sentences were passed at five trials involving desertion, but on each occasion these were commuted to terms of penal servitude ranging from three to ten years. The following officers were subject to trial by court martial:

18.9.14   Captain C.A.C. Bentley – drunk – severe reprimand, later quashed.

10.12.15   Lieutenant C. Hoare-Archibald – drunk and two charges under Section 40 – dismissed from the service. (Section 40 – conduct prejudicial to good order).

23.5.16   Second Lieutenant Lord E.B. Seymour – drunk – dismissed from the service.

18.1.19   Acting-Captain E.J.A. Maunsell – A.W.O.L. – severe reprimand.

16.3.19   Second Lieutenant R.J.W. Feather – drunk – dismissed from the service.[12]

On 1 May the 1st Battalion vacated the trenches at Monchy, and over the following few days marched to Gapennes, a distance of about thirty miles, via St. Amand, Halloy, Neuvillette and Agenville. For the remainder of May it remained in the Gapennes area for training. By 14 June it had returned to the Mailly-Maillet area, and four days later was back in the trenches in the Auchonvillers sector.

By June 1916 the German line across Belgium and France formed a salient, the apex of which was near Albert. Plans were drawn up for the Allies to make this a point of attack. The objective was to penetrate the maze of trenches which had been constructed after the war had lost its "mobility" during the early days of 1915.

A group of unknown officers of the 1st Battalion, c.1916. (Royal Warwickshire Rgt. Museum)

From Switzerland to the North Sea, neither the Allied nor German armies held a favourable position from which to advance in any direction. To attempt a frontal attack meant crossing open ground, cutting through barbed wire entanglements often up to fifty feet deep. Behind this were trenches and dug-outs up to thirty feet deep which, in turn, had machine-gun emplacements positioned to enfilade any assailants who managed to make some progress. Any possible attempt to attack required the support of an artillery bombardment which, of course, destroyed any element of surprise. Tomes recalls one soldier commenting that even if the German front line was overrun, the enemy were so thorough in their planning that the attacking forces would be confronted by a series of well-established strong-points in villages and woodland to the rear. Nevertheless, the British took the decision to carry out a frontal assault, and among many of

Capt. M.C. Harrison, M.C. and another unknown officer from the 1st Battalion, Royal Warwicks. An image probably taken during summer 1916. Harrison was killed in action 12 October 1916. ((Royal Warwickshire Rgt. Museum)

the young officers and men there was a great feeling of optimism. The troops were fed up with the stalemate and a "gung-ho" attitude of "Let's get on with it!" prevailed. As an unnamed optimist put it, "… any change from mud, lice, rats and flies which we had endured for fifteen months was preferable."

Thus, on 1 July 1916 the Somme Offensive was launched, running along a line north of the Somme between Amiens and Peronne. It eventually involved nearly ¾ million Allied troops confronting 16 frontline divisions of the German Second Army. It was preceded by a bombardment lasting eight days with the intention of annihilating the enemy's forward defences.

Up until 26 June, the 1st Battalion held the 4th Division's trenches; on 25 and 26 June gas attacks were made on the enemy. On the previous day (24 June) the gas had had little effect upon the enemy, and their artillery was especially active in causing damage to the Warwicks' trenches.

Casualties were heavy, mainly attributed to the German 5.9" shells and "Whizz Bangs", however some were also caused by British gas being blown back into the Battalion's lines.

On 25 June a similar turn of events transpired, with the Battalion trenches coming under heavy fire. The use of gas was dangerous and unpredictable, as the Battalion war diary recorded:

> At about 10.30 pm one of the gas cylinders leaked owing to having been hit by a piece of shell. At 10.45 pm the wind dropped completely and a very light breeze E.S.E. came up, [and] brought the gas back. The trench was also filled with gas from the leaking cylinder![13]

Three companies had to put on their rudimentary "smoke helmets". The Special Brigade, under Lieutenant Jones, which was responsible for discharging the gas, was badly gassed, two of them dying. Sergeant Keeley received a special mention for his fine work. There is also a note in the war diary stating "Old men very tired after nine days shelling and gas."

On the night of 26 June it was time once again for Shute and Gorton to lead a raiding party into the German trenches, but this time the enemy "… put such a heavy barrage up in front of and on our line that the party were unable to leave our own line and the raid was abandoned." The following day the 1st Battalion moved to Bertrancourt for rest and a change of clothing, remaining there until 30 June, when it was transferred to the assembly trenches at the front.

Orders were received indicating that the Allies were preparing for a major attack. Under the heading "Equipment", the Operation Order specified:

> Every man will carry rifles and equipment [packs and greatcoats were not included], 1 Bandolier, SAA [small-arms ammunition], 170 rounds in all, except grenade groups, who will carry 120 each, 2 Mills grenades [incl. officers], waterproof sheet, Cardigan jacket, 2 sand-bags per man, 6 sandbags per man placed folded on the back under the braces, 2 smoke helmets [gas masks], food for 48 hours in haver-sack as follows: mess-tin filled with small biscuits, 3 ozs. cheese, 1 tin beef, 1 tin Machonachie, iron rations of tea and sugar, and 5 large biscuits. In addition every fourth man will carry a tin of jam.[14]

On 1 July, the 10th Brigade began its advance as ordered. The 2/Royal Dublin Fusiliers and 2/Seaforth Highlanders led across open ground, with the 1/Royal Warwicks and 1/Royal Irish Fusiliers in support. At 9.15 a.m. the 1st Battalion received an order to halt and reform at Tenderloin Trench. Lieutenant-Colonel Bannerman recorded:

At 1.02 p.m. received an order to make an attempt to reach German line and Point 27 as British troops were reported in and about Point 27. I sent a patrol under Lieutenant R. R. Waters from "A" Coy. to try and make a lodgement at Point 27 – moving across Watling St.[15]

The patrol was initially successful, but was then pinned down by enemy machine-gun fire from Beaumont-Hamel and forced to return at about 2.15 p.m. By early evening it was obvious that the advance of the 10th Brigade was not going to achieve the desired results, so the Warwicks were moved back to a safer position. They remained in the trenches until relieved on 7 July.

Whilst the action of the Allies further south was considered a great success, that in the north involving the 4th Division was according to Kingsford a "splendid" failure. The corps commander, General Sir Aylmer Hunter-Weston, congratulated the division on its "indomitable pluck", assuring the men that though they had found the German strength too great, they had made a valuable contribution to the whole offensive by closely engaging and holding up such a formidable enemy force.

The field report covering the period 22 June to 1 July 1916 shows that the 1st Battalion's casualties from shellfire and gas were 8 officers and about 250 other ranks. On 1 July alone Kingsford indicates that the casualties were 61 other ranks. Neither give a breakdown of these numbers, but the Battalion's roll of honour records Lieutenant T. F. Breene and 13 other ranks killed on this day. On 1 July alone the army suffered 60,000 casualties, of whom one-third were killed. Following this slaughter there followed a stalemate lasting several weeks. The 1st Battalion was soon transferred from this area of the front.

Fighting was still raging in many other areas of the front, and it was to one of these that the 4th Division was now directed. In the early hours of 22 July the 4th Division entrained at Candas station, en route for Belgium. By 10 a.m. the same day the 1st Battalion had arrived at "K" camp, sited on the road between Poperhinghe and Watou. The following day the Prince of Wales visited the camp. Kingsford considered the next few weeks a period of rest, but some of the time was spent in trenches around the Ypres area. Much of the time was occupied in training and cleaning-up. In early September the men were issued with the new small box respirator.

By 16 September it was time for the 1st Battalion to move south again, where intensive fighting had been taking place for a couple of weeks. The Battle of Flers-Courcelette had taken place on 15 September, during which tanks were introduced to the field of battle for the first time. The Warwicks entrained at Proven, en route for Coisy, which is situated near Amiens. The journey via Hazebrook, Calais, Boulogne, took fourteen hours. After the men had detrained at Longeau they marched to Coisy, where they were

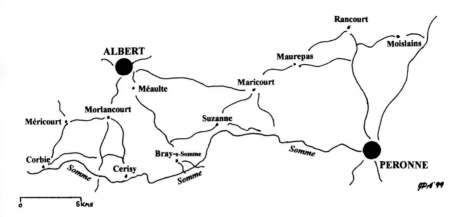

The 1st Battalion, Royal Warwickshire Regiment, September 1916 – March 1917.

billeted for the night. Following a further period of training exercises in the vicinity of Daours and Corbie the 4th Division moved north a few miles and by 8 October was settled at Mansell Camp, near Mametz.

Next day the 1st Battalion marched to Guillemont, moving into trenches east of Lesboeufs in the late afternoon. These had previously been occupied by the London Rifle Brigade. The remainder of 10th Brigade was also in the vicinity. During the night enemy artillery was very active, and the war diary records that Second Lieutenant Lovelace-Taylor was killed. The following two days saw an increase in action from both sides. On 11 October two Germans surrendered to the Battalion and were sent to Brigade headquarters for interrogation. Orders were given to prepare for an attack on the enemy's lines.

The diary records that "… the men had had a heavy shaking by constant shelling on 10th and 11th but the morning of the 12th was luckily fairly quiet and shelling was only intermittent." The attack began with a creeping barrage, under cover of which all the companies left the assembly trenches and moved across no man's land with little or no loss. At 3 p.m. it was reported that the 1/Royal Irish Fusiliers, together with some of the 1st Battalion's "D" Company, had run into trouble from their own barrage, forcing that part of the line to return to their original trenches. The initial advance gained over 300 yards, and the men dug-in. By mid-evening, however, it was obvious that other elements of the attack had not been so successful. Without flanking support the 1st Battalion was forced to reorganise and consolidate. It remained in the trenches most of the next day before being relieved by the 2/Royal Dublin Fusiliers at 10.30 p.m.

On the evening of 22 October the Battalion moved into trenches east of Lesboeufs.

Men wounded in France were encouraged to exercise whenever possible during their convalescence. (David Vaux Collection)

Due to the atrocious state of some billets, life under canvas was sometimes preferable. (David Vaux Collection)

The next assault on enemy lines was intended to begin on the morning of 23 October, the 1st Battalion being supported by the Dublin Fusiliers. However, because of poor visibility the attack did not get underway until 2.30 p.m., "Barrage fire opened – attack launched." Progress was good, and the first casualties did not occur until the attackers were well into no man's land. Covering fire was good, and by 4 p.m. the first German prisoners were brought back. An hour later some frontline strongpoints had been secured, but according to a wire from the Royal Dublin Fusiliers to the commander of the Warwicks, the advance was now being seriously held up by intense machine-gun fire, with casualties becoming heavy. Ammunition was running out; any German counter-attack would meet little opposition. By now, the attackers were beginning to break up into isolated groups and, where possible, dug-in. The shortage of ammunition was critical. At midnight Lt.-Col. G.N.B. Forster, 1st Battalion C.O., received a message from his counterpart in the Somerset Light Infantry that " "H" Coy. [Somerset L.I.] went forward to gun pits and delivered bombs and ammunition and found sufficient R. War. R. and R. Dub. Fus. there so withdrew." However, the Battalion requested a report, and it was found that the ammunition had not been delivered. Things began to quieten down, and one group in the trenches reported that "... Rifle fire this morning stopped a feeble attempt at a counter-attack with bombs." At 2 a.m. on 25 October the 1st Battalion was relieved by 20/Royal Fusiliers, 33rd Division.

The casualty figures for October 1916 were: Captain S.J. Riley, Captain M.C. Harrison, Second Lieutenant A.I. Glyka, Second Lieutenant D.W.A Hankey [16], Second Lieutenant Lovelace-Taylor and Second Lieutenant F.H. Cox killed in action. Captain R.R. Waters and Captain G.F. Irvine both died of wounds. 7 other officers were wounded. There were 175 casualties in the other ranks. Although the war diary does not break this figure down, other sources indicate 139 men were killed.

The Battalion returned to its camp in Trones Wood and, after a short rest, marched to Mansell Camp, where the men were accommodated under canvas. On 27 October, they moved to billets at Corbie. After cleaning themselves up the following day, the men were visited by the commander of 10th Infantry Brigade, who congratulated them on their fine performance during October's heavy fighting:

Both the Division and Corps were proud of the Battalion. All ranks showed great gallantry and now we shall be out of the line for one or two months and new drafts would join us, and they should be imbued with the same spirit. [17]

CHAPTER 7

With Tenacity and Valour: The 1st Battalion, Royal Warwicks, November 1916–June 1919

On 30 October 1916 the 1st Battalion entrained at Corbie for a 4 ½ hour journey to Airaines, from where it marched to Huppy, a few miles south of Abbeville. Two days later it travelled south to Tours and spent a month training there. On 8 November, Corporal H. Williams of "C" Company was awarded a Military Medal for his actions the previous month. The 15 November was, in some ways, a sad day for the Battalion and Brigade, as it saw the departure of the men of the 2/Royal Dublin Fusiliers. The Warwicks' drums played them through the village, closing with "Auld Lang Syne" as they finally departed. The Brigade's strength was once more brought up to par with the addition of the House-hold Battalion – a composite of surplus troops from the three regiments of the Household Cavalry.

On 3 December, the 1st Battalion was en route for the Somme once again, leaving Oisemont at 1 p.m. before arriving at billets in Morlancourt, north-east of Amiens, in the early evening. It moved into very poor frontline trenches near Sailly-Saillisel on 8 December, at a time when enemy artillery was very active. Relief came after eight days, and the pattern of a few days in the trenches followed by a few days in reserve was to continue for the next couple of months. The Somme offensive had petered out by the end of the year due to increasingly bad weather. Casualties had been heavy on both sides but the offensive had relieved pressure on the French at Verdun. In all, 12 battalions of the Royal Warwickshire Regiment had participated in the offensive. Overall, the British had suffered just over 400,000 casualties, a large majority of these being from "volunteers" battalions. The French casualties were about half this figure. The enemy lost about 500,000 men, including a high percentage of officers and non-commissioned-officers.

As winter approached the Allies had manoeuvred the enemy into a salient between the rivers Scarpe and Ancre. The German commanders then implemented a new strategy by consolidating and establishing a fresh defensive position some twenty miles to the rear of their current frontlines. This new position, sited further east of the northern and central areas on the Western Front, was not a solid defensive line but a cleverly planned system of linked fortifications, strategically spaced so that if necessary they could support each other. They stretched from the northern coast of France, south to Verdun, and were known collectively to the Allies as the Hindenburg Line. The planned German withdrawal began in early March, the enemy operating a scorched earth policy. W. Douglas Newton wrote:

> The German retreat in itself has been characterised by many evil German qualities. The Teutonic instinct for destruction appears to have had full sway; villages were burnt and plundered wantonly, wells were choked – and, what is abominable, poisoned – and at certain places young girls were carried off.[1]

G.H. Greenwell recorded:

> The Huns certainly did put arsenic in the wells at Basleux, and they left all sorts of little booby-traps behind them. The cunning dogs half-sawed through some bridges across the Somme and put bombs underneath which promptly blew up. They have left stoves in the dug-outs all ready for lighting which also blew up – in fact, they have done this retreat as throughly as they do everything else.[2]

The New Year of 1917 was greeted with a draft of 199 other ranks joining the 1st Battalion which, at the time, was encamped and training near Bray, between Amiens and Peronne. There was no heavy fighting during this period, and according to the Battalion war diary, casualties were very low. On 8 January the Battalion lost a semi-final football match in the General Lambton Cup Competition 4–1 to the Royal Irish Fusiliers. On 14 January, 4196 Lance Corporal F. Wilson was presented with a Military Medal. On 10 February 1917 the Battalion occupied new frontline trenches north of Bouchavesnes, where things began to "warm up". Two days later 1 man was killed and 5 wounded. Aircraft were much in evidence, and on 15 February British artillery shot down an enemy aircraft south of Bouchavesnes. The next day the Battalion was relieved by the Household Battalion. On 3 March the 1/Battalion Royal Irish Fusiliers played the 10th Field Ambulance, R.A.M.C., in the final of the General Lambton Cup, the R.A.M.C. winning 3–1.

On 5 March, the 1st Battalion began what was to be a long march north from Corbie. The first stage of thirty miles was completed two days later at Mezerolles and there, between 8 and 12 March, the various companies underwent training. The next stage of twenty miles to Savy-Berlette took place on 13–14 March. On 15 March an officer and 50 men from "B" Company retraced their steps to Penin, where they were employed in repairing roads. Another officer with 60 men marched west to undertake similar work at Ligny-St. Flochel, the location of the Third Army Trench Mortar School, situated five miles east of St. Pol-sur-Ternoise, on the main road between St. Pol and Arras. Similar work and training continued until 21 March, on which day the Battalion marched ten miles north to Camblain-Châtelain, fifteen miles south-west of Bethune. Here the Battalion rested, cleaned up and continued training. On 26 March "The 4th Division Follies" began a six-night season at the Knowle Church Army Hut, no doubt playing to a packed house each night. By the end of the month more officers and men had been added to the Battalion's strength. By now the men were well-rested, relaxed and without doubt fit from all the marching, road repairs and training. The war diary records that the officers of the 1st Battalion at the end of March were as follows:

Name and Rank	*Remarks*
Lieutenant-Colonel G.N.B. Forster, D.S.O.	
Captain (T. Major) Sir G.H.A. Lacon, Bt.	
Captain G.W. Cox	No.4 I.B.D. from 23.3.17
Captain A.J. Roberts	
Captain Strevens, M.C.	
Captain S.H. Holley	
Lieutenant H.T.Elliott	
Lieutenant Evezard	
Lieutenant E.J.A. Maunsell	
Lieutenant G.E.M. Marston	
Second Lieutenant I.H. Iles	
Second Lieutenant C.H.I. Jackson	
Second Lieutenant I.B. Hornblower	10th Brigade H.Q.
Second Lieutenant F. Denis	
Second Lieutenant J.K. Field	
Second Lieutenant W.G.B Edmonds	Wireless Tele. Cse. 17.3.17
Second Lieutenant K.L. Mole	
Second Lieutenant F.W. Arthurton	
Second Lieutenant S.H. Dowson	10th Brigade H.Q.
Second Lieutenant S.V. Figg	

Second Lieutenant (T. Lieut.) D.H. Willis
Second Lieutenant C.C. Oakey
Second Lieutenant R.H. Jeffrey
Second Lieutenant F.B. Dawson
Second Lieutenant H.J. Dixon
Second Lieutenant C.B. Riley
Second Lieutenant F.A. Smith
Second Lieutenant J. Parker
Second Lieutenant F.P. Dolley
Second Lieutenant J.H. Rushton
Second Lieutenant J. Hughes
Second Lieutenant N.R. Lowder
Second Lieutenant C.A. Price
Captain and Quartermaster T.H. Harwood

Officers Attached

Captain P.L.E. Walker — 7th Hussars Senior Officer Training School, Aldershot 28.3.17

Lieutenant H.B. Stutfield — General List
Captain D.A. Warren — R.A.M.C. (T.)
Captain Rev. S.C. Waldergrove C.F, C.E.

It was now becoming obvious that "something was on the cards" in the near future. On 1 April training began to take place on a larger scale, the 1st Battalion marching off at 7 a.m. to participate in 10th Brigade manoeuvres on the training ground near Moncy-Breton. The exercise, which included two-way communication with reconnaissance aircraft, was a success. Training continued for a few more days. On 6 April the G.O.C. 4th Division visited the camp and met the men in their billets, where he briefed them on the nature of the forthcoming operations, adding that he was in no doubt that the Battalion would live up to the fine reputation it had already gained on the Somme. The plan was for the 9th (Scottish) Division and South Africans to attack the St. Laurent – Blangy and Athies areas of Arras. They would then move on to Fampoux, a few miles east of the town. The Warwicks would be attached to the second wave of this attack.

At 6.45 a.m. on 9 April the 1st Battalion followed its preliminary orders and moved forward, taking ground and some German prisoners. The following day all went to plan, and by early evening the Battalion was settled in trenches east of Fampoux.

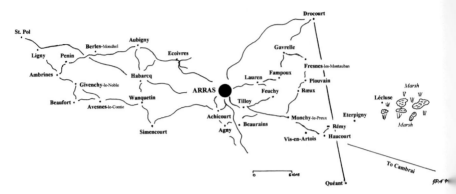

The 1st Battalion, Royal Warwickshire Regiment, May–June 1917, October 1917–April 1918, and August–October 1918.

The main attack began at midday on 11 April, by which time the 1st was on the outskirts of Fampoux. The day's objective was to secure a line from the railway embankment at Plouvain to a local château. The 1/Royal Irish Fusiliers and 2/Seaforth Highlanders began their advance, with the Warwicks following in support of the former. However, even before setting off from the assembly trenches enemy shells caused several casualties. The enemy shellfire was accompanied by heavy machine-gun fire from the chemical works and railway embankment, which further delayed the advance. Two 1st Battalion officers and a few men managed to get to within 100 yards of the railway station, but were soon forced back to a trench held by men of the 12th Brigade. There was no alternative but to dig-in. By nightfall the 1st Battalion was in the centre of the line, with the Royal Irish Fusiliers on its right flank and 2/Seaforths to its left. It remained in this forward position until 16 April, after which it retired to support trenches.

The war diary for 17 April recorded:

> Enemy were active during the morning on "B" Coy's trench. Enemy aircraft inactive. Enemy shelled support trenches in the evening. Battalion found working party of 4 officers and 160 other ranks. Party had to withdraw owing to enemy putting barrage down on Sunken Road.[3]

One of those killed at this time was Private Amos Twigger, from Nuneaton. He was only 22 years of age, and had worked for the Griff Colliery Company at their "Clara Pit", from which over 100 men had given their lives for their country. Twigger's father received details of his son's death in the usual sparsely-worded communication, and as with the majority of relatives of those killed in action, the Twigger family were eager to discover further details of their loved one's death. As a result, the following interesting story appeared in a local newspaper, written by one of Private Twigger's comrades:

My Dear Friends,

As regards news of your son Amos. Well, all that I can tell you [is] that he was killed instantly by a German shell on 17.4.17. During the bombardment, and just before he got hit one of our fellows said to him, 'Come along the trench a little, Amos,' so he said, 'Oh, I shall be all right here,' and the next we heard was that he was killed, so I take those to be his last words and concerning his photos and cigarette case, I saw the fellows today that buried him and they were unable to take anything from him owing to the intense shelling, so you can gather from this that all his belongings were buried with him. Well, friends, I am sure you have my deepest sympathy, and the fellows in his section send same, as he was very well admired by all who knew him, both officers, N.C.O.'s and men. So now I think this is as much as I can possibly tell you, and I hope to hear from you again in the near future, also Dinah. Give my best love to Norman and the rest of the children, and accept same yourself.

From your sincere friend, Corporal Leach,
"B" Coy., 1st R. War. R., B.E.F., France.[4]

On 20 April the 1st Battalion was relieved by the 8/Lincolnshire Regiment, and returned to the brigade reserve area near St. Nicholas, a little north of Arras. After cleaning up and resting, they transferred to Ambrines next day, before marching to Beaufort for further training. Returning to Arras again the following day, they prepared for another spell in the trenches.

In his "Narrative of Operations", Major Lacon considered...

... the failure of the attack was partly due to the fact that we were in view of the enemy practically the whole way from the fourth German system of trenches to the assembly area, also enemy aeroplanes which flew over the sunken road, (about 1000 ft. high), just before zero hour.[5]

The casualties amongst the officers were second lieutenants F. Devis and R. H. Jeffrey killed; Second Lieutenant P.H. Iles wounded and missing; Lieutenant H.T. Elliott and second lieutenants K.L. Mole, F.W. Arthurton, F.B. Dawson and C.A. Price wounded. Of the other ranks 43 were killed or died of their wounds.

Two views of the stark and battered landscape of Ypres, 1917. (Private collection)

The following day the 1st Battalion was transferred by motor transport to Ambrines. It then marched to Beaufort for further training, before returning to Arras on 29 April and preparing for another spell in the trenches. As the French were concentrating their offensive action along the River Aisne, it became necessary to occupy as much of the enemy's strength as possible in the Arras area. Consequently, at 12.30 a.m. on 3 May a general thrust was launched along the six mile line between Fresnes-les-Montauban and Plouvain.

The 10th Brigade, together with one battalion from the 11th, occupied the right flank of the 4th Division's attack. The Operation Order stated that,

> 10th Infantry Brigade and Somerset Light Infantry will attack between boundaries shown on map; 1st R. Warks R. on left, Household Battalion in centre, 1st Somerset Light Infantry on the right. 1st Royal Irish Fusiliers follow R. Warks. R. and 2nd Seaforth Highlanders – Household Battalion and Somerset L.I.[6]

Initially the advance, conducted in two waves, went as planned, but then became pinned down by heavy enemy machine-gun fire. By 5.15 a.m. "D" Company had begun to penetrate the first German line of trenches, and enemy-occupied houses, but as casualties were high it was forced to retreat. The Household Battalion was also held up. An enemy counter-attack later in the day caused stalemate.

At the end of the day Captain H. Strevens resumed the attack with four lines of troops, each being composed of 20 men. The first line mainly consisted of bombers, the third of Lewis gunners. Lieutenant A.W. Dacombe led the first line, and managed to gain a portion of enemy trench, only to be bombed out before supports arrived. Dacombe launched another attack using the second and third lines, but again was driven back by machine-gun fire and rifle grenades. Similarly, Captain Strevens and the fourth line were driven back. The Battalion war diary indicated that the trench would have been taken and held if the attack had received more support. At midnight on 4 May the 1st Battalion was relieved by the 1/Hampshire Regiment.

Since 1 January 1917 the Battalion had lost 1 officer killed, 6 wounded and 4 missing; 5 other ranks killed, 78 wounded and 109 missing. When the relief was completed the Battalion marched a short distance to dug-outs and shelters, remaining there for a few days whilst undertaking repair work.

At 7 p.m. on 8 May a ten minute feint attack, popularly known as a "Chinese bombardment", was launched at the enemy's front line trenches. This was intended to divert attention from more serious activity taking place elsewhere. Later that same evening the 1st Battalion relieved the 2/Seaforths and a section of the Royal Irish Fusiliers in the trenches. The next action occurred at 7.30 p.m. on 11 May, when an attack on Rœux was renewed. At 8.20 p.m. the commander of the Household Battalion reported that he believed the objective had been achieved, although casualties were high. An hour later he reported that he was being held up, so "B" Company, 1st Battalion, now only 28 men strong, was sent to assist. At about this time a serious gap opened between the 10th and 11th brigade positions, which was closed by "C" Company, now about 30 men strong. Darkness fell, and it was not until the moon rose that positions could be firmly established. At midnight "A" Company was sent forward to complete what turned out to be a successful movement. By 7 p.m. on 12 May many German prisoners had been taken. A few hours later the 10th Brigade secured Rœux. During these actions the 1st Battalion lost 1 officer (Captain C. Evezard), and 3 other ranks killed and 21 wounded. On the afternoon of 11 May the Battalion's strength had only been 8 officers and 165 other ranks. By the following day this had been further reduced to 7 officers and 141 other ranks.

The 1st Battalion was relieved by the 1/5 Seaforths during the early hours of 12 May. By 3 p.m. next day it was billeted in houses and barns at Houvin-Houvigneul, some 20 miles west of Arras. Here it rested and further training took place. On 25 May the brigade paraded before the corps commander for the presentation of the following decorations: Captain D.A. Warren, R.A.M.C., attached to the 1st Battalion, – M.C.; 1266 Lance-Corporal H. Guest – Military Medal (M.M.); 2428 Lance-Sergeant H. Williams – D.C.M.; 11286 Lance-Corporal C.H. Wilson – M.M.; 1076 Sergeant S. Murrell – M.M.; 942 Sergeant J. Hems – M.M.; 30161 Private H. Lyons – M.M.; 6372 Private E. Lampert – bar to M.M. A later 10th Infantry Brigade Message indicated that 1773 Sgt. A. Village was awarded the French Medaille Militaire, and 645 Corporal H. Williams the M.M. The ceremony was followed by a 10th Infantry Brigade Sports Afternoon.

June opened with the 4th Division Horse Show, followed by some days of training. On 10 June the above-mentioned men of the 1st Battalion received their medals from Major General the Hon. W. Lambton, 4th Division C.O.

The Battalion returned to the trenches and the all-too-regular pattern of a few days at the front, and a few out. On 9 September a Special Divisional Order from Major General Lambton was received by the Warwicks, thanking it for the hard work carried out by all ranks in holding the line in the Scarpe Valley. The poorly-built trenches captured in June had been replaced by a properly-organised line, with continuous support and reserve trenches, and good dug-out accommodation. All this work had been carried despite the considerable difficulties imposed by bad weather and "… is a testimony to the hearty co-operation and good spirit shown by all ranks." Major General Lambton concluded by saying that he " … felt sure the same spirit will be shown in the forthcoming training, and that all ranks will do their utmost to fit themselves for battle, during the short time available." On 19 September the 1st Battalion entrained for Proven, northwest of Poperhinge, Belgium, from where it moved into Palma Camp and, after a few days training, to Wolff Camp, near Ypres.

On 3 October the 1st Battalion was being held in reserve. At 6 a.m. the following day a major offensive was launched, involving the 2/Seaforth Highlanders and 3/10 Middlesex regiment, who had replaced the Royal Irish Fusiliers in 10th Brigade. The intention was to advance some 1,200 yards. Besides having to cover open ground, the attackers were faced with the natural hazard of Laudetbeek Marsh. In the early afternoon the 1st Battalion receive orders to reinforce the Seaforth Highlanders. It arrived at Eagle Trench at about 3.30 p.m., suffering few casualties despite the enemy's heavy barrage. The commander of the Seaforths reported that his left flank was "unsupported and in the air." "A" and "B" companies advanced to reinforce the Seaforth Highlanders, "C" company providing close support. On reaching the frontline the men were ordered to capture Hill 19, but were confronted by heavy enemy machine-gun fire before they had even reached their objective.

Two supporting patrols from the 1st Battalion were sent out under Lieutenant J.S. Morris, and two pill boxes and a machine-gun were captured along with eight prisoners. A short while later Lieutenant Morris was killed by a sniper. The troops then made a further advance, positioning themselves on the reverse slope of Hill 19. By sending out patrols the Battalion hoped to establish contact with the troops on both flanks. They were subsequently successful in contacting the 2/East Lancashire Regiment to the right, and the 1/Royal Dublin Fusiliers, now part of the 29th Division, on the left flank. Further efforts were made to link up with the 2/Seaforths and 3/10 Middlesex, but enemy machine gun-fire restricted further movements. Orders were then received to consolidate, abandoning a further advance. During the night of 5/6 October the 1st Battalion relieved the 2/Seaforths and 3/10 Middlesex Regiments; the 2/South Wales Borderers moved into the 1st Battalion's old positions, eventually making contact with the 1/Rifle Brigade. The 1st Battalion was later relieved, arriving at Hull's Camp at 3 a.m. on 7 October.

It was decided by Sir Douglas Haig to continue efforts to advance. The weather remained inclement, and on 10 October the 1/Royal Warwicks and Household Battalion were placed under the orders of the 12th Infantry Brigade commander, resuming their frontline duties. Two days later it was the turn of the 1st Battalion to join the battle at a point east of Poelkapelle, where it relieved the 2/Lancashire Fusiliers. Casualties were low. The British artillery laid down a heavy barrage, enabling the 1st to

The 1st Battalion, Royal Warwickshire Regiment, April–August 1918.

advance and take several important positions to the north-east of the village, although the brewery at the end of the village remained in enemy hands.

At 5.20 p.m. it appeared that the enemy was preparing to make a counter-attack, but an S.O.S. was sent up and the British artillery responded almost immediately, thus preventing any German attack. In the early hours of the 13 October the 26/Northumberland Fusiliers attempted to relieve the Warwicks' but, due to the pitch black night and poor weather conditions, this proved impossible until later in the day. The 1st Battalion then marched to bivouac shelter at Leipzig Camp. The following message was received from Major General T.G. Matheson, commander of 4th Division:

> Nobody will ever forget the part taken by the 4th Division in the great battle of Flanders 1917. In eight days you have had three fights in the most trying conditions that any troops have had to endure, and in the words of the army commander 'the performance was marvellous.'

The demands made on the artillery have surpassed all previous records and the gallantry and determination of the infantry have been beyond all praise. Machine-gun companies and light trench mortar batteries have materially assisted the infantry and in spite of heavy losses have shown the finest spirit throughout. As usual the gallantry of the linesmen and devotion to duty of all the signal service have been splendid. But for the unceasing energies of the R.E. and pioneers the movement across country and the transport of material up to the front would have made the operations impossible. Last but not least a great debt of gratitude is due to the R.A.M.C. personnel with the attached infantry stretcher bearers for their never ceasing efforts to bring in the wounded and save them from unnecessary suffering. Nobody could be more proud than I am of commanding such troops. I thank and congratulate you all.[7]

On 18 October the 1st Battalion entrained at Hopoutre Siding and travelled to Aubigny, twelve miles north-west of Arras. On 23 October they marched to Achicourt, on the outskirts of that town. Next day they relieved the 6/Buffs Regiment at Brown Line (Mackenzie Trench). After regular training sessions, several companies spent the remainder of the month making coils of barbed concertina wire which were taken up to the front at night. On 1 November the 1st Battalion moved into support trenches.

On 8 November orders were issued to prepare a raiding party. This was part of a plan to divert the enemy's attention to enable a larger, main offensive, to be launched by the Third Army. The intention was that the Warwicks, together with other regiments in the area, show as much activity as possible and harass the enemy by simulating preparations for an attack. The raid actually took place on 20 November, and a subsequent message from Lt. General C. Fergusson, commanding XVIII Corps, thanked all ranks for their co-operation. He wrote:

… the raiding and patrol work of the infantry with the support of the artillery have done exactly what was needed. The enemy has been worried night and day, has suffered casualties, has lost prisoners and machine-guns and has been generally uncomfortable. This activity has entitled us to claim at any rate a small share in the success of the Third Army.[8]

Several weeks were spent in the Arras area. At times the front was active, at other times relatively quiet, but casualties were very low. On 23 December the enemy sent out two raiding parties. The first was quickly repulsed by Lewis gun fire, but the other succeeded in entering the sap and 6 men from "A" Company were reported missing. The raid was followed by an enemy gas shell bombardment, which caused several casualties and badly damaged the trenches. Christmas celebrations for the Warwicks did not take place until 31 December at Schramm Barracks, where there was a special performance by the "4th Division Follies", music being provided by the division band. On 1 January 1918 all of the Battalion's officers dined at the Hotel de Univers in Arras.

Kingsford sums up the activities of 1917 by saying that,

> ... the Great Offensive had in the end been robbed of the prospect of more far reaching results by bad weather. The fighting in its last phases at Ypres and Cambrai had been costly, and consequent gaps in the British forces in France had still to be made good.[9]

The task of relieving other troops in the trenches was always a precarious business, and on 3 January a N.C.O. and 8 other men were wounded as the Battalion relieved the 1/East Lancashires. On 10 January R.Q.M.S. Poste was awarded a D.C.M., the citation for which is given in Appendix VIII. By the time the men went into the front line on 18 January large sections of the trenches were up to three feet deep in water due to the incessant rain over previous days. Under such conditions it would not be unreasonable to expect that illness would be rife, especially chest complaints and pneumonia. However, the war diary makes the point that there was little sickness at the time.

More decorations were forthcoming for the 1st Battalion on 2 February, when A/Sergeant Gunter, A/Sergeant Hemmings and Corporal Brain were awarded the Belgian Croix de Guerre. On 8 February, 8 officers and 250 other ranks joined the 1st Battalion from the 11/Royal Warwicks, which had been disbanded. That same day, the 3/10 Middlesex Regiment left the 10th Brigade prior to being disbanded. Apart from these events life carried on for the 1st Battalion in what, for want of better words, was "the usual way". At the end of February another congratulatory message was delivered to all ranks, this time from Lt. Col. H. Carslake, General Staff, 4th Division thanking them for,

> ... the splendid way they have worked during the last few weeks the Division was in the line. The destruction of the trenches caused by the thaw was enough to dishearten anybody, but instead of it having that effect, everybody set to and worked magnificently.

> The spirit evinced by all ranks of all arms during this period could not have been better. It has once more shown that the spirit which enabled the 4th Division to save the old Expeditionary Force from disaster during the retreat from Mons is still present, and should the

necessity arise, the Germans will once more find to their cost that the 4th British Division will once again defeat their efforts.[10]

On 28 March the enemy mounted a massive attack on Arras. Although British losses were high the offensive was halted. On this occasion the 1st Battalion was not involved, as it did not arrive at the frontline until two days later. On 30 March orders were received to push on and occupy "India" and "Iceland" trenches. "A", "C" and "D" companies achieved their objectives, but "B" was pinned down by heavy machine-gun fire and had to retreat to its original position; later "D" had to do the same. "C" was attacked with rifle-grenades and it, too, had to retreat. By the following night Lieutenant J. Preedy had been killed, Lieutenant C.J. Gittings and Second Lieutenant P.M. Carpendale wounded, and 25 other ranks either killed or wounded. On 1 April Second Lieutenant N.A. Kingston was killed.

By 10 April the pressure exerted by the enemy indicated that the line across the Lys required reinforcement, and this task fell partly to the 4th Division. During the afternoon of 12 April the 1st Battalion was transported to Lillers, north-west of Bethune, and two days later they were in Hinges. Early that morning a patrol from "C" Company captured two enemy machine-guns along with one prisoner. Later the same morning a German artillery officer, accompanied by a signaller, was seen close to "C" Company. The signaller was shot and the officer taken prisoner, and another machine-gun was also captured. During the evening the British launched a heavy artillery bombardment concentrated on Riez-du-Vinage and Pacault, and the 11th Brigade successfully took Riez. During this action the 1st Battalion's headquarters received a direct hit, and Captain F.N.H. Beamish, M.C., was wounded. Probing attacks were launched along the road running through Pacault Wood, but the enemy was well-established and the troops were forced to retreat.

After an early conference on the morning of 15 April, orders were issued for the 1st Battalion, along with the 2/Duke of Wellington's Regiment, to attack and capture Pacault Wood and other strategic enemy positions north of the wood. At 5.15 p.m. a covering artillery barrage began, the Battalion taking up positions to advance at 5.45 p.m. The two companies on the right were to cross the Canal d'Aire by the Pont d'Hinges; the two companies on the left were to cross the canal by means of a pontoon bridge.

When the British artillery barrage commenced at 5.15 p.m. it was so short in distance that it fell behind the two companies on the left. The enemy artillery then took the initiative and opened up. When the British artillery resumed its fire it was still off-target, and its creeping barrage fell on 1st Battalion's headquarters, as well as the two companies positioned on the left who were waiting to cross the pontoon. Even though the enemy response was ferocious and British casualties high, the men stood their ground. The pontoon was temporarily out of use due to a direct hit by enemy fire. Matters were not helped when it took another direct hit, this time fired by the British artillery. The Royal Engineers were commended for their instant action in repairing the pontoon, despite being under intense enemy shell and machine-gun fire.

By 5.40 p.m. the situation had improved, and the British artillery barrage was ahead of the advancing troops. Although there was heavy German fire the two left-hand companies successfully crossed the pontoon, and despite suffering heavy losses, were able to launch their attack. The enemy were positioned throughout Pacault Wood, which contained several buildings. Enemy cavalry was also seen in the area. The attack appeared to have caught the enemy in the act of forming for a counter-attack, preparations for which were halted. Try as they might, the British were only able to penetrate a short way into the wood, and strong enemy resistance resulted in the two left-hand companies having to dig-in on the edge of the area.

At 5.45 p.m. the companies positioned on the right crossed the Pont d'Hinges, but due to the failed advance of their neighbours to the left they were enfiladed and suffered high casualties. Their progress was also impeded by wire. Second Lieutenant P.J. Bowden's party did achieve their first objective at high cost, as he and all but 5 men from his platoon fell to enemy fire. Other groups reached the perimeter of the wood but casualties were high here, too, and as it was impossible to get any reinforcements forward, their only option was to retire. Second lieutenants G.S. Bourke and W.T.L. Terise were killed, as were all the men in their party. During the same attack second lieutenants A.H. Murch, H.J. King and E.H. Fisher were wounded and over 50 other ranks killed. Amongst them was 267316 Private Charles William Bradley, who only three days before had written the following letter to his wife Doris:

> Dearly Beloved Wife,
> I now take the pleasure of answering your lovely letter which I received quite safe and also thank you for the fags which came in very handy. I am also very glad to hear that you and all at home are in the best of health as it leaves me at present. I am very glad to hear that you have got plenty of work but for God's sake do not overdo yourself or you will only make yourself bad as I do not want to hear that as it is worse out here. Dear, I will look out for the cocoa when it comes I will let you know when I have it. Dear, do not worry your head about me as I shall look after myself and come home and make you happy, as I think more of you now as I did before and I hope that it will soon be

During the war the Warwicks won several sports competitions, football being the most popular. (David Vaux Collection)

Membership certificate for the Old Contemptibles belonging to W.W. Milner, D.C.M., 1st Btn. Royal Warwicks. (David Vaux Collection)

all over as I am sick of it all. I dare say you do not have much time at home now, but let Gladys do her share in the house-work as you have enough to do, but I tell you that if I was at home you would not go to work but now it is all for the good of the cause. I am sending you our Dad's letter, and write and let me know what do you think about it. I am also sending you a card which I hope you will like. Dear, tell A. Overton that I am sorry that I could not write to him as I lost his address. Well Dear, I think I can now come to a smash [?] wishing Mrs. Howard and jolly old Dick, Dad and Gladys and you the best of health and love.

From your loving husband, Bill

xxxxxxxxxxxxxxxxx (one at a time please)

Write back soon[11]

This simple, yet poignant, letter is typical of the many thousands sent home by men on active service. All too often, they were followed a few days later by another, written by an officer on Army Form B104–82, informing the beloved wife that it was his duty to inform her that she was now a widow.

The battle for the Canal d'Aire and Pacault Wood continued throughout the following day. The activity on 18 April began at 2.30 a.m. when enemy artillery put down a prolonged and heavy bombardment. This was an overture to a renewed German attack passing through the wood and up to the banks of the canal, where the Germans attempted to float a pontoon across it. The British retaliated with Lewis and machine-gun fire which drove the enemy back. Enemy casualties were high and some 130 prisoners were taken. The 4th Division had won the day, but not without suffering heavy losses, especially amongst the 2/Seaforth Highlanders. After being relieved by the 1/Rifle Brigade on 19 April, the 1st Battalion marched to billets in Gonnehem.

The break at Gonnehem only lasted for a few hours, and on the evening of the following day the 1st Battalion was once again back in the area of the canal, giving support to the 12th Brigade. It remained here until being relieved by the 1/Somerset Light Infantry, and then marched to billets in Busnettes. This particular offensive had seen the Germans employ over one hundred divisions in their attempt to destroy the British. No praise can be too high for the manner in which the B.E.F. faced such strong opposition. A press communiqué dated 22 April praised all those involved. It emphasised the distinguished role played by the 4th Division, which of course included the 1/Royal Warwickshire Regiment and other regiments of the 10th Brigade.

After four days rest the 1st Battalion relieved the 2/Lancashire Fusiliers in the trenches. On 9 May the Battalion came under attack from enemy gas shells, which lay especially heavy in the rear areas. The Medical Officer and his staff had to be evacuated suffering from gas poisoning. Lieutenant W.H. Joyce (M.O.R.C.) was taken to hospital, where he died on 17 May. The action around the canal bank area continued the following day. Early that morning Lieutenant J. de C. Stretton and CSM R. Gibson were killed in the trenches by a 'whizz-bang.' On 15 May the Battalion was relieved by the 1/Rifle Brigade, returning to billets in Busnettes.

On 16 May, Captain E.J.A. Maunsell and second lieutenants J. de C. Stretton and A.H. Murch were awarded the M.C., and Sergeant J. Webb of "D" Company received the D.C.M. Three days later further awards were made to other ranks who had distinguished themselves in the recent fighting. The 1st Battalion relieved the 2/Lancashire Fusiliers later that same day (19 May). The next seven days were spent in the trenches; there was little activity from either side. On 30 May, when the men were back in Busnettes, a number of enemy shells fell in the village. 1 man was killed and 4 wounded. That evening the "Divisional Follies" returned with a show for the troops.

The next spell in the trenches began on 3 June, when there were several sightings of enemy aircraft. Two days later one of these dropped propaganda into the British lines. British aircraft later brought down an enemy observation balloon. Throughout this period there were intermittent periods of heavy artillery fire from both sides. On 12 June, Second Lieutenant F.N. Martin and a patrol of 8 men were bombed and subjected to machine-gun fire. Martin was wounded, 1 other rank killed, 2 mortally wounded, 1 man missing and another wounded. While back in billets on 14 June the 1st Battalion's strength was increased by 91 other ranks. On 30 June a raiding party of 4 officers and 108 other ranks penetrated the enemy's trenches. According to orders the object of this exercise was "to obtain identifications".

The first wave of the raiding party experienced very little difficulty in moving forward, as the accompanying artillery barrage had made impressive gaps in the wire. The first few Germans they encountered were either killed by rifle fire or by running into the artillery barrage as they bolted away. The second wave passed through the first, finding the enemy retreating from their frontline, many Germans being shot as they ran away. Five prisoners were taken and other men were killed either by rifle fire or the box barrage. The official report shows that a total of 50 of the enemy were killed, it was believed none escaped. There was very little German resistance, 1st Battalion casualties were only 2 badly wounded, 12 slightly wounded, and 1 man was missing, although it was reported later that he was in a dressing station belonging to another regiment. The operation had gone smoothly and was a success. Due to a change in wind direction smoke from the British barrage began to drift across the Battalion's front, but this was not considered to be a major problem.

On the night of 17 July, "C" Company placed steps over its front line parapet and cut gaps in the wire. This was to enable a raiding party to be launched from the Warwick's trenches at 2.30 p.m. by the 2/Duke of

The 1st Battalion, Royal Warwickshire Regiment, October 1918–January 1919.

Wellington's Regiment. It was impossible to launch it from this unit's section of the front. The opening British artillery barrage was soon answered by the enemy, who shelled the 1st Battalion's front and support lines, resulting in 4 men being killed and 6 wounded. 29 enemy prisoners were taken during the raid. "C" Company later repaired the gap in the wire. The 1st Battalion was relieved by the 1/Rifle Brigade on 20 July. As the 1st Battalion was relieving the 2/Lancashires on 27 July 7 men from "D" Company fell into the canal as the barrel bridge they were crossing overturned – 1 of them was drowned.

A few days earlier the great German Spring Offensive began to falter, with the French success at the Second Battle of the Marne. The enemy began to retreat, and it then became the Allies turn to take the initiative on the Western Front. The war was becoming mobile once again. The first victory of the counter-offensive took place east of Amiens on 8 August. The Warwicks were not involved as they remained in the northern part of the line, near Lys. But progress was soon made in that area, too. On the morning of 6 August "A" Company advanced towards the enemy's assumed front line but discovered that it had already been evacuated. The next day the company achieved two of its three objectives. During this fighting Second Lieutenant R.W. Thorowgood, M.C., was killed. Battalion headquarters were set up east of Riez-du-Vinage.

Between 10 and 15 August the 1st Battalion was billeted at Busnettes. On 10 August the Warwicks had formed part of a guard of honour along the Lillers-Bourecq road during a visit by King George V to France. On 15 August the Battalion returned to the trenches, this time relieving the 2/Essex Regiment. On the morning of the following day, 5 men from "A" Company were slightly gassed and, throughout 16 and 17 August there was heavy artillery fire from both sides in the area of Pacault Wood. On 17 August the enemy opened an accurate close-range fire with rifles and machine-guns. Next day news was received that the enemy was preparing to retreat a distance of nearly two miles. On 18 August the 4th Division was able to approach and occupy the villages of Pacault and Paradis.

On 25 August the 4th Division was transferred from the Fifth Army to the First. The advancing Third Army had created a salient before Arras, and enabled the First Army to extend the attack. Within two days Monchy-le-Preux, Gavrelle and Rœux had been captured from the enemy.

The 1st Battalion entrained at Pernes and arrived a few hours later at Petit Houvin, near St. Pol. It then marched to very poor billets at Buneville; accommodation was so poor that 100 men had to bivouac in the open air. On 28 August orders were issued for the 1/Royal Warwickshire Regiment to relieve the 5th Canadian Mounted Rifles. After a short journey by bus the Battalion assembled at Fuechy Chapel. At 6.30 p.m. it moved forward and some eight hours later was in its designated position in front of the village of Vis-en-Artois. The relief had not gone smoothly, and amongst the casualties was the wounded Second Lieutenant G.R. Pocklington. Next morning a further advance was made, with the capture of Rémy. The 1st Battalion now saw heavy action.

On 30 August the 1st was met by a substantial enemy artillery barrage and concentrated machine-gun fire as it attempted to advance. "B" and "C" companies bore the brunt of this fire, and suffered severe casualties. Lieutenant A.J. Adams was killed; Captain P.H. Hicks, M.C., and Lieutenant J.B. Coventry were wounded, and Second Lieutenant T.F. Hyde was gassed. Captain E.J.A. Maunsell's "D" Company managed to reach its objective with only slight casualties. The attack was renewed at 4 p.m. when the 1st Battalion advanced alongside the 2/Duke of Wellington's Regiment. Under the leadership of Captain Maunsell the men from again moved forward. They were faced with two natural obstacles, a river and a swamp, which necessitated some of the men wading through muddy water, at times waist deep. Though this slowed them down their objective was reached without much resistance from the enemy, many of whom were shot as they attempted to flee. During this attack casualties included Lieutenant L.J.C. Seaman killed; Lieutenant C.W. Rowntree and Second

Lieutenant F.G. Kitching wounded; Second Lieutenant J.E. Hosking gassed. Because of the unavoidable delay in crossing the river and swamp the covering creeping barrage had moved too far ahead, which, together with the serious shortage of men at the front, prevented further objectives being taken.

Captain W.G.B. Edmonds, M.C., took the initiative and, together with some 60 stragglers, moved up to reinforce Captain Maunsell, who had occupied a position west of the second objective. Support was later received from a company of Seaforth Highlanders, who relieved the 1st Battalion. Due to heavy losses the companies were reorganised next day. 14 other ranks had been killed, and 4 officers and 147 other ranks were wounded or missing. Because of this reduced strength, "A" and "C" companies were merged, as were "B" and "D". They were designated numbers 1 and 2 composite companies. At this time British artillery was concentrating its fire on a sixteen mile line running from Drocourt, north-east of Arras, to Quéant, directly east of Cambrai and south of Arras. This line held highly concentrated pockets of enemy troops whose resistance had to be broken.

On 4 September, the 1st Battalion boarded buses at Tilloy and was transported to billets at Bailleul-aux-Cornailles. Next day the 4th Division commander visited the camp to congratulate the officers and men on their success during the previous weeks. Until 18 September the men's time was spent cleaning-up and training, and an inter-company football competition was played. At 12.20 p.m. on 18 September the Battalion was once again en route to the trenches, and after being taken by bus to Vis-en-Artois, it relieved the 1/1 London Regiment in the line near Lécluse – "C" and "D" companies were in the frontline, with "A" and "B" in support. The marshy area around Lécluse was covered with many lakes and meres. The British artillery remained active throughout this period. During the night of 25 September, Second Lieutenant P.L. Smith, M.C., led a patrol through the marshes and was confronted by enemy sentries, although the men managed to evade them and avoided any casualties. Second Lieutenant L.W. Adams and his patrol were fired upon by the enemy whilst moving along a flooded road at Etaing. Although they experienced difficulty in returning to their lines they managed to avoid suffering any casualties.

On the night of 28 September Second Lieutenant R.B. Hall and his party acquired a boat and attempted to cross a flooded area but, as they reached marshland on the opposite side, they were subjected to heavy machine-gun fire. In trying to escape, the boat hit an obstacle in the river and sank in eight feet of water. Eventually, the men reached the relative safety of a small island, and one of the party managed to swim back to the lines. A

Members of the 1st Battalion, Royal Warwickshire Regiment, plus band, at Binche station, June 1919. (David Vaux Collection)

rescue party with another boat was sent out and all returned safely. Two days later the Battalion was relieved by the 1/Hampshire Regiment. It proceeded to trenches and dug-outs in the area around Eterpigny, and took up a reserve position near to the 11th Brigade. There was little enemy activity, and although the 1st Battalion remained in the trenches, regular baths could be taken and a limited amount of training was possible. Relief came during the evening of 6 October, when the 8th Battalion Canadian Infantry took over. The Warwicks then marched to Arras, where they were billeted in the Museum and Granary. Next morning, following an inspection and parade, the men marched to Simencourt, where the Battalion was placed in army reserve.

On 11 October, the 1st Battalion was transported from Wanqetin, south-west of Arras, to St. Olle, on the outskirts of Cambrai. This town was classed as "out of bounds" to the troops. Once again the men were going into action. After marching through Cambrai on 13 October, they arrived in Naves. During this march the war diary notes "... the country through which we marched showed few signs of the battle fought two days ago. Two delayed-action mines exploded as we passed through." On arrival at Naves the billets were found to be in a poor state, mainly due to shellfire, and the following day was spent cleaning and making them habitable. Ambulances passed through, transporting civilians who had been rescued from Saulzoir, four miles to the north-east. The Battalion

165

relieved the 4th Duke of Wellington's Regt. in the trenches at a point in front of Villers-en-Cauchies. At 11 p.m. on 23 October, the Battalion took up its battle positions – "B" and "D" companies in the front line, the former on the left, the latter on the right. "C" Company formed the left-hand support, "A" the right.

At zero hour, 4 a.m. on 24 October, events got off to a bad start when the covering artillery barrage fell short, causing the 1st Battalion a few casualties. The River Ecaillon was crossed without opposition, and as the Battalion moved into the village of Verchain large numbers of the enemy surrendered. It took only an hour for it to achieve its first objective. Achieving the second, an area of high ground north-east of the village, was not so easy, and the attackers were confronted by a trench line supported by enemy machine-guns. "A" and "C" companies were forced to regroup some 200 yards short of their objective. They were in close contact with the 1/Somerset Light Infantry to their left and the 2/Duke of Wellington's Regt. to their right. During this phase of the advance Second Lieutenant F.N. Martin was killed, and Second Lieutenant J. Harrison and Lieutenant F.A. Smith, M.C., wounded. Later that evening the Battalion was relieved by the 1/King's Own Regt. from the 12th Brigade, and moved into billets at Saulzoir. The total number of casualties was 95 killed or wounded and, in addition to those officers already mentioned, Second Lieutenant H.H. Carter was wounded. The Battalion captured 2 light mortars, 8 heavy machine-guns, 10 light machine-guns and approximately 150 men.

The extremes of daily life in the Royal Warwicks were astonishing. Days of hell in the trenches were often, but not always, followed by a break in a totally different environment, although still relatively close to the front. Football competitions were very popular, but there were also other events which one would hardly have expected to take place in the middle of a war. After the Battalion had reached Saulzoir, where the men bathed and changed their clothes, 7 men were presented with medals which had been won at the brigade's horse show three months earlier. The officers from the Shires were certainly not going to let a war interfere with their traditions! On the last day of October preparations were made to occupy fresh positions in the forward area at Artes.

Around the end of October 1918, the commander of 4th Division, Major General T.G. Matheson, was appointed commander of the Guards Division. When he relinquished his command, he thanked the officers and men of the 4th Division for their distinguished service whilst serving under him. The basis of his statement provides a fitting summary of the role played by the 1st Battalion Royal Warwickshire Regiment during the last twelve months of the war. After distinguishing themselves in Flanders during the latter months of 1917 they continued to do so in March 1918 when "… sheer tenacity and valour alone could stem the overflowing enemy tide." The 4th Division had proved its worth at Arras, where it halted a hostile enemy advance. This had had far reaching results. After a rapid transfer to a sector north of Bethune the division was once again in the frontline, and immediately advanced to take Riez-du-Vinage. This was followed by intense and stubborn fighting around Pacault Wood, where a large number of the enemy were captured. After the wood had been taken, "… there were many defensive works to create, and this work was carried out in a manner worthy of the best traditions." Then came a period during which untiring patrols had seized the initiative from the enemy, who, after severe fighting, was forced to withdraw.

By August 1918 the division had returned to Arras, where the Allies had enjoyed a great victory in breaking the Drocourt – Quént line, albeit only after several days of continuous fighting, during which hundreds more of the enemy were taken prisoner. Finally, Major General Matheson paid tribute to the thousands of men who had made the ultimate sacrifice with their lives. The 4th Division, along with the 8th, held the unique position of being a Regular Division who were representative of the "Old British Army" as it stood at the outbreak of the war. By the time the war ended the original B.E.F. had been sadly depleted, and there were very few Old Contemptibles "left to tell the tale".

The first few days of November saw all six battalions of the Royal Warwickshire Regiment in the sector south of Valenciennes. On the first day of the month the 1st Battalion supported the Seaforth High-landers in taking Presau, where they were based when the Armistice was declared.

On 11 November 1918 the war diary for the 1st Battalion closed and a new peace diary opened. On 19 November the men marched back to Saulzoir. Ironically it was only a few miles north of the point where the Warwicks had begun their war four years earlier.

The final casualty statistics show that between 1914 and 1919 the number of officers in the Royal Warwickshire Regiment who were killed or died in service was 585, of which 62 (10.6%) were from the 1st Battalion. The figure for other ranks was 10,891 killed or died in service, of which 1,397 (12.8%) came from the 1st Battalion.

That was not quite the end of the story for the 1st Battalion. It remained where it was until January 1919 before moving north to Binche in Belgium. Its service finally came to a close when, after embarking at Antwerp, it arrived home at Tilbury on 10 June 1919. It is left to Old Bill to have the final word!

Old Bill, en route to a "far, far better 'ole". (Mr and Mrs T. Holt)

Appendices

Appendices

APPENDIX I

Statement by Lt.-Colonel Arthur Edward Mainwaring

This Statement is only made for my friends, of whom I find there are many more than I thought. I rely on my friends not to use it to try and get any redress for me until Peace had been declared.

Monday, August 24

We arrived at Le Cateau at about 10 a.m., and detrained. After a short rest we marched to Beaumont (five miles), where the Brigade bivouacked in a field.

General Haldane informed me that we should most probably be marching north, to cover the retirement of our first and second armies.

I did not get any sleep whatever, as I had to see that everything and everybody was ready to move.

Later on orders to march north arrived, and I was again busily employed supervising matters, and in arranging for the withdrawal of our company on outpost duty.

Tuesday, August 25

We marched at 2 a.m., and continued to do so till about 6 a.m. Shortly afterwards General Haldane directed the Brigade to take up positions. The men spent the day digging themselves in, and remained in their positions till late in the afternoon. Then I received orders to draw them nearer in for night positions. The frontline was drawn to within 200 yards of the farm. At about 5 p.m. the enemy began shelling the farm and our trenches, the Seaforths suffering a few casualties.

General Haldane sent for me, and explained that the Brigade had to remain where it was until the whole of our troops in front had passed through.

Soon after this it became dark, shortly after which some sharp bursts of musketry fire from companies in front broke out.

We remained thus till about 10 p.m., when orders were issued for the Brigade to march on Honcourt [Haucourt], a long night march, and our second consecutive one.

After the march commenced I never saw the general again, nor any member of his staff, with the exceptions referred to later, nor did I get another order of any sort from the brigadier, except an answer to a note I sent him at 8.35 a.m., explaining the situation.

Wednesday, August 26

Finally we arrived at Honcourt [Haucourt], (where I understood the 4th Division was in reserve) at about 5 a.m. I sent the adjutant to seek for orders. He returned to say that there was no sign of the Brigade staff, but that he had seen Colonel Edmunds, of the divisional staff, who said we were to march again at 7 a.m. another 12 miles. I went to Colonel Edmunds myself, and he confirmed the order, adding that the men were to consume their iron ration, AND ASKING ME IF THE MEN COULD DO IT. I replied that they could, after a couple of hours' rest and some tea.

I returned to the Battalion, and at about 6 a.m. a furious fire[fight] broke out on a small hill about 1,000 yards to the north-east, the result being no food for the men.

Suddenly a wave of men of another corps came pouring in confusion back over the hill towards us. I fell in the Battalion, and directed Captain Clarke to extend his company along the road, facing the firing, and Captain Higginson to do the same, slightly in echelon behind Captain Clarke, and left Major Shewan in charge of these two companies.

By this time the other two companies and various platoons of other battalions had got away rather too far to the rear. For some time I could not get my horse, but as soon as I did so, managed to stop the movement. I took command of all the infantry I met, directing them to take up positions, and finally, getting hold of Captain Conlan's and Captain Wheeler's companies, placed them in position, and remained in a central place on the road myself.

By this time the action, confined in our part of the field to artillery, became general, and there was nothing to be done but lie still and await the infantry attack, which was momentarily expected, everyone, of course, being directed to dig themselves in.

During the first part of the action I received two messages from the divisional staff, both verbal, and sent the one already referred to above to the 10th Brigade, in which I described our positions.

The first was delivered by the A.D.C. to the G.O.C. IV Division. Captain Allfrey said to me, "The General says he wishes you to hold on here to the end." Then, turning in his saddle, he added, "General Snow told me to say that this is a personal message from him to the regiment." I answered that the General might rely on us to do what he said.

Later on Captain Burnett-Hitchcock, of the same staff, said, "It's only going to be a case of long bowls; no retirement." Again I said there should be none.

I myself had already told my men that we could not possibly retire as long as the two batteries remained in front of us.

Then came a lull. I occupied the time in conference with Captain Conlan, in directing the digging of further trenches for details who had joined us, and improving those we had already dug.

The shrapnel fire that followed was, for some two and a half hours, by common consent, something all together out of the common. Although shrapnel does little harm in comparison with its volume, the moral effect of lying still without being able to fire a shot in reply is very hard on even the strongest nerves.

At about 5 p.m. infantry which had been slowly withdrawing for some time had all passed away from the front and left front of our positions.

About 5 p.m. one of the batteries in front brought up their horses, and got their guns away at full gallop. The other battery had suffered severely. We were told that two of its guns were out of action, and I could see that the men could not remain behind the shields.

The behaviour of our men had been splendid throughout. They were so dog-tired that many of them slept through the infernal fire, as one could hear them snoring. But not one other sound of any sort did I hear during that eleven hours. The Adjutant and I were so sleepy that, since it was imperative to look out for the infantry attack, we determined, not to fall asleep at the same time.

But now, since it was evident that there was no one left in front of us but the disabled battery, I wrote a note to General Snow, explaining the situation, and asking for instructions. The Adjutant, Captain R.M. Watson, volunteered to carry it. In about 20 minutes he was back, and told me that General Snow and the Divisional Staff had gone, that no one remained to give an order of any sort, and that we were left alone.

On this information I decided to retire, and, passing the word to everyone within sight to get ready, we, at about 5.30 p.m. retired through the village [Caullery].

Here I found Major Burrowes, Royal Irish Fusiliers, and Captain Frankland, of my regiment, who had been General Haldane's staff captain. They assisted us to get the men into artillery formations, in which we passed slowly away to the rear. Captain Frankland gave me his horse, as I was nearly done.

Unfortunately, owing to woods, wire, farms, etc., the other files did not keep in touch with me, and when I reached Malencieux [Malincourt], I had only 40 men of the Battalion with me.

We reached Malencieux [Malincourt], at dusk, and the men being thoroughly exhausted, I got them into a barn, told them they might consume their iron ration, and go to sleep.

I then went to try and find somebody to give an order or direction of some sort. I met Major Daniell, Acting Brigade-Major of our Brigade. He expressed great joy at seeing me, asked how many men I had, attached 60 of the Warwicks, under a Special Reserve lieutenant, to me, and promised to send me orders. I pointed out the house we were in to him, put a sentry on the gate, so that an orderly should find him, and spent most of the time there myself. I did not dare lie down, as all the rest did, as I had nobody on whom I could possibly depend to wake me up. This was my third night without one wink of sleep of any kind.

After some two hours or less I again went to see if I could find why no orders had reached me. I found a cavalry regiment just leaving, the last troops in the village, with the exception of ourselves. The cavalry colonel told me the retirement, his, at least, was on two villages, L'Empire, [Lempire] and Rossay [Ronssoy], and left me. Consulting my map, I determined to march on the latter, as being the more southerly, and waking the men myself, started somewhere a little before midnight.

Thursday, August 27

At 3 a.m. we reached the village of Beaurevoir, which showed me we had missed the road in the night. I put the men into barns, but again stayed up myself. The strain was cruel, but I could trust no one else.

At 5 a.m. we marched towards Estreé [Estrées]. I determined to march on St Quentin by Jongcourt [Joncourt] and Le Vergies [Levergies]. Shortly after making this resolution we met Lieutenant-Colonel Elkington, with about 100 men of his regiment, the Warwicks, and joined forces, he, being the senior, taking over the command. He told me he had already made up his mind to march on St. Quentin. I very much doubted our ability to get them as far as St. Quentin, but by dint of encouragement and pointing out that stragglers must become prisoners, and marching very slowly, and with many halts, we managed to reach that place between 12 midday and 1 p.m.

Colonel Elkington sent me on to see what could be done, and I met General Smith-Dorrien in the town, and told him the men were done. He told me it was a marvel that any of us had got away, that we had been up against four and a half to five German Army Corps, and that he would give us a train to Noyan [Noyon], if I could get one, and that if I could not he advised me to march some five miles further on the road to Ham, and join the 3rd Division. A member of his staff reminded him that it had marched from there, when he said, "There are some details there; you had better try and join them." I said I doubted if our men could do it, and that I would at all events try for a train first.

I sent this information to Colonel Elkington, asking him to march to the station, and proceeded there myself, only to find that all the railway staff had fled, and that there was no chance of a train. Colonel Elkington then arrived with the party, and we determined to try and make the men make an effort to get on towards Ham.

At this moment General Hobbs arrived in a motor-car. He said that the mayor would probably be able to get us a train, and certainly some food, so Colonel Elkington directed me to go and see him. I did so, taking an interpreter with me. The mayor told me there was no chance whatever of a train, but that he would send us some food, which I asked him to expedite.

At this moment a breathless messenger handed a note to the mayor, who, on reading it, became very excited, throwing up his hands, and exclaiming it was the end, all was lost. The room was full of excited Frenchmen, so I told my interpreter to tell me exactly what was in the note. He said that the town was surrounded, all exits blocked, that people in motor-cars were coming back, unable to get through, and that the mayor was waiting to surrender the town. I was leaving the room when the mayor caught sight of me and said, "Ah! your troops will spoil all. The Germans will shell the town now, and the women and children will be killed," or words to that effect. I said, "You need not fear; if we cannot get our men away, we will not fight in the town. I must go and see my commanding officer." We neither of us doubted the authenticity of the mayor's statement, for we had ourselves seen shells bursting only some seven or eight miles north of St. Quentin, more than three hours before.

Colonel Elkington agreed that we must not endanger the safety of the inhabitants by fighting in the town. I addressed my men, and he addressed his. I told mine that I would lead them out then and there, and try to get to Noyan [Noyon], a distance of 25 miles, if they would make the attempt, BUT NOT ONE MAN OFFERED TO COME. Colonel Elkington has also stated on oath that he made the same offer to his men with a similar result. The fact is that the men could do no more for the time being. Their limit of endurance was reached. I considered it my duty to protect these men, who so nobly had done theirs. I still consider that it was so, and my conscience is quite clear. Their condition was admitted by the Court, by mouth of the President.

He therefore directed me to surrender, and while I was doing so he disarmed the men, putting their rifles and ammunition in one railway shed, and them in another.

As I rode back to the *Mairie* I saw terrified women dragging their children indoors, and everyone putting up their shutters. Everyone but ourselves and a few stragglers had fled, and as I rode up, my brain became obsessed with the one idea that our duty was to save nameless horrors overtaking these poor, defenceless creatures. It was Thursday afternoon; I had not slept once since Monday morning; I had seen villages burning and others shelled. I could think of nothing else, and that is the whole truth, to which I have sworn on oath. The consequence was that when I came to sign the paper I felt my duty was to make our purpose quite clear. I wrote the names of the officers and the strength of the party, and I said as the men were unable to march away we would "surrender unconditionally." Even as I wrote the words I paused; but the state of my brain was such that I felt if I argued as to conditions it might leave an opening for the Germans to shell the town and kill the civilian population, and I then felt my duty was to make no attempt at terms. Prostrated with physical and mental exhaustion, I wrote those words, convinced I was doing my duty and a noble act. This upheld me and was my one feeling throughout, and that, as to all else I have written here, I swear to on oath.

I returned to the station. At about 4 p.m. a cavalry subaltern rode into the station yard, calling upon the men to turn out and follow him. They utterly refused to. I explained the situation. He abused them and left. As time passed on it became evident that something had delayed the German advance, and I began to pray for darkness. I heard afterwards that the cavalry came from somewhere, and held them back.

Later on a cavalry captain arrived, accompanied by the same subaltern. He told me he could guide us out, when I at once said every man would thankfully come. By now I was in command, as Colonel Elkington had left.

I said I must get the paper back from the mayor. The cavalry officers said they meant to have that. I said I did not mind who had it as long as it was recovered. The cavalry subaltern accompanied me to the *Mairie*, and, pushing on in front, demanded the paper. I was too proud to argue with him for possession of it, as I was still upheld with the conviction that I had done my duty. They took it and sent it to their general.

I returned to the station, told the men the situation had changed, and called upon them to follow me. After a couple of minutes they fell in, got their arms and ammunition, filled their water-bottles, and awaited orders. At 9 p.m. we started, but only to be again halted for another hour in the town. This was my fourth night without sleep, and twice I fell down when standing up.

At about 10 p.m. we moved on; two or three large wagons had been provided for the men who could not walk, and they were immediately filled. We moved very slowly, with a cavalry escort, and about 2 a.m. halted at a farm and village named Roupy. Here the cavalry left us, and after blocking the road and putting wagons across it, posting piquets on it, I lay down and slept till dawn, the first sleep I had been able to get since Monday morning.

Friday, August 28

Soon after daybreak the cavalry rejoined us, and escorted us some way, till, telling us to make for St. Surplice [Sulpice], they left us. I must say here that before the two officers withdrew both of them shook hands with me, and said I had done everything a man could do.

We marched all that day, coming up with the 3rd Division, until, at evening, we reached Noyan [Noyon], where we were entrained and taken to Compiegne.

Author's Note

There is an epilogue to the *Statement* by Lt. Colonel Mainwaring which reads:

What the men think of the matter may be judged from the following extract from a letter from an officer in my late regiment, who, unsolicited by me, is collecting evidence in the hope that it may be of use when peace is declared: 'There is not a man here that does not believe implicitly in you and what you did to save them. There are several men in other regiments now swear that you alone saved them, so I am collecting as much information as possible which will assist in bringing things to light when this show is over.'

APPENDIX II

Statement by Lt.-Colonel John Ford Elkington

On 25 August 1914 my Battalion left their bivouac near BOSIGNY about 4 a.m. forming the Advanced-Guard of the 10th Infantry Brigade until a line of railway was reached about 9 a.m. this was not considered a good position, the 10th Infantry Brigade then fell back (my Battalion forming the rear-guard) to a position on high ground in the vicinity of a large farm. Trenches were dug, the 10th Infantry Brigade taking up a position to cover the retirement of other troops during the afternoon the enemy's artillery opened on us but there were few casualties. At about 1 a.m. (26 Aug) the 10th Infantry Brigade left this position falling back on LIGNY, the Brigade marching once more through the night and reached the vicinity of LIGNY about 6 a.m. where a halt was made. No sooner had the men taken off their equipment and were getting ready for a rest than heavy artillery fire was heard and wagons were seen rushing down a hill opposite us and slightly to our left many of them being overturned. I immediately got the Battalion together, 2 companies I formed up in a ditch by the side of the road just in front of us, the 2 remaining coys. about 200 yards in the rear. I then looked at the situation and decided that the best way to relieve the pressure was to make a counter-attack against this hill. This I did with my Battalion but once having gained the top of the hill we came under heavy maxim and shrapnel fire and I considered it necessary to fall back. I fell back slowly to my old position and entrenched. We stayed in these trenches all day exposed to heavy shrapnel fire during parts of the day.

Towards evening we commenced to fall back, each trench being held as long as possible, the Battalion falling back in batches, we then got separated. I fell back with the men in a sunken road towards the village of LIGNY where a better position could be obtained and from there after dark we followed a main road. I did not know in which direction we were supposed to retire. During the retirement in the dark it was impossible to keep the same men together for any length of time, there being so many stragglers and the men were continually falling out from exhaustion. About 2 a.m. (27 Aug.) I halted on the outskirts of a village and collected another 60 men of my Bn. by 4 a.m. I then continued my march, these men having little to eat for 24 hrs my first thought was where to get them some food. I continued my march in the direction of ST.QUINTON [St. Quentin], which I knew to be a railway junction and at about 8 a.m. I met Col. [Mainwaring], (with some men of his Battalion and some of mine). We continued our march together and managed in one village to obtain some loaves for the men which gave them a small piece each. We were in all about 250 men. During our march we constantly heard guns firing and reports were brought to us that the Germans were close. Along the road we came across the discarded ammunition of some British artillery which extended for at least a mile, this did not have a cheering effect on our men who were tired and worn out.

On reaching the vicinity of ST. QUINTON *(sic.)* I halted and put out outposts and observed two German cavalry patrols. I sent Col. [Mainwaring] into ST.QUINTON *(sic.)* in order that he might make arrangements for feeding the men and getting train accommodation. Col. [Mainwaring] sent me a note telling me to march into the town and meet him at the Railway Station which I did, arriving there about 2 p.m. (27 Aug) there I halted and let the men rest as they were in a state of collapse. I met a staff officer, (General Hobbs), who was leaving the town, he told me the *Maire* [mayor] would make arrangements for food and a train. I sent Col. [Mainwaring] to interview the *Maire*, where he arranged for food which we received about 3 p.m. On Col. [Mainwaring's] return he told me the *Maire* was in a terrible state owing to the close proximity of the Germans and that the *Maire* had told him the town was surrounded, that he was preparing to surrender, that all the motor cars leaving town were being sent back, and that the presence of British troops were a danger to the town, as the Germans might shell the town causing great danger to the women and children. We then went to arrange for a train but all the offices were closed and the staff had fled. I then consulted with Col. [Mainwaring] and told him to go and pacify the *Maire* and tell him I would not fight in the town but our men must have rest and food. There was never the slightest intention in either of our minds to surrender to any one nor did we do so, we fully intended to leave ST. QUINTON *(sic.)* and continue our march on NOYON directly the men were rested. If surprised by the Germans my intention was to fight at the back of the station and not in the streets so as to save unnecessary slaughter of the women and children of whom the town was full.

Col. [Mainwaring] proceeded to the *Maire* with an interpreter and signed a paper to the *Maire*. This paper I never saw till the trial and did not know till then how it was worded. I am sure that when Col. [Mainwaring] signed it he did so under great mental and physical strain and did not realize the consequences. I thought at the time the *Maire* was exaggerating the situation. I then marched the men into the station yard and spoke to my men, Col. [Mainwaring] to his men and told his men that two courses were open to them:

1. To march in the direction of NOYON a distance of 40 kilos., where I would lead them.
2. To remain with the risk of becoming prisoners of war.

Not a single man volunteered to continue the march, in fact they were exhausted and could not. I then put the men in one shed to rest and feed and their arms and ammunition by squads in another shed close by where they could be easily got in the case of need. About an hour after this I was washing and we heard a noise in the yard Col. [Mainwaring] rushed out and I followed, we found a cavalry officer addressing the men, they were taking no notice of him. Col. [Mainwaring] at once spoke to the men and said if they remained with him he would see them through. I saw the situation had changed and that all was clear. I urged the men to fall in and come out with me but they would not. As I saw the danger was passed and they could get out when they chose I left the yard about 5.30 p.m. as I was anxious to get on and collect more stragglers. I found a deserted horse on the square and some discarded British saddlery, I saddled the horse and rode out of ST. QUINTON *(sic.)* exactly at 6 p.m. with Major [?] On the way I collected a large number of stragglers from different battalions and marched towards NOYON. I caught up with the 5th Division and got some wagons for the exhausted soldiers and rode on myself and joined my own Division (4th) at about 5 p.m. (28 Aug) having been more or less without food or rest since 4 a.m. 25 Aug. Col. [Mainwaring] with the men left ST.QUINTON *(sic.)* at 7 p.m. 27th and every man got safely away, not one man surrendered or was lost. Wagons had to be got to get these tired troops along.

The paper which Col. [Mainwaring] unfortunately signed to the *Maire* without my authorization was got by a staff officer after I left ST. QUINTON*(sic.)*. On 28th I took over command of my Battalion which had collected at NOYON and commanded them through the remainder of the retreat and on two days in the advance and was once more in action with them. I was then arrested. I was slightly wounded at the fight at LIGNY by shrapnel in the foot and shoulder but did not report sick as I was anxious to remain with my Battalion. I was taken straight to my trial after a long day's march and tried on the following charges:

1. Cowardice, of which I was acquitted.
2. Conspiring to surrender, of which I was found guilty.

I had no one to help me in the defence of myself and the other Colonel and was not in a fit state to think clearly, as senior officer I took the full blame of any mistakes made and asked for Col.'s [Mainwaring] acquittal as I was sure he was not in a fit state to be tried. After the trial we were two days under shell fire unarmed before being sent home.

Author's Note

This document, originally written in pencil, may well have originated as an *aide-mémoire* to be used at the court-martial, after which it was typed up into the form above.

APPENDIX III

1st Battalion
Royal Warwickshire Regiment
Key to Commemorative/
Burial Locations

AC   Abbeyville Communal Cemetery, France
ACE   Abbeyville Communal Cemetry Extension, France
AG   Aubigny Communal Cemetery Extension, France
AI   Aire Communal Cemetery, France
AL   Allonville Communal Cemetery, France
AP   Abney Park Cemetery, UK
AR   Arras Memorial, France
AS   Aston (SS Peter and Paul) Churchyard, UK
AT   Athies Communal Cemetery Extension, France
AU   Aubigny Communal Cemetery, France
AV   Auchonvillers Military Cemetery, France
BA   Bailleul Communal Cemetery, France
BAX   Bailleul Communal Cemetery Extension, France
BC   Bard Cottage Cemetery, Belgium
BE   Beuvry Communal Cemetery Extension, France
BH   Birmingham (Handsworth) Cemetery, UK
BI   Bienvillers Military Cemetery, France
BL   Berlin South-Western Cemetery, Germany
BLH   Birmingham (Lodge Hill) Cemetery, UK
BN   Bertrancourt Military Cemetery, France
BO   Boulogne East Cemetery, France
BR   Bray Military Cemetery, France
BS   Brown Copse Cemetery, France
BT   Battersea Cemetery, UK
BUR   Buffs Road Cemetery, St. Jean-les-Ypres, Belgium
BV   Beauval Communal Cemetery, France
BW   Birmingham (Witton) Cemetery, UK
BY   Birmingham (Yardley) Cemetery, UK
CA   Cabaret-Rouge British Cemetery, Souchez, France
CB   Cite Bonjean Military Cemetery, France

CC	Chocques Military Cemetery, France
CE	Coates (Holy Trinity) Churchyard Whittlesey, UK
CF	Canada Farm Cemetery, Belgium
CG	Cologne Southern Cemetery, Germany
CH	Cement House Cemetery, Belgium
CL	City of London Cemetery, UK
CM	Crump Trench British Cemetery, France
CO	Charleroi Communal Cemetery, Belgium
CR	Carnoy Military Cemetery, France
CT	Caterpillar Valley Cemetery, France
CV	Coventry (London Road) Cemetery, UK
DB	Derby (Normanton) Cemetery, UK
DE	Denain Communal Cemetery, France
DH	Duhallow Ads. Cemetery, Belgium
DN	Duisans British Cemetery, France
DO	Douai Communal Cemetery, France
DR	Dover (St. James) Cemetery, UK
DU	Doullens Communal Cemetery, France
DY	Dury Crucifix Cemetery, France
DZ	Dozinghem Military Cemetery, Belgium
EP	Eterpigny British Cemetery, France
ES	Essex Farm Cemetery, Belgium
ET	Etaples Military Cemetery, France
EX	Exhall (St. Giles) Cemetery, UK
FE	Feuchy Chapel British Cemetery, France
FI	Fins New British Cemetery, Sorel Le Grand, France
FM	Fampoux British Cemetery, France
FN	Fontaine-au-Pire, Communal Cemetery, France
FO	Ferme-Oliver Cemetery, Belgium
FR	Forceville Communal Cemetery Extension, France
GH	Gonnehem Churchyard, France
GN	Gonnehem British Cemetery, France
GR	Grove Town Cemetery, France
GS	Glasgow Western Necropolis, UK
GU	Guards Cemetery, France
GZ	Gezaincourt Communal Cemetery Extension, France
HA	Haute-Avesnes British Cemetery, France
HB	Harbourne (St. Peter) Churchyard, UK
HI	Hinges Military Cemetery, France
HN	Honnechy British Cemetery, France
HO	Hoogsteade Belgian Military Cemetery, Belgium
HP	Houplines Communal Cemetery, France

HU   Humbercamps Communal Cemetery, France
HV   Happy Valley British Cemetery, France
HZ   Hazebrouck Communal Cemetery, France
IP   Ipswich Cemetery, UK
IN   Inkpen, (St. Michael's), UK
LA   La Brique Cemetery, No. 1, Belgium
LC   La Creche Communal Cemetery, France
LD   London Cemetery, France
LF   La Ferte-sous-Jouarre Memorail, France
LG   Le Grand Beaumart, British Cemetery, France
LK   Liverpool Kirkdale Cemetery, UK
LM   Loos Memorial, France
LN   La Neuville Communal Cemetery, France
LO   Longuenesse (St. Omer) Souvenir Cemetery, France
LP   La Pugnoy Military Cemetery, France
LR   London Rifle Brigade Cemetery, Belgium
LS   Lijssenthoek Military Cemetery, Belgium
LV   Le Vertannoy British Cemetery, Hinges, France
LX   Level Crossing Cemetery, France
LY   Ligny St Flochel, British Cemetery, France
MB   Monchy British Cemetery, France
MC   Montigny Communal Cemetery, France
MG   Mont-Bernanchon Brit. Cemetery, Gonnehem, France
MH   Mont Huon Military Cemetery, France
MM   Mailly-Maillet Communal Cem. Extension, France
MR   Miraumont Communal Cemetery, France
MT   Meteren Military Cemetery, France
NE   Nuneaton (Stockingford) Cemetery, UK
NI   New Irish Farm Cemetery, Belgium
NL   Nikolai Cemetery, Latvia
NO   Nottingham General Cemetery, UK
NZ   Niederzwehren Cemetery, Germany
OO   Oossttaverne Wood Cemetery, Belgium
PB   Pernes British Cemetery, France
PC   Portsdown (Christ Church) Military Cemetery, UK
PD   Porte-de-Paris, Cemetery, France
PJ   Point-de-Jour Military Cemetery, France
PL   Ploegsteert Memorial, Belgium
PO   Poelcapelle British Cemetery, Belgium
PP   Poperinghe Old Military Cemetery, Belgium
PR   Preseau Communal Cemetery Ext., France
PW   Prowse Point Military Cemetery, Belgium

QC   Queant Communal Cem. Brit. Extn., France
QR   Queant Road Cemetery, France
RC   Richmond Cemetery, UK
RG   Rugby (Clifton Rd.) Cemetery, UK
RG2 Rugby (Croop Hill) Cemetery, UK
RM   Ramilles British Cemetery, France
RO   Roulers Communal Cemetery, Belgium
RT   Ration Farm (La Plus Douve) Annexe, Belgium
RU   Rue Petillon Military Cemetery, France
RW   Railway Dug-outs Burial Ground, Belgium
SA   St. Aubert British Cemetery, France
SC   St. Catherine British Cemetery, France
SF   Seaforth Cemetery, Belgium
SH   Sherbourne Cemetery, UK
SK   Sunken Road Cemetery Fampoux, France
SM   St. Marie Cemetery Le Havre, France
SN   St. Nicholas British Cemetery, France
SO   Southampton (Hollybrook) Cemetery, UK
SR   Strand Military Cemetery, Belgium
SS   St. Sever Cemetery Rouen, France
ST   St. Souplet British Cemetery, France
STH St. Hilaire Cemetery, France
SU   Sucerie Military Cemetery, France
SV   St.Venant-Robeco Rd. Brit. Cem., Robeco, France
T   Terlingthun British Cemetery, France
TA   Trois Arbres Cemetery, Steenwerk, France
TC   Tyne Cot Cemetery, Belgium
TCM Tyne Cot Memorial, Belgium
TH   Thiepval Memorial Cemetery
TV   Thiepval Anglo-French Cemetery, France
TL   Talana Farm Cemetery, Belgium
TN   Tournai Communal Cemetery Allied Extn. Belgium
TQ   Torquay Cemetery and Extension, UK
TY   Tilloy British Cemetery, France
VA   Valenciennes Communal Cemetery, France
VC   Verchain British Cemetery, France
VCN Vieille Chapelle New Military Cemetery, France
VE   Vis-en-Artois British Cemetery, France
VEM Vis-en-Artois Memorial, France
VMC Vlamertinghe Milit. Cemetery, Belgium
VXB Vauxbuin French National Cemetery, France
W   Walsall (Ryecroft) Cemetery, UK

WDM Windmill British Cemetery, France
WH   White House Cemetery, Belgium
WM   Wimereux Communal Cemetery, France
Y   Yate (St. Mary) Churchyard, UK
YPR Ypres (Menin Gate) Memorial, Belgium
YTC Ypres Town Cemetery, Belgium

N.B.: Entries which are annotated WG in the appendices indicate that the names of those individuals appear only in information supplied by the War Graves Commission and are not shown in any other rolls of honour consulted.

APPENDIX IV

1st Battalion Royal Warwickshire Regiment Roll of Honour 1914–1918 – Officers

Officers belonging to or serving with 1st Battalion, who were killed or died on service.

Name and Rank	Died	Buried/ Commrtd.	Notes
Adams, A. J., Captain	30.8.18	VE	
Bentley, C. A. C., Captain	25.10.14	CB	Indian General Service Medal 1908
Black, F. H., Captain	25.4.15	–	
Bloomfield, C. G. M., Major.	9.6.15	TL	
Bowden, P. J., Second Lieutenant	15.4.18	PL	
Breene, T. F., Lieutenant	1.7.16	TH	
Christie, W. C., Major	13.10.14	MT	
Coatsworth, A. H., Second Lieutenant	8.9.16	–	Attached M.G.C.
Cockburn, J., Second Lieutenant	25.4.15	YPR	
Cooper, S. G., Second Lieutenant	17.9.15	YPR	
Cox, F. H., Second Lieutenant	23.10.16	–	
Cox, G. W., Captain	3.5.17	TH	
Devis, F., Second Lieutenant	11.4.17	–	
Edinger, W. M. V., Second Lieutenant	23.8.18	–	
Evezard, G., Captain	9.5.17	AU	
Fiddler, F., Captain	26.4.15	–	Attached 1/Hants.
Forster, G. N. B., Brigadier-General	4.4.18	–	D.S.O., C.M.G.
Gamble, J. F., Second Lieutenant	24.6.16	AV	
Glyka, A. I., Second Lieutenant	12.10.16	TH	
Hamilton, T. K., Lieutenant	1.6.15	NI	
Hankey, D. W. A., Second Lieutenant	12.10.16	TH	
Harrison, M. C., Captain	12.10.16	TH	Military Cross
Hornblower, P.B., Second Lieutenant	4.18	–	Military Cross

Hunt, F. H., Lieutenant	25.4.15	–	
Irvine, G. F., Captain	24.10.16	TH	
Jeffrey, R. H., Second Lieutenant	11.4.17	–	
Johnson, J. C., Second Lieutenant	8.7.15	BC	
Jowitt, A., Lieutenant	25.4.15	YPR	
Kingston, N. A., Second Lieutenant	1.4.18	CA	
Knapton, O. A., Lieutenant	18.9.14	VXB	
Lancaster, J. C., Major	8.5.15	OO	
Loring, W. L., Lieutenant-Colonel	23.1014	YPR	
Lovelace-Taylor, A. G., Second Lieutenant	9.10.16	TH	
Lukey, C. X., Second Lieutenant	24.6.16	AV	
Maclaglan, G. C., Lieutenant	25.4.15	YPR	
Martin, F. N., Second Lieutenant	24.10.18	VC	
Marwood, C. P. L., Captain	24.11.15	–	Attached Nigeria Regt.
Mason, H. H. L., Second Lieutenant	12.10.17	DZ	
Morris, R. H., Lieutenant	5.10.17	TCM	
Mould, D., Second Lieutenant	13.6.16	SU	Attached T.M.B.
Nicolai, R. C., Lieutenant	25.4.15	YPR	
Partington, C., Second Lieutenant	30.8.18	–	
Payne, J. O., Lieutenant	25.4.15	NI	
Preedy, L. J., Second Lieutenant	31.3.18	–	Ex-King Edward School, Birmingham
Rees, L., Lieutenant	4.10.17	TCM	
Riley, S.J., Captain	12.10.16	TH	
Seaman, L. J. C., Lieutenant	30.8.18	VE	
Simpson, A. H., Lieutenant	1.2.15	BO	
Spencer, R. M., Lieutenant	22.1.16	SU	
Strandring, B. A., Second Lieutenant	19.12.14	–	
Stretton, J. de C, Second Lieutenant.	11.5.18	LV	Military Cross
Stretton, W. S. de C., Second Lieutenant	4.9.16	–	
Thorowgood, R. W. T., Lieutenant	7.8.18	ME	Military Cross
Tillyer, R. B. B., Lieutenant	25.4.15	YPR	
Terrise, H. L., Second Lieutenant	15.4.18	PL	
Walker, H. J. I., Captain	25.4.15	YPR	
Wasey, C. W. C., Captain	28.10.17	–	R.F.C.
Waters, R. R., Captain	24.10.16	TH	
Welch, S. L., Second Lieutenant	20.7.17	ACE	

Officers attached to 1st Battalion, who were killed or died whilst serving.

Name and Rank	Died	Buried	Notes
Bourke, G. S., Second Lieutenant	15.4.18	–	Liverpool Regiment
Briscoe, E. V., Captain	26/7.8.16	–	Adjutant 10/Royal Warwicks
Lewis, G.A.D., Second Lieutenant	8.7.15	–	South Staffs. Regiment

N.B.: In compiling this data the writer has cross-checked wherever possible. However, because of the complexity of the exercise and differing research sources, there may be occasional errors.

APPENDIX V

Officers from 1st Battalion Royal Warwickshire Regiment who were taken prisoner or interned, 1914–1918

Rank and Name	Date Missing	Interned	Repatriated
Day, Major D.A.L.	1.10.14	Holland 22.1.18	18.11.18
Meiklejohn, Major R.	4.9.14	Switzerland 30.5.16	24.3.18
Besant, Capt. P.E.	30.9.14	Switzerland 9.12.17	14.6.18
Haddon, Capt. J.B.	18.12.14	Holland 24.2.18	18.11.18
Knight-Bruce, Capt. J.H.W.	1.10.14	–	11.9.17
Chichester-Constable, Lt. C.H.J.	4.9.14	–	1.9.19
Nathan, Second Lt. G.S.M.	3.5.17	–	11.1.19
Maunsell, Lt. C. F.	26.8.14	Switzerland 9.12.17	6.12.18
Willes, Second Lt. A.H.	3.5.17	–	31.12.18

APPENDIX VI

1st Battalion Royal Warwickshire Regiment Honours/Decorations List 1914–1918 – Officers

Name	Rank	Honour/Decoration
Forster, G. N. B.	Brigadier-General	D.S.O., C.M.G.
Poole, A. J.	Brigadier-General	C.M.G.
Elkington, J.F.	Lt.-Colonel	D.S.O.
Bannerman, J.A.M.	Major	D.S.O.
Kennington, J.	T/Major	D.S.O. (ex-Lincolnshire Regt.)
Marriot, G.B.	Major	D.S.O., awarded whilst Commanding 8/LN Lancs. Regt.
Tomes, C. T.	Major	D.S.O., M.C.
Beamish, F.N.H.	Captain	M.C.
Burnard, C.F.	Captain	D.S.O.
Harrison, M.C.	Captain	M.C.
Jackson, A.H.K.	Captain	D.S.O., M.C.
Montgomery, B. L.	Captain	D.S.O., Citation: "For conspicuous gallantry leading on 13th October, (during the 4th Divn. attack on Meteren 1914) when he turned the enemy out of their trenches with the bayonet. He was severely wounded."
Strevens, H.	Captain	D.S.O., M.C.
Warwick, A. M.	T/Captain	M.C. (ex-R.A.M.C.)
Watkins, W.	A/Captain	M.C., Citation: "For conspicuous gallantry when in command of a company during the attack near Verchain on 24th October, 1918. He led his company with great skill over the River Ecaillon, reorganised them on the other side and pushed on, cleared the village of Verchain of machine gun posts and rounded up a number of prisoners. He showed marked initiative, his bearing throughout was a great incentive to his men."
Dowson, P. H.	Captain	M.C.
Figg, S. V.	Lieutenant	M.C.

Maunsell, E.J.A.	Lieutenant	M.C., Citation: "For conspicuous gallantry and devotion to duty. The far end of a position over a canal which was under heavy shell fire was blown up. He volunteered to go into the position and report the damage. Later he repeatedly led his men into a wood through heavy fire in his endeavour to force a way through the enemy line. His fine leading and cool behaviour were an example to all."

Bar, Citation: "For conspicuous gallantry and able leadership east of Arras on 30th August, 1918. In spite of hostile machine gun and artillery fire he got his company into position and led them into attack on the ridge north of St. Severins Ridge. He was the only officer of the Battalion who reached the second objective, where he took charge of all the scattered companies, reorganising them and getting in touch with the units on the flank."

Shute, J.L.	Lieutenant	M.C., Citation: "For conspicuous gallantry. He led a raiding party into the enemy's trenches and after accounting for several of the enemy skilfully withdrew with only one slight casualty."
Thorowgood, R.W.T.	Lieutenant	M.C., Citation: "For conspicuous gallantry and devotion to duty on. His coolness and disregard for danger whilst leading carrying parties through intense enemy shelling were very valuable to all ranks. In spite of heavy shell fire and continued sniping, he was always to be seen in the most exposed part of his trench encouraging and assisting his men."
Willis, D. H.	Lieutenant	M.C.
Edmunds, W.G.B.	T/Lieutenant	M.C., Citation: "For conspicuous gallantry and devotion to duty in action. When the troops on the right were forced to withdraw, exposing the flank, he led a party of about 60 men from various units and counter-attacked. He obtained a footing on high ground, when our artillery put down a heavy barrage, and he was forced to withdraw owing to casualties among his men. He showed great dash in taking the ridge."
Dixon, H.J.	T/Lieutenant	M.C.
Hornblower, P.B.	T/Lieutenant	M.C., Citation: "For conspicuous gallantry and devotion to duty. He was in charge of an ammunition carrying party which came under heavy shell fire, causing casualties. By his personal example he reorganised his men and delivered the supplies in time to meet the demands of the situation."

Collins, W.T.	T/ Second Lieutenant	M.C., Citation: "For conspicuous gallantry and ability to command during the attack near Verchain on the 24th October, 1918. He personally led an attack on two hostile machine guns, killing some of the teams and capturing the remainder. He then led his platoon to the first objective and assisted another company to take the second. His example and leadership were excellent."
Hall, R.B.	T/Second Lieutenant	M.C., Citation: "For marked gallantry and initiative during the attack near Verchain on 24th October, 1918. The bridge for the River Ecallion being too short, he immediately jumped into the river and assisted the whole of his platoon to cross, remaining in the bed of the river the whole of the time, helping his men and carrying guns and equipment across. He then organised his platoon and led them to their objective, effectively rounding two hostile machine guns and their teams."
Harrison, J.	T/ Second Lieutenant	M.M., M.C., M.M. Citation: "He displayed fine courage and leadership during the attack near Verchain on 24th October, 1918. He led his platoon with great dash, and effectively silenced and rounded up machine gun posts, personally capturing two machine guns and about thirty prisoners. When the advance was checked he supervised the organising and digging-in of his platoon, during which he was severely wounded."
Murch, A. H.	T/ Second Lieutenant	M.C., Citation: "For conspicuous gallantry and devotion to duty during an attack. He was in charge of an advanced post feeling that the advancing troops would be held up by the wire in front, he went out with one man under heavy machine gun fire and commenced to cut it. He continued his work until badly wounded."
Stretton, J. de C.	Second Lieutenant	M.C., Citation: "For conspicuous gallantry and devotion to duty. He led his platoon with the utmost dash, and succeeded in getting through the enemy defences, capturing a machine gun and killing all the crew. He also attacked and took a strong fortified house. When forced to withdraw he collected all the men he could find of other units, and took up a position and dug-in. His work throughout was an example to all."

N.B.: In compiling this data the writer has cross-checked wherever possible. However, because of the complexity of the exercise and differing research sources, there may be occasional errors.

APPENDIX VII

1st Battalion Royal Warwickshire Regiment Roll of Honour 1914–1918 Other Ranks

Name	Service no.	Rank	Died of wounds or killed in action	Bur./ comm.	Medals and former service in other regiments
Accleton, W.C.	648	Pte.	12.10.16	TH	
Adams, C.H.	7050	Pte.	25.4.15	YPR	
Adams, H.	2537	Pte.	14.10.16	GR	9997 Ox. Bucks. L.I.
Adamson, A.	27293	Pte.	3.5.17	AR	
Adcock, W.	9402	Pte.	25.4.15	YPR	
Adkins, A.C.	21459	Pte.	13.5.17	NZ	
Ainscough, W.F.	20561	Pte.	15.4.18	MG	10120 Army Cyclist Corps
Ainsworth, G.	33013	Pte.	10.7.18	LY	GS25503, D.G.
Albrighton, T.C.	24136	Pte.	3.9.18	LY	
Alcock, F.	30428	Pte.	3.5.18	AR	
Allder, L.	2365	L/Cpl.	11.4.17	BS	
Allen, A.	138	Pte.	24.5.15	YPR	
Allen, A.	11186	Pte	20.6.16	BN	
Allen, J.T.	27602	Pte.	12.10.16	GR	5526 Sth. Staffs. Regt.
Allen, W.J.	12278	Pte.	25.6.16	AV	53145, R.G.A.
Allen, W.R.	23951	Pte.	5.7.17	CM	
Allton, W.	15280	Pte.	21.6.16	AV	
Amey, W.	438	Pte.	25.4.15	YPR	
Amos, F.	27607	Pte.	10.12.16	TH	5595 Sth. Staffs. Regt
Amos, S. WG	1106	Pte.	15.7.16	BLH	
Amy, G.S.	36210	Pte.	15.9.18	–	
Anderson, W.	34182	Pte.	30.8.18	DY	8199 Dragoons
Andrews, E.	33185	Pte.	20.11.17	AR	23647 Lancers
Andrews, G.	9810	L/Cpl.	12.10.16	TH	
Andrews, T.W.	1101	Pte.	13.10.14	MT	
Andrews, W.	14291	Pte.	26.6.16	TH	

Angus, D.	9384	Pte.	25.4.15	YPR	
Antley, J.	9183	C.S.M.	23.10.16	TH	
Arculus, J.	267481	Pte.	14.4.17	ET	
Armfield, J.	9071	Pte.	25.4.15	YPR	
Armstrong, W.	33014	Pte.	22.4.18	SV	GS/21997, Dragoon Guards
Arthurs, W.	2386	Pte.	26.8.14	FN	
Ash, A.D.	16124	Pte.	11.4.17	BS	
Ashford, A.H.	8132	Pte.	1.12.14	PL	
Astell, B.T.	9887	Pte.	25.4.15	YPR	
Astill, A.	9509	Sgt.	3.5.17	AR	
Atherton, J.W.	33012	Pte.	16.4.18	LP	GS/21488 Dragoon Guards
Atkins, A.	2334	Pte.	25.4.15	OO	
Atkins, W.	2258	Pte.	23.10.16	TH	
Austin, C.	34801	Pte.	30.8.18	VE	
Austin, F.J.	25409	Pte.	12.10.17	CH	
Austin, J.	4025	Pte.	9.5.15	YPR	
Austin, W.H.	10190	L/Cpl.	11.4.17	–	
Ayres, W.	40145	Pte.	11.6.18	GN	
Bacon, J.	1840	Pte.	25.4.15	YPR	
Bailey, G.	4508	Cpl.	5.4.16	BI	
Baines, A.W.	2427	Pte.	19.9.14	–	
Baker, A.	765	Pte.	30.8.18	VEM	
Baker, C.L.	9768	Pte.	19.10.15	SU	
Baker, J. WG	3441	Pte.	18.12.18	BLH	
Baker, J.	1830	L/Cpl.	8.7.15	YPR	
Baker, J.A.	7511	Pte.	20.10.14	PL	Indian General Service Medal 1908
Baker, S.	20602	Pte.	12.10.16	TH	11247, Army Cycle Corps
Baker, W.	6314	Pte.	25.4.15	YPR	
Baker, W.A.	34803	Pte.	25.8.15	T	
Baldwin, F.	34804	Pte.	20.7.18	LM	
Ball, A.	21049	Pte.	18.10.18	QC	
Ball, G.T.H.	2387	Pte.	29.4.15	FN	
Ball, J.J.	3839	Pte.	10.5.15	YPR	
Ballard, E.	4114	Pte.	25.4.15	YPR	
Barclay, A.	1485	Pte.	25.4.15	YPR	
Barefoot, C.H.	2572	Pte.	19.6.15	YPR	
Barnbrook, R.	15976	Pte.	12.10.16	TH	R.F.A.
Barley, F.	2288	Pte.	26.4.15	YPR	
Barnes, A.W. WG	2427	Pte.	19.9.144	VXB	
Barnes, G.E.	7273	Pte.	13.10.14	MT	

Barnett, G.	9562	Pte.	9.7.15	YPR	
Barnett, H.	9614	Pte.	18.12.14	PW	
Barnickle, H.	276	Pte.	3.1.15	PW	
Barrett, C.	9167	Sgt.	25.4.15	NI	
Barrett, W.A.	18516	Pte.	30.8.18	VE	25301 Som. L.I.
Barrow, R.H.	33186	L/Cpl.	30.8.18	VEM	7056 Lancers
Basnett, T.	3424	Pte.	7.11.15	SU	
Batchelor, C.	21511	Pte.	11.4.17	AR	
Batchelor, F.	626	Pte.	18.10.14	HP	
Batchelor, J.	2362	Pte.	26.8.14	LF	
Batchhelor, R.	761	Pte.	6.6.15	VMC	
Batchelor, S.	10559	Sgt.	1.12.17	DN	
Bate, F.C.	20856	Pte.	28.10.18	ET	
Bates, A.	412	L/Cpl.	13.10.14	MT	
Bates, H.	2433	Pte.	26.8.14	LF	
Bates, T.H.	9074	Cpl.	31.3.18	CA	
Batho, R.T.	24525	L/Cpl.	12.10.17	CH	
Battin, C.	3027	Pte.	19.6.15	YPR	
Battin, H.A.	11067	Pte.	28.4.16	BI	
Baugh, J.	528	Pte.	26.4.16	YPR	
Baughan, H.	23124	Pte.	30.8.18	VEM	
Baxter, W.	1982	L/Cpl.	16.4.18	LP	140411 Gnr. R.F.A
Bayliss, E.F.	9991	Pte.	13.10.14	MT	
Bayliss, F.	1682	Pte.	19.6.15	YPR	
Bayliss, H.	3578	Pte.	11.5.15	YPR	
Beach, C.T.	9458	Pte.	25.4.15	YPR	
Beachham, C.J.	1723	Pte.	6.8.15	BN	
Beacher, L.G.B.	2276	Cpl.	14.10.14	LO	
Beale, G.J.	9939	Pte.	30.1.15	BO	
Beale, J.A.	8966	Pte.	25.4.15	YPR	
Beales, W.	16391	Pte.	17.4.17	SK	
Beasley, A.	41119	Pte.	18.7.18	RU	
Beck, F.	1964	L/Cpl.	2.7.16	TH	
Beddington, W.H.	581	Sgt.	26.8.14	FN	
Beech, G.E.	5096217	Pte.	19.8.21	AS	
Beechham, P.R.G.	34809	Pte.	16.4.18	LP	
Beesley, J.E.	9240	Pte.	26.4.15	YPR	
Beeson, R.	1285	Pte.	8.6.15	TL	
Beezley, W.	9051	Pte.	31.8.18	VE	
Bembridge, H.	3342	Pte.	25.4.15	YPR	
Bench, C.W.	6266	Sgt.	23.7.17	CM	

Bench, J.	1558	Sgt.	11.4.17	AR	
Bennett, H.	33093	L/Cpl.	27.4.18	LP	19140 Dragoons
Bennett, W.	4304	Pte.	25.5.15	LA	
Benson, W.E.	9482	L/Cpl.	25.4.15	YPR	
Bentley, W.T.	931	L/Cpl.	9.12.14	PL	
Berry, A.	16579	Pte.	4.10.17	TCM	
Berry, W.H.	6501	Pte.	13.10.14	MT	
Betteridge, H.W.C.	36221	Pte.	13.8.18	VE	
Betts, F.G.	9473	Sgt.	25.11.16	TQ	
Bickley, A.	1922	L/Sgt.	25.4.15	YPR	
Biddle, A.E.	IO/8	Dmr.	20.8.14	FN	
Bidwell, C.	12272	Pte.	23.10.16	TH	53927 R.G.A.
Biffin, A.S.	2782	Pte.	25.4.15	YPR	
Billett, L.J.	306675	Pte.	26.4.18	ET	
Billingham, A.	1388	Pte.	11.4.17	ABS	
Billington, S.	2035	Pte.	13.10.14	MT	
Bilke, B.	9610	Pte.	9.7.15	YPR	
Bird, Harold	1786	Pte.	3.5.17	AR	
Bird, Harry	971	Pte.	12.4.18	PL	
Bird, Harry	36222	Pte.	30.8.18	VE	
Bird, S.	2245	L/Sgt.	27.4.18	LP	
Birtley, A.	787	Pte.	11.10.16	TH	
Bishop, C.E.	1898	Pte.	14.10.14	T	
Bishop, H.V.	17881	Pte.	15.4.18	CC	
Bishop, L.	2172	Pte.	5.11.14	SR	
Bishop, O.C.S.	38819	Pte.	30.8.18	VE	
Bishop, T.	2005	L/Cpl.	15.4.18	GH	
Blackmoor, J.	2356	Pte.	13.10.14	MT	
Blake, T.H.A.	32445	Pte.	30.8.18	VEM	R/4/111060 R.A.S.C.
Blakemore, M.	1608	Pte.	12.10.16	TH	
Blamire, R.	42502	Pte.	9.11.18	PR	
Blewitt, J.	7211	COMS	5.5.188	ET	
Blick, W.J.	7020	Pte.	25.4.15	YPR	
Bloomer, G.	1502	Pte.	11.7.15	LS	
Bloxham, G.	15622	Pte.	19.4.18	PB	
Blundell, A.H.	12746	Pte.	12.10.16	LD	
Boase, F.T.	25441	Pte.	30.8.18	VE	
Bocock, G.F.	19491	Cpl.	15.4.18	PL	
Boden, F.	4590	Pte.	10.12.16	TH	
Bodfish, H.	4974	Pte.	24.7.15	ET	
Bodman, W.	16885	Pte.	12.10.16	TH	

Bolton, W.J.	7364	Pte.	17.1.15	PW	
Boneham, H.	1450	Pte.	29.10.14	PL	
Booth, C.	9288	Pte.	1.7.16	TH	
Boswell, G.	431	Pte.	27.4.18	LP	
Bosworth, W.	1365	Pte.	19.6.15	YPR	
Botterill, J.	1373	Pte.	22.6.16	GZ	
Boucher, A.H.	8609	Pte.	1.7.16	TH	
Boulter, R.H.	11362	Pte.	30.9.15	SU	
Bousfield, S.R.	2446	Pte.	26.4.16	YPR	
Bovey, A.A.	20601	Pte.	23.7.17	CM	11239 Army Cyclist Corps
Bowden, P.	803	Pte.	26.11.15	SS	
Bowen, P.J.	267565	Pte.	9.1.18	ET	
Bowers, C.	27849	Pte.	2.5.18	IN	24671 Shrops. L.I.
Bradburn, R.	21705	Pte.	15.4.18	PL	29925 Glos. Rgt.
Bradbury, E.	2562	Pte.	16.6.15	YPR	
Bradley, A.	14840	Pte.	25.10.16	–	
Bradley, C.W.	267316	Pte.	15.4.18	PL	
Bradley, E.	4570	Pte.	27.7.17	SN	
Bradley, G.	7935	Pte.	23.11.14	PW	
Bradley, G.	10971	Pte.	2.11.15	SU	
Bradshaw, L.	1858	Pte.	25.4.15	YPR	
Brain, O.J.	25339	Pte.	15.4.18	PL	
Branford, F.	21324	Pte.	18.4.17	AR	26764 R. Berks. Regt.
Brassington, H.	2118	Pte.	13.10.14	MT	
Bratton, C.H.	1117	Pte.	12.10.16	TH	
Bray, F.J.	16684	Pte.	11.10.16	TH	
Brice, H.	9007	Pte.	3.11.14	SR	
Bridgwood, H.	41945	Pte.	26.10.18	RM	
Bright, E.	16193	Pte.	28.8.16	–	
Brimble, R.	4807	Pte.	25.4.15	YPR	
Brimble, W.	36226	Pte.	30.8.18	VE	
Brinkworth, F.G.	28245	Pte.	3.5.17	AR	27264 Hussars
Broadfiled, G.	9073	Sgt.	12.10.17	TCM	
Broadfield, O.	2358	Pte.	26.5.15	YPR	
Brookes, G.	9666	L/Cpl.	26.8.14	FN	Indian General Service Medal 1908
Brookes, J.J.	28542	Pte.	30.8.18	VEM	
Brooks, C.	815	Cpl.	13.10.14	MT	
Brown, A.B.	7206	Pte.	3.5.17	AR	
Brown, A.	9955	Pte.	13.10.14	MT	
Brown, C.	28319	Pte.	12.4.17	HA	27332 Hussars

Brown, F.G.	WG	27968	Pte.	15.4.18	LP	
Brown, G.A.		306608	Pte.	15.4.18	PL	
Brown, H.		1616	Pte.	25.4.15	BUR	
Brown, H.A.	WG	939	Pte.	23.5.15	AR	
Brownlow, A.		4792	Pte.	30.8.18	VE	
Brueton, T.		4000	Pte.	12.10.16	TH	
Bryan, E.F.		16/1385	Cpl.	12.6.18	MG	
Bryan, W.		3923	Sgt.	12.10.17	CM	
Buckley, J.U.		10183	Pte.	6.7.15	YPR	
Buckley, T.		20343	Sgt.	26.4.15	YPR	
Bullock, J.		27954	Pte.	25.2.17	WM	
Bullock, W.T.		1651	L/Cpl.	25.4.15	YPR	
Bunn, J.F.		777	A/Cpl.	23.3.15	RT	
Burden, O.		3992	Pte.	19.6.15	YPR	
Burford, A.		201964	Pte.	18.7.18	SV	
Burgess, A.	WG	3163	Pte.	20.2.19	BW	
Burnett, D.		402	Pte.	3.5.17	AR	
Burnett, S.		10637	Pte.	3.5.17	AR	
Burrows, A.		9762	Pte.	13.10.14	MT	
Burton, A.E.		10516	Pte.	13.10.16	TH	
Bush, J.H.	WG	59337	Pte.	10.8.19	SO	
Busson, W.		609	Pte.	26.8.14	LF	
Butler, H.		13071	Pte.	11.4.17	AT	
Butler, M.		1683	Pte.	26.415	YPR	
Butler, W.E.		1028	L/Cpl.	19.6.15	YPR	
Butt, T.		9800	Pte.	11.4.17	AR	
Buxley, J.A.		50823	Pte.	30.8.18	VE	
Byron, J.		2418	Pte.	19.6.15	YPR	
Caines, E.B.		2345	Pte.	8.9.14	HN	
Cairns, W.		2148	Pte.	13.10.14	MT	
Calderbank, J.		804	Pte.	13.10.14	–	Indian General Service Medal 1908
Callant, A.		2460	L/Cpl.	25.1.15	LR	
Cann, H.		50822	Pte.	30.8.18	VE	
Canning, W.J.		1277	Pte.	5.4.16	BI	
Carey, G.		6803	L/Sgt.	23.10.16	–	
Carlow, H.		2040	Pte.	3.5.17	CM	
Carr, F.W.		16451	Pte.	25.6.16	AV	
Carter, B.		27952	Cpl.	3.5.17	AR	
Carter, E.J.		33060	Pte.	15.4.18	PL	5535 Dragoons
Carter, G.A.		11353	Pte.	6.8.15	SU	

Carter, G.H.	927	Pte.	21.12.14	LR	10116 Worcs. Regt.
Carter, G.H.	1535	Pte.	25.4.15	YPR	
Carter, H.	1701	Pte.	1.7.16	TH	
Carter, H.B.	9759	Pte.	9.7.15	LS	
Carter, P.	9991	Pte.	12.10.17	TCM	
Carter, W.E.	34132	Pte.	21.11.17	–	8522 Lancers
Carter, W.J.	2047	Pte.	2.4.16	HV	
Carvell, E.H.	10442	Pte.	30.4.18	ET	
Carver, B.	1575	Pte.	7.10.17	DZ	
Casey, A.E.	2379	L/Cpl	29.10.14	LF	
Cashmore, J.	66	Pte.	29.4.15	BO	
Cassell, J.	4260	Pte.	25.4.15	YPR	
Casterton, A.	30102	Pte.	30.11.17	WDM	9019 Leics. Regt.
Cattermole, H.	307820	Pte.	26.7.17	CM	
Cavit, S.N.	267663	Pte.	4.10.17	CH	
Chamberlain, S.	11372	L/Cpl.	11.4.17	–	
Chance, T.	267672	Pte.	26.8.14	AR	
Chandler, A.W.	6822	Sgt.	29.10.14	LF	Indian General Service Medal 1908
Chandler, W.	36231	Pte.	26.10.18	QR	
Chapman, J.	164	L/Cpl.	4.5.15	BO	
Chappell, S.	27317	Pte.	15.4.18	PL	388 West Rdg. Regt.
Chapple, W.E.	16/1454	Pte.	9.5.17	AR	
Charles, A.E.	1239	Sgt.	8.7.15	YPR	
Charles, L.	330863	Pte.	26.7.17	CM	
Charlwood, J.	2352	Pte.	25.4.15	YPR	
Charnell, W.J.	20716	Pte.	1.4.18	AR	
Chatland, W.G.	229	Pte.	25.4.15	YPR	
Checkley, J.	9671	Pte.	27.10.14	SR	
Cherry, A.	3072	Pte.	25.4.15	YPR	
Childs, G.H.	9689	Pte.	9.12.14	PL	
Chinn, J.W.	27870	Pte.	3.5.17	AR	
Chivers, F.	203817	L/Cpl.	19.9.18	MH	Military Medal
Church, S.C.	18469	Pte.	29.3.18	CA	24310 Somerset L.I.
Clark, P.J.	25712	Pte.	14.5.18	AP	019212 Army Ord. Corps
Clarke, A.	1247	Pte.	29.10.14	PL	
Clarke, A.	1029	L/Cpl.	18.9.14	LF	
Clarke, F.	42383	Pte.	25.10.18	RM	
Clarke, G.H.	4351	Pte.	15.4.18	PL	
Clarke, J.W.	7536	Pte.	25.4.15	YPR	
Clarke, O.J.	1943	L/Cpl.	15.7.16	TH	

Clarke, S.F.	34823	Pte.	15.4.18	PL	
Cleal, E.C.	27961	Pte.	8.2.17	BR	
Cleaver, A.H.	9222	L/Cpl.	25.4.15	YPR	
Cleaver, J.	225	Pte.	13.10.14	MT	Indian General Service Medal 1908
Cleaver, J.V.	17860	Pte.	11.4.17	PJ	
Cleaver, W.E.	9477	Pte.	17.1.16	MM	
Clemens, J.	7557	Pte.	25.4.15	YPR	
Clements, S.S.	1125	Lsgt.	16.2.17	FI	
Clements, T.	694	Pte.	25.4.15	YPR	
Cleton, J.	6324	Pte.	25.4.15	YPR	
Clews, C.	5661	Pte.	11.4.17	BS	
Clifford, F.	11669	Pte.	14.10.16	GR	
Clifford, N.	1420	L/Cpl.	26.4.15	YPR	
Clover, B.	378	Pte.	7.7.15	BC	
Coates, B.	7242	Pte.	25.4.15	NI	
Coates, F.	306	Pte.	25.4.15	YPR	
Coates, J.	9641	Pte.	11.5.15	YPR	
Cockerell, H.R.	34825	Pte.	1.9.18	VE	
Cockerell, H.	2424	Pte.	25.5.15	SF	
Cockerill, G.	4581	Pte.	7.7.15	YPR	
Coldicott, T.	2119	Pte.	13.10.14	MT	
Cole, D.	7535	Pte.	12.11.14	PL	
Cole, R.	8925	Pte.	25.4.15	TC	
Collett, A.H.	23199	L/Cpl.	16.9.18	MH	
Collett, T.	9821	Pte.	3.7.17	LX	
Collier, E.J.	36234	Pte.	24.10.18	RM	
Collier, F.H.D.	23959	Pte.	11.4.17	FM	
Collins, C.	2789	Pte.	26.4.15	YPR	
Collins, C.H.	8828	Pte.	9.6.15	HZ	
Collins, C.	36235	Pte.	5.8.18	MG	
Collins, G.	28381	Pte.	30.8.18	VE	
Collins, J.L.	1144	L/Cpl.	26.4.15	YPR	
Collins, W.	462	Cpl.	12.10.16	TH	
Compton, W.	10421	Pte.	20.10.16	GR	
Conboy, D.	7487	Pte.	3.5.15	PP	
Congrave, J.	26246	Pte.	24.10.18	VC	
Connor, J.	9695	Pte.	25.4.15	YPR	
Cook, A.	2242	Pte.	25.4.15	SF	
Cook, C.E.	27851	Pte.	2.9.18	VE	24792 Shrops. L.I.
Cook, F.	18738	Pte.	15.10.16	AL	24050 Soms. L.I.

Cook, W.A.	34828	Pte.	15.4.18	SV	
Cook, W.W.	9223	Pte.	16.6.15	YPR	
Coombes, A.	1788	Pte.	30.6.15	RG2	
Cooper, E.	1601	Sgt.	24.6.15	–	
Cooper, G.	8131	Pte.	27.4.18	LP	
Cooper, J.W.	9806	Pte.	26.6.16	TH	
Cooper,T.	7791	Pte	13.10.14	MT	
Cope, T.	6838	Pte.	22.12.14	BA	
Cormell, A.	18127	Pte.	12.10.17	TCM	
Cornishh, S.F.	28984	Pte.	26.4.18	PB	
Cort, A.	1072	Pte.	25.4.15	YPR	
Cosford, G.	419	Cpl.	26.4.15	OO	
Cotton, F.C.	28322	Pte.	10.5.18	–	27354 Hussars
Cotton, F.	2350	Pte.	2.7.15	YPR	
Cox, F.J.	9410	L/Cpl.	13.10.16	GR	
Cox, G.	6886	Sgt.	11.4.17	AR	
Cox, G.B.	36236	Pte.	8.8.18	LM	
Cox, G.W.	9712	Pte.	14.11.14	CG	
Cox, J.	2120	Sgt.	6.8.18	AI	
Cox, W.	4826	L/Cpl.	22.6.15	BC	
Coxhill, H.	27872	Pte.	11.4.17	AT	
Coyne, P.	1940	Pte.	25.4.15	YPR	
Cracknell, J.	4080	Pte.	26.4.15	YPR	
Craddock, R.	1614	Pte.	25.4.15	YPR	
Cramp, W.	157	Pte.	13.10.14	MT	
Cranbrook, W.	6340	A/Sgt.	25.4.15	YPR	5289 West Riding Regt.
Crane, H.E.	50807	CQS	30.8.18	VE	13387 Ox. and Bucks L.I.
Crane, J.J.	468	L/Cpl.	2.11.14	CB	
Creeper, F.W.C.	34831	Pte.	15.4.18	PL	
Cross, B.R.	15973	Pte.	23.10.16	TH	
Cross, G.W.	21345	Pte.	11.4.17	AR	27090 Ryl. Berks. Regt.
Crowe, W.	4081	Pte.	19.6.15	YPR	
Crump, T.	9381	Pte.	20.10.14	BO	
Crumpton, C.	8958	Pte.	25.4.15	YPR	
Crumpton, W.	2397	Pte.	20.12.14	PW	
Curtis, H.	9577	Pte.	13.10.16	TH	
Cussack, E.	4438	Cpl.	31.1.16	SU	
Daft, H.	717	Pte.	13.10.14	MT	
Dale, J.A.	7687	Pte.	25.4.15	YPR	
Darby, W.H.	1271	Pte.	3.5.17	AR	
Darby, W.T.	2097	Pte.	19.5.15	BAX	

Daubney, R.	21116	Pte.	11.4.17	AR	146058 R.A.S.C.
Davidson, J.	33065	Cpl.	1.4.18	AR	9792 Dragoons
Davies, F.	6273	L/Cpl.	10.5.18	H	
Davis, C.	43365	Pte.	30.8.18	VE	P/681 M.M.P.
Davis, G.	28704	Pte.	2.5.18	–	
Davis, H.	6126	Pte.	9.12.14	PW	
Davis, J.A.	4793	Sgt.	11.10.16	TH	
Davis, R.W.	27754	Pte.	19.4.18	LP	5313 Glos. Regt.
Davis, W.	707	A/Sgt.	24.10.15	SS	
Davis, W.	4087	Pte.	25.4.15	YPR	
Daw, J.L.	831	Pte.	25.4.15	SF	
Dawson, W.	7613	Pte.	25.4.15	YPR	
Day, A.J.	25446	Pte.	15.4.18	PL	
Day, A.J.	9876	Pte.	21.5.15	WH	
Deeley, A.	9843	Pte.	1.4.15	LR	
Deeley, D..N.	9597	Pte.	13.4.17	SN	
Delve, J.	35978	Pte.	9.8.18	MG	
De Meza, G.	23988	Pte.	24.12.17	DN	
Dennis, H.	9779	L/Cpl.	25.4.15	YPR	
Denny, A.	7361	Sgt.	25.6.16	AV	
Denny, J.	9510	Pte.	12.10.16	TH	
De Ville, S.	33023	L/Cpl.	27.6.18	PB	GS/13059 Dragoon Gds.
Dewis, J.H.	16842	Sgt.	15.4.18	PL	
Dignan, J.	11966	Pte.	12.10.16	TH	
Dix, H.	9837	Pte.	20.5.15	BAX	
Dixon, S.F.	20604	Pte.	23.10.16	TH	11352 Army Cyclist Corps
Dixon, W.	9418	Pte.	26.5.16	WH	
Dobinson, W.	511	PTE.	25.4.15	YPR	
Dobbs, G.N.	16093	L/Cpl.	12.10.16	TH	
Dodd, A.J.	9393	CSM	1.2.15	SU	
Dodd, H.	28323	Pte.	18.2.17	–	23803 Hussars
Dodd, W.	16/2000	Cpl.	15.4.18	RU	140414 R.F.A.
Dolan, J.	1609	Pte.	9.5.15	RO	
Doughty, J.H.	6790	Pte.	25.4.15	YPR	
Downing, J.H.	27940	Pte.	3.5.18	ET	
Draper, A.	9767	Pte.	11.10.16	GU	
Draper, G.	28255	Pte.	11.4.17	BS	27459 Hussars
Driver, H.	29866	Pte.	12.10.17	TCM	
Duckerin, F.W.	2413	Pte.	25.4.15	YPR	
Duddy, T.	1912	Pte.	10.8.18	PB	
Dunkley, L.	305871	Pte.	9.8.17	CM	

Dunn, H.L.	9200	Pte.	1.7.16	TH	
Dunn, J.	8996	L/Cpl.	13.10.14	MT	Indian General Service Medal 1908
Dunne, J.	8851	Pte.	25.12.15	SU	
Dutton, P.	10077	Sgt.	15.4.18	PL	
Dyde, J.	9668	Pte.	4.10.17	TCM	
Dyke, O.	7701	A/Cpl.	12.10.16	TV	
Eadon, G.E.	13066	Pte.	1.7.16	SU	
Eadon, H.	2393	Pte.	25.4.15	PR	
Eames, M.	36245	Pte.	29.8.18	VEM	
Easey, H.C.	9361	Sgt.	13.10.14	MT	
Eaton, J.C.	3560	A/Sgt.	22.7.16	DB	
Eden, J.A.	2463	Pte.	4.2.15	PW	
Edge, J.W.M.	10682	L/Cpl.	12.10.17	TCM	
Edmonds, H.	1890	Sgt.	12.10.16	TH	
Edmunds, W.	1244	Sgt.	12.4.17	AU	
Edwards, E.	506	Pte.	21.4.17	CA	
Edwards, J.	3108	Pte.	25.4.15	YPR	
Edwards, J.H.	4122	Pte.	23.10.16	TH	
Edwards, J.	7672	Sgt.	3.5.17	CM	
Edwards, P.	2246	Pte.	19.9.14	–	
Edwards, T.	9726	Pte.	20.9.14	VXB	
Elliott, F.E.	18735	Pte.	12.10.16	TH	23088 Somerset L. I.
Elliott, J.O.	1262	Pte.	7.11.15	SU	
Elliott, P.W.	16090	Pte.	16.2.17	FI	
Elwell, A.	4836	Pte.	12.10.16	TH	
Elyard, R.J.	19966	L/Cpl.	15.4.18	PL	
England, C.E.	9782	Pte.	12.12.15	SU	
Ensor, S.	9707	Pte.	14.4.17	AU	
Evans, C.W.	2255	Pte.	23.10.16	TH	
Evans, F.	26187	Pte.	25.7.18	GN	
Evans, J.	2183	Pte.	12.10.16	–	
Evans, R.J.	20989	Pte.	19.4.17	SN	
Evans, T.	2546	L/Cpl.	12.10.16	TH	
Everitt, A.T. WG	39471	Pte.	10.5.19	ACE	
Evetts, R.A.	16012	Pte.	26.6.16	TH	
Fairbrother, J.W.	10510	Pte.	1.7.15	–	
Fall, W.G.	2448	Pte.	3.5.17	CM	
Fallon, H.	33025	Pte.	30.8.18	VE	
Fane, E.J.	9617	Pte.	25.4.15	YPR	
Farmer, A.	9969	Pte.	12.10.16	TH	

Faulkner, C.H.	3685	Pte.	3.6.15	NI	
Faulkner, G.F.	3390	Pte.	5.6.15	NI	
Faulkner, J.	2786	Pte.	25.4.15	YPR	
Fawson, H.A.	459	Pte.	30.4.16	BI	
Fellows, F.H.	33918	Pte.	30.12.18	BY	
Feltham, W.E.	2298	L/Cpl.	25.1.16	SU	
Fereday, J.A.	19551	Pte.	18.4.17	AU	
Fevers, W.	8377	Pte.	11.4.17	AR	
Field, A.	12797	L/Cpl.	9.10.17	TCM	
Field, A.L.	2423	Pte.	2.10.15	SU	
Finch, A.C.	28260	Pte.	23.7.17	CM	27451 9th Reserve Cavalry Regt.
Finch, W.	366	Pte.	25.4.15	YPR	
Fincham, A.T.	16922	Pte.	3.5.17	AR	
Fish, H.	27538	Pte.	30.8.18	VE	Notts. and Derby Regt.
Fiske, H.	14320	L/Cpl.	12.10.16	TH	
Fitzer, A.	6878	Pte.	19.6.15	FO	
Fitzgerald, J.	9259	Pte.	8.2.15	–	
Fitzgerald, R.	11325	Pte.	10.10.15	–	
Fletcher, A.C.	19348	Pte.	11.4.17	PJ	
Fletcher, G. WG	5348	Pte.	28.4.19	Y	
Fletcher, I.	4477	L/Cpl.	31.10.17	MH	
Fletcher, W.	4528	Pte.	24.5.15	YPR	
Foden, H.	1227	Pte.	25.4.15	YPR	
Ford, I.	146	L/Cpl.	23.7.15	NI	
Forrest, M.	4484	Cpl.	12.10.16	TH	
Forrest, R.	11470	Pte.	12.10.16	TH	
Fortey, B.	10969	Pte.	16.2.17	FI	
Foster, F.C.	267682	Pte.	3.5.17	BS	
Foster, W.	9359	Pte.	18.9.14	LF	
Fox, A.E.	5219	Pte.	1.4.18	TY	
Fox, T.	9546	Pte.	8.7.19	YPR	
Fox, N.H.	2123	Pte.	21.3.15	RT	
Foy, J.	3368	Pte.	11.10.16	TH	
France, A.	33082	Pte.	15.4.18	SV	21551 Dragoons
France, W.H.	9169	Pte.	5.3.15	BL	
Francis, F.C.	266894	Pte.	30.8.18	VE	
Francis, H.	4979	Pte.	9..5.17	TN	
Francis, J.	33010	A/Cpl.	20.11.17	WDM	GS/5414 6th Dragoon Guards

Franklin, A.	18380	Pte.	7.5.17	CO	23357 Somerset Light Infantry
Fraser, H.	3719	Pte.	25.4.15	YPR	
Freeman, J.	9325	Pte.	25.4.15	YPR	
French, W.C.	10660	Pte.	12.10.17	–	
Fry, E.	4296	Pte.	10.10.16	TH	
Fuller, J.	9634	Pte.	21.3.16	BI	
Fynn, G.	20630	Pte.	23.10.16	TH	11115 Army Cycle Corps.
Gadbsy, J.	23279	Pte.	11.4.17	PJ	
Gahan, L.	7519	Pte.	26.4.15	YPR	
Gains, S.	27955	Pte.	12.10.17	CH	2145 Hants. Regt.
Galloway, J.	932	Pte.	25.4.15	YPR	
Ganley, T.	9721	A/CSM	23.12.17	DN	
Gardener, G.	9453	Pte.	6.6.15	VMC	
Gardener, H.	2137	Pte.	16.11.14	CB	
Gardner, C.H.	11163	Pte.	21.4.17	ET	
Gardner, G.H.	28836	Pte.	24.10.18	ST	S/2016961 R.A.S.C.
Gardner, W.	10169	Pte.	8.6.15	TL	
Garland, W.	1951	Pte.	8.7.15	YPR	
Garland, W.E.	11680	Pte.	8.8.16	YPR	
Garratt, J.	11912	Pte.	14.4.18	CC	
Garrison, B.R.	14780	Pte.	11.4.17	FM	
Gartenfield, C.R.	3274	Pte.	25.4.15	YPR	
Garvey, W.H.	6861	Pte.	25.4.15	YPR	
Gathercole, C.B.	29499	Pte.	30.8.18	VE	61988 Cheshire Regt.
Gear, C.J.	6921	Pte.	25.4.15	YPR	
Gibson, R.	503	CSM.	11.5.18	LV	M.M.
Gifford, W.H.	2157	Pte.	25.4.15	YPR	
Gilbert, G.	6748	Pte.	11.2.15	BW	
Gilderson, W.C.	1872	Pte.	18.6.15	YPR	
Gilderthorpe, H.	9771	L/Cpl.	2.5.15	YPR	
Giles, H.	33158	Pte.	30.8.18	VEM	27416 Hussars
Gilks, W.G.	384	Sgt.	6.1.16	MR	
Gill, E.	22907	Pte.	24.10.18	VC	
Gill, J.T.	1422	Cpl.	3.5.17	AR	
Gillard, F.G.	36382	Pte.	30.8.18	VEM	
Gilliver, H.H.	11880	Pte.	28.4.18	ET	
Golding, F.H.	36260	Pte.	30.8.18	VEM	
Goode, W.E.	17027	Pte.	25.4.18	CC	
Goodhead, J.	2371	Pte.	20.12.14	PW	
Goodley, G.M.	23566	Pte.	12.10.17	TCM	174190 Royal Engineers

Goodman, W.G.	228	Pte.	27.8.14	HN	
Goodyear, J.	7739	Pte.	26.4.15	YPR	
Copsill, A.	27881	Pte.	23.6.17	BS	
Gordon, E.L.	2574	Pte.	11.12.16	TH	
Gordon, W.P.	2575	Pte.	25.4.15	YPR	
Gordon, J.	273	Pte.	11.4.17	BS	
Gough, B.G.	9935	Pte.	25.4.15	YPR	
Gough, W.	2871	Pte.	27.12.15	SU	
Gould, G.	6835	Pte.	17.1.15	PW	
Govett, A.B.	10410	Pte.	25.4.15	YPR	
Graves, A.	4325	Pte.	17.10.16	ET	
Gray, W.C.	1204	Pte.	25.4.15	YPR	
Greatrix, H.	1468	Pte.	14.3.15	PW	
Greatrix, W.	171	Pte.	26.4.15	YPR	
Gregory, R.C.	35286	Pte.	8.9.18	ACE	
Green, A.E.	2133	Cpl.	13.10.14	MT	
Green, E.T.	13251	Pte.	16.7.16	DU	
Green, P.	268875	Pte.	18.12.17	TY	
Green, P.T.	203707	Pte.	12.4.18	PL	
Greening, A.	9238	Pte.	20.4.15	–	
Greenslade, R.	34849	Ptre.	2.4.15	WM	
Greenway, E.J.	2139	Pte.	19.7.15	WM	
Greenway, W.	11668	L/Cpl.	12.10.17	TCM	
Grice, H.	1876	L/Cpl.	25.4.15	YPR	
Griffin, E.	4235	Pte.	18.11.15	SU	
Griffiths, A.	9197	Pte.	25.4.15	YPR	
Griffiths, H.	1000	Pte.	5.4.18	DN	
Grimes, R.	22837	Pte.	7.5.17	DO	
Gubbings, S.	7608	Pte.	20.6.17	SN	
Guest, A.	10014	Pte.	12.10.16	TH	
Gunn, W.H.	2457	Pte.	10.4.15	–	
Gurney, J.T.	316	L/Cpl.	25.4.15	NI	
Guttery, A.	4054	Pte.	24.8.15	MM	
Gwinnett, A.	1949	Pte.	25.10.14	PL	
Hackett, E.W.	2096	Pte.	4.12.14	LG	
Haddock, J.M.	41358	Pte.	25.10.18	RM	
Hadley, A.	9549	Pte.	6.9.15	SU	
Hadley, F.W.	8781	Pte.	3.5.15	BO	
Hadley, T.	29624	Pte.	6.10.17	DZ	
Hale, S.J.	940	Pte.	31.10.14	CB	Indian General Service Medal 1908

Hales, H.	2105	Pte.	13.10.14	MT			
Hall, A.	7954	Pte.	27.10.14	PL			
Hall.A.A. WG	9619	Pte.	4.10.15	SU			
Hall, C.	2393	Pte.	26.4.15	YPR			
Hall, F. WG	9619	Cpl.	25.4.15	NI			
Hall, R.	24121	Pte.	16.4.18	LP			
Hammond, J.	734	Pte.	25.4.15	YPR			
Hancox, C.J.	1685	Pte.	26.4.15	YPR			
Hand, W.	27038	Pte.	3.5.17	AR	M.M.	3802	4/Lincolnshire Regt.
Hands, J.	2067	Pte.	1.11.18	BL			
Hankinson, T.	11381	Pte.	11.10.16	TH			
Hanks, J.H.	646	Pte.	31.10.18	RM			
Hanson, C.	1817	Pte.	7.7.15	YPR			
Hanson, R. WG	2520	Pte.	11.2.16	RC			
Hardman, J.	448	Pte.	17.12.14	PW			
Hardiman, W.	10665	Pte.	3.5.17	–			
Harley, A.	3503	Pte.	29.3.18	CA			
Harris, A.E.	9919	Pte.	31.7.15	SU			
Harris, C.O.	675	Pte.	10.10.15	TH			
Harris, F.	9158	Pte.	13.10.14	MT			
Harris, F.E. WG	9639	Pte.	20.3.19	BY			
Harris, G.A.	9052	Pte.	10.4.15	RT			
Harris, T.	4432	Pte.	27.7.15	BO			
Harris, W.C.	7257	Pte.	25.4.15	YPR			
Harrison, J.A.	683	L/Cpl.	5.1.16	SU			
Hart, J.T.	2486	Pte.	25.4.15	YPR			
Hartshorne, W.	4715	Pte.	7.11.15	SU			
Harvey, J.	2295	Pte.	12.4.17	NL			
Haseldine, S.	36395	Pte.	30.8.18	VEM			
Haskey, S.	8971	Pte.	13.10.14	MT			
Hastings, F.	9648	Pte.	29.10.16	ET			
Hastings, J.C.	9255	Pte.	25.4.15	YPR			
Hateley, I. WG	9866	Pte.	20.5.19	W			
Hatfield, P.G.	267622	Pte.	31.5.17	CG			
Havard, G.	4883	Sgt.	11.4.17	AR			
Hawker, E.J.	8715	L/Cpl.	7.3.15	PW			
Hawkes, F.G.	6984	Pte.	25.4.15	YPR			
Hawkwswood, A.E.	1553	Pte.	9.6.17	BY			
Hawley, G.A.	9774	Pte.	1.5.16	BI			
Haywood, C.H.	1636	Pte.	7.11.15	SU			

Haywood, H.	62	Pte.	11.10.16	TH	
Haywood, W.	10882	Pte.	17.11.15	SU	
Hazelton, A.C.	33045	Pte.	25.7.18	GN	6591 7th Dragoon Guards
Healey, J.T.	8995	Pte.	25.4.15	YPR	
Heard, A.	9257	Pte.	25.4.15	NI	
Heath, R.	2238	Pte.	18.11.15	W	
Heath, W.T.	42331	Pte.	17.12.15	ET	
Hedges, R.	7490	Pte.	17.4.18	LM	
Height, H.	244	Dmr.	29.4.16	DU	
Hemmings, J.W.	7205	L/Cpl.	1.9.18	VEM	
Hewins, J.	1648	L/Cpl.	12.10.16	CR	
Hewitt, G.	1610	Pte.	26.4.15	YPR	
Hibbert, H.W.	9085	L/Cpl.	1.7.16	TH	
Higgerson, A.	2489	Pte.	26.4.15	YPR	
Higham, A.C.	1992	L/Cpl.	8.7.15	YPR	
Highley, A.E.	34857	Pte.	15.4.18	PL	
Hill, C.G.	2230	A/Cpl.	28.10.14	BA	
Hill, G.J.	1936	Pte.	25.4.15	YPR	
Hill, H.	9752	Pte.	25.4.15	YPR	
Hill, J.	38944	Pte.	8.8.18	GN	
Hill, J.	10015	L/Cpl.	12.10.17	CM	
Hill, R.B.	9574	Pte.	4.7.15	BC	
Hill, W.	34165	Pte.	1.4.18	AR	GS/14701 Dragoon Guards
Hirons, G.	50866	L/Cpl.	3.9.18	VE	
Hitchman, W.	796	Sgt.	1.5.17	AR	
Hobbs, G.	1924	A/Sgt.	17.4.16	BI	
Hobson, H.	2162	Pte.	27.8.14	HN	
Hoden, W.O.	9066	Pte.	13.10.14	MT	
Hodgkiss, G.	7896	L/Cpl.	11.4.17	PJ	
Hogg, J.	2194	Pte.	26.8.14	LF	
Hogg, V.	4560	A/Cpl.	17.4.16	BI	
Holden, C.	9055	Sgt.	9.8.18	LM	D.C.M.
Holdom, J.	941	Sgt.	12.10.16	TH	
Hollands, J.	8620	Pte.	30.8.18	VE	Hussars
Holland, T.	7823	Pte.	25.6.16	AV	
Hollingsworth, H.	37583	Pte.	31.5.18	–	236229 R.A.S.C.
Holmes, B.	1664	L/Cpl.	20.11.17	AR	D.C.M.
Holmes, S.	41980	Pte.	16.9.19	W	
Holtham, G.	1454	Sgt.	20.6.17	AR	
Holtom, F. WG	280	A/Sgt.	9.4.17	SC	
Hone, J.	721	Pte.	24.10.18	ST	

Honner, J.	400	L/Cpl.	25.4.15	YPR	
Hoomans, B.	1046	Pte.	17.4.16	BI	
Hornsby, A.	7752	Pte.	29.10.16	DR	
Hornsby, R.	2402	Pte.	26.10.16	–	
Hornsey, S. WG	2783	L/Cpl.	23.4.17	AR	
Horton, J.	9687	Pte.	24.10.14	CB	Indian General Service Medal 1908
Hoskins, H.	9423	C/Sgt.	24.5.15	YPR	
Howell, W.A.	10905	Pte.	15.12.15	BT	
Howes, H.J.	1069	Pte.	8.9.14	LF	5490 Scots. Gds. 747 R. Highr.
Howlett, G.	201390	L/Cpl.	30.8.18	VE	
Hubball, A.R.	742	Pte.	26.4.15	YPR	
Hubball, F.	7603	L/Cpl.	11.4.17	FM	
Hubbard, J.	9728	Pte.	24.9.14	NZ	
Hudson, J.	6911	Pte.	9.7.15	LS	
Hughes, A.	835	Pte.	12.10.16	TH	
Hughes, S.F.	1975	Pte.	7.3.15	LR	
Hull, G.	3066	Sgt.	12.10.16	TH	
Hurden, F.J.	34855	Pte.	17.4.18	CC	
Ingram, F.	9831	Pte.	25.4.15	YPR	
Ingram, G.J.	9301	Pte.	19.9.14	VXB	
Ingram, W.	1878	Pte.	25.4.15	YPR	
Inman, W.H.	2282	Pte.	11.10.16	TH	
Irons, S.	30260	L/Cpl.	11.4.17	BS	954 Hunts. Cycl. Battn.
Ives, J.F.	50868	Pte.	30.8.13	LY	
Jackson, A.W.	9628	Pte.	31.3.18	AR	
Jackson, G.R.	898	Pte.	23.11.14	PW	
Jacques, A.W.	41769	Pte.	24.10. 18	VC	
James, J.H.	17100	Pte.	12.12.16	GR	
Jauncey, J.	2033	Pte.	24.3.16	BI	
Jarratt, J.	1760	L/Cpl.	9.5.15	YPR	
Jarvis, A.E.	8611	L/ Sgt.	28.8.14	MC	Indian General Service Medal 1908
Jasper, E.G.	25529	Pte.	12.10.17	TCM	
Jay, Arthur.	8136	Cpl.	12.10.17	TCM	
Jeery, A.G.	20578	Pte.	12.10.16	TV	10718 Army Cyclists Corps
Jeavons, A.J.	24804	Pte.	30.8.18	VEM	
Jelf, J.	8853	Pte.	26.4.15	YPR	
Jennings, E.	1758	Pte.	6.8.16	LS	
Jennings, J.	1969	Pte.	4.10.17	TCM	

Jennings, W.	9427	Pte.	1.7.16	TH	
Jephcott, O.	425	Pte.	13.10.14	MT	Indian General Service Medal 1908
Jeynes, E.T.	9982	Sgt.	25.4.15	YPR	
Johnsey, A.E.	9405	Pte.	20.9.15	SU	
Johnson, E.P.	16/1778	Pte.	1.12.17	MB	
Johnson, W.	11173	Pte.	26.6.16	BN	
Jolly, J.	6976	Pte.	1.3.18	LR	
Jolliffe, E.R.	33064	Pte.	15.4.18	PL	25696 Dragoon Guards
Jones, A.	31	Pte.	9.5.15	YPR	
Jones, A.E.	6334	Pte.	29.5.15	YPR	
Jones, A.V.	16574	Pte.	12.10.16	TH	
Jones, A.	2117	L/Cpl.	25.4.15	YPR	
Jones, A.	609	L/Cpl.	12.4.17	SN	
Jones, A.T.	28332	Pte.	4.10.17	TCM	27404 Hussars
Jones, C.	27933	Pte.	1.4.18	AR	
Jones, J.	6230	Pte.	20.6.18	LV	
Jones, P.	26656	Pte.	31.10.19	–	
Jones, R.J.	2233	Pte.	26.8.14	LF	
Jones, R.	2015	Pte.	25.4.15	YPR	9370 Coldstream Guards
Jones, W.	323	CQS	25.4.15	YPR	
Jones, W. WG	11076	Pte.	2.9.18	NE	
Jones, W.E.	23086	Pte.	3.5.17	AR	
Juggins, W.L.	50830	Pte.	31.8.18	LY	
Keeling, J.J.	23214	Sgt.	25.10.18	QR	
Kelly, A.	3564	Pte.	9.5.17	LX	
Kelly, R.	7095	Pte.	25.4.15	YPR	
Kemp, A.	8548	Pte.	26.8.14	LF	Indian General Service Medal 1908
Kemp, W.A.	1768	Pte.	3.6.15	YPR	
Kendall, R.G.	16504	Pte.	14.7.16	ET	
Kennett, H.T.	16042	Pte.	10.10.16	TH	
Kenyon, H.	33029	Pte.	15.4.18	PL	GS/21982 Dragoon Guards
Kerr, H.	34192	Pte.	23.12.17	MB	4209 Hussars
Ketteridge, W.	13106	Pte.	5.10.17	TCM	
Key, A.	13317	Pte.	4.7.16	AC	
Kiff, J.F.	284	Pte.	31.3.15	RT	
Kimberley, T.	42394	Pte.	24.10.18	VC	
Kinchin, H.	57	Cpl.	9.10.16	TH	
King, T.	30485	Pte.	30.8.18	VEM	S/4/087052 R.A.S.C.
King, W.G.	2280	Pte.	17.4.18	LP	

Kirkoff, G.	7393	Pte.	25.4.15	YPR	
Kitching, W.	9599	Pte.	21.10.14	CB	
Knight, A.	983	L/Cpl.	13.10.14	MT	
Knight, A.	16736	Pte.	23.10.16	TH	
Knight, T.	79	Pte.	13.10.14	MT	
Knott, J.H.	40539	Pte.	29.6.18	GN	
Kyte, F.A.	9405	Sgt.	27.8.14	HN	Indian General Service Medal 1908
Lacey, N.	36278	Pte.	31.8.18	VEM	
Lakin, C.F.	1798	Pte.	26.4.15	YPR	
Lamb, T.	1615	Pte.	23.10.16	TH	
Lane, E.B.	8883	Pte.	25.4.15	YPR	
Lane, F.C.	50869	Pte.	4.12.18	VA	
Lane, W.A.	15520	Pte.	23.10.16	–	
Langford, H.	307408	L/Cpl.	20.5.18	–	
Lapham, C.R.	1448	L/Cpl.	25.4.15	YPR	
Latham, G.H.	9184	L/Cpl.	11.11.14	SR	
Law, C.	2478	Pte.	12.10.17	TCM	
Lawrence, F.	27566	Pte.	12.10.17	TCM	3792 Notts. and Derby Regt.
Lawrence, M.	20480	Pte.	13.4.17	AT	
Layland, A.	1000	Pte.	11.6.18	LM	
Lazonby, A.	513	Pte.	25.4.15	YPR	
Lea, F.	2496	Pte.	27.8.14	HN	
Leach, H.	849	L/Cpl.	8.9.14	LF	
Leaton, T.H.	884	Pte.	15.9.14	PD	
Leech, J.H.	7650	Sgt.	12.10.16	TH	
Lee, F.	25424	Pte.	12.10.17	CM	3952 Army Pay Corps.
Lee, T.	3277	Pte.	15.4.18	CC	
Lee, W.T.	2836	Pte.	5.6.18	RG	
Leedham, H.	397	Sgt.	25.10.16	TH	
Lees, H.	3660	Pte.	30.8.18	VE	
Leonard, W.S.	28798	Pte.	15.4.18	GH	
Lettington, S.	33101	Pte.	18.6.18	LP	11864 Dragoons
Lewis, E.	2264	Pte.	8.7.15	YPR	
Lewis, T.	3335	Pte.	25.4.15	YPR	
Lilley, W.G.	9620	Pte.	24.5.15	YPR	
Lincoln, R.M.	1652	Pte.	3.5.17	AR	
Line, S.	4850	Pte.	12.10.16	TH	
Lines, E.	1189	Sgt.	4.10.17	TCM	
Ling, H.	2453	Pte.	8.7.15	YPR	
Ling, J.A.	28276	Pte.	27.4.18	LP	27430 Cavalry

Link, J.E.	10720	Pte.	11.4.17	AT	
Linsdale, W. WG	33066	Pte.	1.5.19	CL	
Lionett, P.H.	868	Pte.	1.11.17	WDM	
Lionett, S.N.	935	L/Cpl.	28.4.15	HZ	
Liversage, W.	8155	Pte.	9.5.15	YPR	
Lloyd, A.E.	9281	Pte.	25.4.15	YPR	
Lloyd, J.E.	571	Pte.	25.4.15	SF	
Lockley, E.	3100	Pte.	12.10.16	TH	
Long, A.	10614	Pte.	15.4.18	PL	
Long, F.E.	6922	Pte.	3.12.14	PW	
Longdon, W.H.	27591	Pte.	15.4.18	SV	
Lowndes, B.	7626	Pte.	26.4.15	YPR	
Loynes, C.E.T.	8875	Pte.	6.5.15	YPR	
Lucas, A.W.	241621	Pte.	1.11.19	CV	
Lucas, L.	1603	Pte.	14.10.16	GR	
Luckett, G.E.	2633	Pte.	25.4.15	YPR	
Ludford, C.H.	21110	Pte.	6.10.17	DH	
Lyons, D.D.	19002	Pte.	24.5.17	AU	
Mace, C.S.	1457	Pte.	3.5.17	AR	
Magson, S.	2199	Pte.	13.10.14	MT	
Maidstone, A.V.	17505	Pte.	15.4.18	CC	
Mainwaring, J.	705	A/Sgt.	11.10.16	GU	
Maley, E.	16–1681	Pte.	4.6.16	–	
Maley, M.F.	11169	Pte.	15.4.18	CC	
Malin, F.`	150	Pte.	24.5.15	YPR	
Malin, W.	18998	Pte.	30.8.18	VEM	
Mallen, R.J.	2215	Pte.	24.5.15	YPR	
Malley, F.	3852	Pte.	16.1.16	BV	
Manchester, L.	812	L/Cpl.	25.4.15	YPR	
Manners, B.	9356	Pte.	21.10.14	PL	
Manning, J.	5145	Pte.	11.10.16	TH	
Manning, J.C.	1597	Pte.	25.4.15	OO	9822 Royal Welsh Fusiliers
Manning, P.	19401	Pte.	12.2.17	FI	
Mansfield, H.	11662	Pte.	4.11.15	SU	
Marshall, E.	1054	Sgt.	12.10.16	TH	
Marshall, J.	9556	Pte.	30.4.16	BI	
Marshall, T.H.	42395	Pte.	24.10.18	VC	
Marshall, W.	19604	Pte.	3.5.17	AR	
Marshall, W.A.	33167	Drmr.	14.8.19	PC	
Martin, C.E.	9499	Pte.	28.1.15	PW	
Martin, G.S.	1245	A/Cpl.	5.10.17	CM	

Martin, W.E.	17553	Pte.	18.7.18	LM	
Martin, W.G.	11933	Pte.	12.10.16	–	
Mason, C.	13181	Pte.	25.10.18	ACE	
Mason, F.	33031	Pte.	12.5.18	CG	GS/13314 Dragoon Guards
Masters, F.	9759	Pte.	25.4.15	YPR	
Matthews A.E.	19229	Pte.	18.7.18	LM	
Matthews, P.W.	2635	Pte.	25.4.15	YPR	
Matthews, W.	554	Pte.	25.8.16	RW	
Matthews, W.G.	604	Pte.	25.4.15	YPR	
Maughan, A.	1957	L/Cpl.	25.4.15	YPR	
Maund, E.H.	3590	Pte.	8.6.15	TL	
Mawson, M.W.	11428	Pte.	3.5.17	AR	
Mayoll, F.	21967	Pte.	12.10.17	CH	
McCann, M.	28337	Pte.	12.10.17	TCM	27374 Hussars
McCracken, C.	6864	Pte.	25.4.15	YPR	
McGill, A.F.	34179	Pte.	11.6.18	LV	8159 Dragoons
Meade, C.	1708	L/Cpl.	12.4.17	AG	
Mears, H.	8720	A/Cpl.	14.11.15	FR	
Medlam, F.	15	Pte.	25.4.15	YPR	
Meigh, A.E.	2349	Pte.	30.4.15	BO	
Mellor, W.	7759	Pte.	25.4.15	YPR	
Melton, R.	8946	Pte.	25.5.15	HZ	
Merrick, R.F.	35731	Pte.	20.7.18	LM	29327 Worcs. Regt.
Merrick, T.	9522	Pte.	12.10.16	TH	
Merry, J.F.	6356	Pte.	29.3.16	SS	
Middleton, W.	8944	Pte.	25.4.15	YPR	
Miles, F.	205	Pte.	5.2.15	PW	
Millington, W.E.	50833	Pte.	1.9.18	VEM	
Mills, J.	3226	Pte.	31.7.15	SU	
Mills, S.E.	1033	Pte.	2.5.15	YPR	
Mills, W.N.	485	Pte.	25.4.15	YPR	
Millward, A.	38	Pte.	25.4.15	YPR	
Millward, E.	2584	Pte.	26.4.15	YPR	
Millward, H.	278	A/Cpl.	12.10.16	TH	
Millward, J.	9534	Pte.	12.10.16	TH	
Minshull, C.	267683	Pte.	13.4.17	AG	
Mitchell, A.W.	59872	Pte.	9.8.18	LM	
Mitchell, B.	378	Pte.	26.4.15	YPR	
Mitchell, P.	33032	L/Cpl.	3.1.18	WDM	GS/25501 Dragoon Guards
Mole, B.	9773	Cpl.	10.12.14	PW	
Montgomery, F.T.	9945	Sgt.	26.4.15	YPR	D.C.M.

Moody, H.R.	203914	Pte.	29.8.18	VEM	3042 South Mid. R. E.
Moore, A.	2753	A/Cpl.	20.7.18	T	
Moore, H.	451	Pte.	3.5.17	BS	
Moore, J.G.	8724	Pte.	25.5.15	WH	
Moore, T.H.	9480	Pte.	27.7.18	MG	
Morres, F.	25426	Pte.	30.8.18	VEM	
Moreton, W.H.	1639	Pte.	4.10.17	PO	
Morgan, G.	7496	Pte.	12.10.17	TCM	
Morgan, P.D.	21464	Pte.	12.10.17	TCM	
Morrell, H.	8950	Pte.	12.10.16	TH	
Morris, A. WG	166	Pte.	13.10.14	MT	
Morris, C.	1969	Pte.	16.10.14	HZ	
Morris, F.W.	9363	Pte.	25.4.15	YPR	
Morris, H.	23286	Pte.	17.4.17	–	
Morton, T.	8145	L/Cpl.	12.10.16	TH	
Moseley, C.F.	9390	Pte.	13.10.14	MT	Indian General Service Medal 1908
Moseley, H.	16434	L/Cpl.	16.4.18	LP	
Moss, J.	716	L/Cpl.	26.8.14	LF	
Mott, E.	11251	Pte.	20.6.17	AR	
Mould, C.	7497	Pte.	25.4.15	YPR	
Mounce, W.J.	50873	Pte.	30.8.18	VEM	
Muggleston, E.S.	1596	Pte.	3.5.17	AR	
Mulleague, C.H.	8886	Pte.	25.4.15	YPR	
Mullis, F.G.	8999	Sgt.	14.10.16	GR	
Mulliss, S.	6227	L/Sgt.	25.4.15	YPR	
Murphy, S.J.	50	A/Cpl.	25.4.15	–	
Murphy, W.	27384	Pte.	3.5.17	AR	4710 Notts and Derby Regt.
Murrell, S.D.	1871	Sgt.	2.2.16	MM	
Mushens, W.	20588	Pte.	23.10.16	TH	11011 A. C. C.
Myatt, J.	68	Pte.	22.9.14	LF	
Narborough, E.H.	9196	Pte.	13.10.14	MT	
Nash, G.H.	30036	Pte.	15.4.18	–	
Nash, H.	23227	Pte.	3.5.17	BS	
Nash, J.W. WG	9308	Pte.	26.10.16	BW	
Nash, W.	9023	Pte.	14.10.14	HZ	
Naunton, E.W.	16730	Pte.	12.10.16	TH	
Neal, R.D.	8923	Pte.	27.10.14	YTC	
Neal, S.	2060	Pte.	25.4.15	YPR	
Neale, W.H.	3388	Pte.	31.3.18	AR	251466 Royal Engineers
Nelson, E.	21993	Pte.	30.8.18	VE	

Nelson, H.	27914	Pte.	3.5.17	AR	
Nevett, E.	9396	Pte.	20.8.15	GS	
Newey, D.H.	9605	Pte.	5.12.14	BW	
Newey, T.	7340	Pte.	25.4.15	YPR	6390 Royal Welsh Fusiliers
Newman, G.L.	2548	Pte.	1.7.16	TH	
Newman, R.H.	7071	Pte.	25.4.15	YPR	
Newman, T.M.	29467	Pte.	15.5.18	MG	62127 Cheshire Regt.
Newth, L.	27975	Pte.	31.3.18	CA	16867 R. Berks. Regt.
Newton, A.	9573	Pte.	21.10.14	PL	Indian General Service Medal 1908
Newton, E.	8599	Pte.	2.7.16	SU	
Newton, W.I.	2831	L/Cpl.	25.4.15	YPR	
Nicholl, A.J.	1217	Pte.	25.5.15	HO	
Niclolls, E.A.	7466	Pte.	25.4.15	YPR	
Nicholls, H.W.	20552	Pte.	12.10.16	TH	10114 A.C.C.
Nicholls, J.	22081	Pte.	6.5.17	AG	Lancs. Fusiliers
Nolan, B.	357	Pte.	8.3.15	BLH	
Noon, W.	353	Pte.	26.4.15	YPR	
Norbury, A.	1816	Pte.	7.7.15	YPR	
Norbury, C.J.	17659	Pte.	11.4.17	FM	
Norman, A.	7862	L/Cpl.	8.7.15	YPR	
Norman, F.	16623	Pte.	12.6.17	CG	
Nowell, R.H.	330113	Pte.	24.10.18	VC	
Nuthall, H.	7498	Pte.	25.4.15	SF	
O'Brien, P.	870	Pte.	21.4.17	AR	
O'Brien, T.	2235	Pte.	25.4.15	YPR	
O'Callaghan, J.M.	2312	L/Sgt/	26.4.15	YPR	
O'Dell, F.	200	Pte.	25.4.15	YPR	
O'Hern, R.	2048	Pte.	11.4.17	BS	140432 Royal Field Artillery
Oates, A.	27570	L/Cpl.	12.10.16	TH	25007 S. Staffs. Regt.
Oldaker, D.	18582	Pte.	23.10.16	TH	24921 S. L. I.
Oldham, S.	674	Pte.	10.9.15	NO	
Oliver, F.	2083	Pte.	25.4.15	YPR	
Oliver, O.	20306	Pte.	27.12.16	–	
Orton, C.	10757	A/Cpl.	23.10.16	TH	
Osborne, H.L.	27996	A/Cpl.	11.4.17	AR	
Osborne, J.	3344	Pte.	25.4.15	YPR	
Osborne, W.M.	2229	Pte.	10.11.14	CB	
Overton, T.C.	21520	Pte.	2.5.17	DN	
Overy, A.	10	Pte.	25.4.15	YPR	
Owen, A.H.	10555	A/Cpl.	23.10.16	TH	

Owen, D.	1355	Cpl.	13.10.14	MT	
Owen, G.E.	2824	Pte.	25.4.15	YPR	
Owen, J.	27569	Pte.	12.10.16	TH	24799 Sth. Staffs. Regt.
Owen, W.	658	Pte.	18.7.18	LV	M.M.
Owen, W.T.	4574	Pte.	30.4.16	BI	
Oxspring, F.	3209	Pte.	25.6.16	TH	
Packer, J.	3171	Pte.	25.4.15	YPR	
Paddy, F.	22085	Pte.	25.7.18	GN	4108 – 3/2 London Regt.
Padmore, C.	26714	Pte.	29.8.18	FE	
Page, J. WG	3979	Pte.	16.12.17	HV	
Page, S.	2761	Pte.	18.2.15	PW	
Page, W.H.	2153	Pte.	17.4.18	LM	
Paley, W. WG	16/1951	Pte.	12.12.16	TH	
Palfrey, A.H.W.	303006	Pte.	15.4.18	PL	
Palfreyman, B.E.	7118	L/Cpl.	13.10.14	MT	Indian General Service Medal 1908
Palfreyman, B.	9868	Pte.	13.10.14	MT	
Pallett, H.W.	9589	L/Cpl.	3.5.17	AR	
Palmer, A.C.	985	L/Cpl.	3.5.17	AR	
Palmer, F.	27889	Cpl.	15.4.18	PL	
Palmer, F.S.	4954	Sgt.	2.5.15	YPR	
Palmer, H.T.	29963	Pte.	18.4.18	BE	20402 Oxford and Bucks. L.I.
Palmer, R.	30687	Pte.	20.7.18	SV	
Parker, E.	3984	Pte.	25.4.15	YPR	
Parker, F.	15211	Pte.	15.4.18	PL	
Parker, S.	14841	Pte.	3.5.17	AR	
Parkes, C.A.	8720	Pte.	5.11.15	MM	
Parkhouse, F.T.	25460	Pte.	5.10.17	DZ	1854 Army Pay Corps
Parnell, J.W.	4448	Cpl.	23.7.17	CM	
Parry, E.H.	16683	Pte.	3.5.17	–	
Parsons, H.E.	1831	Pte.	24.5.15	YPR	
Parsons, T.	9159	L/Cpl.	25.4.15	NI	
Parton, T.	27597	Pte.	23.10.16	TH	3849 6/South Staffs. Regt.
Pask, T.	27574	Pte.	3.5.17	AR	25033 10/South Staffs Regt.
Patrick, J.	1048	Pte.	13.5.15	JO	
Paybody, H.	10225	Pte.	25.4.15	YPR	
Payne, H.	2031	L/Cpl.	25.4.15	YPR	
Payne, H.	27603	Pte	12.10.16	TH	
Peach, H.H.	20629	Pte.	12.10.16	TH	10546 Army Cyclist Corps.
Pearce, W.J.H.	16/1703	Sgt.	15.4.18	–	
Pearson, C.	28702	Pte.	17.4.18	CC	

Pearson, J.W.	446	Pte.	25.4.15	YPR	
Peers, J.	1414	Pte.	12.10.16	TH	
Peet, C.W.	22170	Pte.	3.5.17	AR	
Pemberton, W. WG	1599	Pte.	18.7.16	TH	
Penn, A.	2369	L/Cpl.	31.10.16	–	
Pennington, C.	27775	Pte.	15.4.18	PL	4922 Worcs. Regt.
Percy, G.F.	34891	Pte.	15.4.18	PL	
Perks, A.	9607	Pte.	11.4.17	AR	
Perks, A.S.	1684	Pte.	23.10.16	TH	
Perrin, P.	754	Pte.	25.4.15	YPR	
Perry, H.	27764	Pte.	12.10.17	TCM	4807 Worcs. Regt.
Perry, J.T.	2344	L/Cpl.	25.4.15	YPR	
Pettengill, F.C.	33132	Pte.	20.11.17	AR	14752 Dragoons
Phillips, A.	7193	Pte.	25.4.15	YPR	
Phillips, J.	3324	Pte.	3.4.15	LR	
Phillips, S. WG	6637	Pte.	30.6.17	BW	
Phillips, W.	12431	Cpl.	9.4.17	SN	54431 R.G.A.
Phillips, W.	7	Pte.	25.4.15	YPR	
Phipps, M.	23984	Pte.	23.12.17	MB	
Pimm, G.	1858	Pte.	26.8.14	FN	
Pink, C.W. WG	424	Cpl.	27.7.16	TH	
Pinner, S.	11417	Pte.	23.10.16	TH	
Piper, E.A.	1676	Pte.	25.4.15	YPR	
Pitman, N.V. WG	269540	Pte.	21.11.20	SH	
Pitt, A.C.	3266	Pte.	25.4.15	YPR	
Poole, J.	3204	Pte.	13.5.15	AG	
Poole, M.	3431	Pte.	3.6.15	YPR	
Poole, R.W.	27760	Pte.	15.4.18	PL	5166 Worcs. Regt.
Popplewell, A.	240	Sgt.	23.10.16	TH	
Potter, A.	11627	Pte.	12.10.16	TH	
Potter, H.	2422	Pte.	24.5.15	YPR	
Powell, A.	18506	Pte.	4.10.17	PO	25284 Somerset L.I.
Powell, A.E.	14-1322	Pte.	23.12.17	MB	
Powell, E.	2291	Pte.	25.10.14	SR	
Powell, E.W.	16053	Pte.	17.2.17	BR	
Powell, L.S.	34193	Pte.	15.4.18	PS	10761 Hussars
Powell, T.H.	14402	Pte.	11.5.17	CM	
Preddy, G.	20499	Pte.	11.10.16	LN	
Price, A.E.	9760	Pte.	23.10.14	PL	Indian General Service Medal 1908

Price, A.W.N.	2010	Pte.	13.10.14	MT	
Price, F.R.	41294	Pte.	6.8.18	MG	
Price, H.W.	1240	Pte.	26.4.15	YPR	
Price, J.M.	27816	Pte.	30.8.18	VEM	2757 Herefordshire Regt.
Priest, J.E.	9346	Pte.	25.4.15	YPR	
Priest, R. WG	867	Pte.	27.7.18	BW	
Priestley, H.	2059	Cpl.	11.4.17	BS	140437 Royal Field Artillery
Pritchard, G.H.	2095	Pte.	27.10.14	SR	
Probert, A.J.	1843 or 1743	Pte.	25.4.15	YPR	
Pryce, D.O.	1677	Pte.	8.7.15	YPR	
Purnell, F.J.	20164	Pte.	11.4.17	BS	
Pursall, W.	28626	Pte.	20.10.18	SA	
Quick, A.	25331	Pte.	9.5.18	ET	
Quinlan, T.L.M.	1877	Pte.	9.4.15	RT	
Quinney, S.	1629	Pte.	24.4.16	BI	
Rachel, G.	3255	Pte.	25.4.15	YPR	
Radford, J.	3979	Pte.	16.12.17	–	M.M.
Rafferty, T.H.	7840	L/Cpl.	25.4.15	YPR	
Ragsdale, M.	21237	Cpl.	12.10.17	TCM	
Ralphs, W.H.	20546	Pte.	11.10.16	TH	8246 Army Cycle Corps
Randall, E.	42488	Pte.	25.10.18	RM	
Randle, C.E.	20201	Pte.	16.4.18	LP	
Rathbone, A.	27991.	Pte.	15.4.18	PL	
Raven, H.W.	2466	Pte.	26.8.14	LF	1475 Royal Warks. Regt.
Ravenhill, P.A.	344	Pte.	8.11.14	PL	
Rawlins, B.	7262	Pte.	25.4.15	YPR	
Ray, W.	1888	Pte.	17.12.14	PW	
Rea, A.E. WG	5094579	L/Sgt.	27.11.20	BY	
Read, C.H.	3882	Pte.	11.4.17	FM	
Read, G.E.	7051	Pte.	26.4.15	YPR	
Reade, S.	27576	Pte.	11.10.16	TH	24619 South Staffs. Regt.
Reader, T.	9342	Pte.	5.11.14	PS	
Redfern, J.W.	638	Cpl.	2.5.15	YPR	
Reeves, A.	9901	Pte.	13.7.16	AG	
Reeves, J.	17455	Pte.	29.4.18	VCN	
Renowden, C.C.	23712	Pte.	15.4.18	PL	35923 Devon Regt.
Revill.H.	8013	A/Cpl.	14.1.16	SU	
Reynolds, J.	9729	Pte.	11.11.14	PL	
Rhodes, G.L.	27577	Pte.	23.10.16	TH	24793 South Staffs. Regt.
Rhodes, J.B.	27578	Pte.	23.10.16	TH	24766 South Staffs. Regt.

Rhodes, L.	8	Pte.	30.11.14	–	
Rhodes, T.H.	23964	Pte.	3.5.17	AR	
Richardson, A.	706	L/Cpl.	11.10.16	TH	
Ricketts, A.T.	1283	L/Cpl.	25.10.16	ET	
Riddle, J.	64	Pte.	3.10.17	CG	
Rider, D.G.	16358	Pte.	3.5.17	AR	
Ridgewell, G.	34176	Pte.	26.10.18	RM	Hussars
Riley, C.	264	Pte.	13.11.14	PL	
Riley, H.H.	16848	Pte.	11.4.17	AR	
Riman, H.	25431	Pte.	28.10.18	QR	
Robbins, T.	9502	L/Cpl.	25.4.15	YPR	
Roberts, A.	9373	Pte.	27.8.14	HN	
Roberts, G.	6826	Pte.	25.4.15	YPR	
Roberts, G.	2570	Pte.	18.2.15	PW	
Roberts, H.	9005	Pte.	4.11.14	PL	
Roberts, W.	8880	Pte.	25.4.15	YPR	
Roberts, W.	8961	Pte.	19.10.14	CV	
Robinson, G.E.	27579	Pte.	23.10.16	TH	25140 S. Staffs. Regt.
Robinson, H.	20594	Pte.	12.10.16	TH	11088 Army Cyclist Corps
Robinson, W.	6806	Pte.	25.4.15	YPR	
Robinson, W.	16034	Pte.	3.5.17	AR	
Rodds, F.	9739	Pte.	25.4.15	YPR	
Rodgers, F.	166	Pte.	13.10.14	–	
Rollason, M.W.	11673	Pte.	23.10.16	TH	
Rollins, H.	18001	Pte.	11.4.17	AR	
Rollins, J.J.	29625	Pte.	12.10.17	TCM	
Rose, F.	9479	Pte.	12.10.16	TH	
Rose, W.A.	28742	Pte.	30.8.18	VE	
Rossindale, H.	8904	L/Cpl..	25.4.15	YPR	
Rouse, C.	445	Pte.	25.11.14	PW	
Rowe, E.	18699	Pte.	25.10.16	GR	22901 Somerset L. I.
Rowland, E.	1264	Pte.	11.4.17	AR	
Rowley, J.	16594	Pte.	24.10.16	TH	
Rowley, J.J.	9463	Pte.	9.5.15	YPR	
Rowley, W.	97	Pte.	13.10.14	MT	
Rudd, S.	1334	L/Cpl.	15.10.16	TH	
Rulton, A.W.	818	Sgt.	6.7.15	LS	
Russell, F.	9631	Pte.	25.4.15	SF	
Russell, F.G.	10082	Pte.	10.5.17	LX	
Russell, G.J.	9925	L/Cpl.	25.11.14	SR	
Russell, W.T.	181	L/Sgt	15.3.15	PL	

Rutter, A.E.	33134	Pte.	29.11.17	WDM	25590 Dragoons
Ryan, J.M.	9853	Pte.	25.4.15	YPR	
Sabell, S.	11295	Pte.	7.7.15	YPR	
Sadler, T.	12165	Pte.	4.4.18	DN	
Sammonds, G.H.	20142	Pte.	11.4.17	BS	
Sanders, E.	132	L/Sgt	31.10.14	BO or PL	
Sanders, F.	2099	Pte.	30.4.15	BO	
Sansome, D.	20082	Pte.	8.5.17	DN	
Saunders, A.T.	35431	Pte.	15.4.18	PL	
Saunders, E.	28714	Pte.	15.4.18	CC	
Saunders, J.	9193	Pte.	26.5.15	BO	
Saunders, T.M.E.	17348	Pte.	14.7.18	HB	
Saunders, W.	10524	Pte.	12.10.16	TH	
Savage, J.P.	2571	Pte.	25.4.15	YPR	
Saward, C.	243	L/Cpl.	25.4.15	YPR	
Scattergood, W.F.	50809	L/Sgt.	30.6.18	LM	21768 Oxford and Bucks. L.I.
Scott, J.	20641	Pte.	30.6.18	LM	11376 Army Cycle Corps
Scragg, A.	11924	Pte.	12.10.16	TH	
Searles, J.	8921	A/Cpl.	26.4.15	YPR	
Sears, C.	28347	Pte.	4.5.17	DN	27377 Hussars
Selby, W.	1784	Pte.	9.5.15	YPR	
Sennett, J.A.	27609	Pte.	8.9.17	AR	5654 South Staffs. Regt.
Setchell, W.H.	9198	L/Cpl.	30.5.18	–	
Seymour, C.H.	3697	Pte.	5.6.15	VMC	
Sharkey, A.	34177	Pte.	13.5.18	MG	1070 Hussars
Shaw, A.E.	1396	Pte.	26.4.15	YPR	
Shears, A.	16713	Pte.	2.5.17	AG	
Sheffield, T.W.H.	1719	Pte.	25.4.15	YPR	
Shell, A.V.	28168	Pte.	12.10.17	TCM	18030 Hussars
Shepherd, F.	9953	Pte.	25.4.15	YPR	
Shepherd, S.H.	3479	Pte.	8.7.15	FO	
Sherbon, A.	–	–	12.8.16	ES	
Shillton, H.H.	12807	Pte.	16.4.18	LP	
Shilton, W.H.	27896	Pte.	11.4.17	AR	
Shilton, W.J.	15602	Pte.	15.5.18	MG	
Shorthouse, W.	193	Pte.	26.8.14	HN	
Sidebotham, H	23977	Pte.	11.4.17	SC	
Sidwell, T.	203788	Pte.	15.4.18	CC	
Silk, F.A.	4011	Pte.	25.4.15	YPR	
Simcox, W.E.	453	Pte.	24.5.15	YPR	
Simmons, A.E.	3656	Pte.	11.10.16	TH	

Simmons, H.	9058	Pte.	13.10.14	MT	
Simmons, H.	17704	Pte.	6.9.16	–	
Simons, J.	1820	Pte.	3.11.15	SU	
Simpkins, R.	33047	Pte.	20.11.17	WDM	921 Dragoons
Siviter, G.H.	7829	L/Cpl.	13.4.17	AT	
Skidmore, W.H.	9395	Sgt.	25.4.15	YPR	
Skinner, A.S.	27857	L/Cpl.	10.12.16	TH	
Skryme, H.J.	25463	Pte.	6.10.17	CH	
Slack, J.	37731	Pte.	15.4.18	PL	
Slade, L.H.	30520	Pte.	15.4.18	–	
Slatcher, A.	16712	Pte.	15.5.18	LP	
Slater, H.	3617	L/Sgt.	26.8.16	RW	
Slaymaker, D.	10420	Pte.	25.4.15	YPR	
Sleet, W. WG	6910	Pte.	14.4.21	BW	
Small, E.	22739	Pte.	11.4.17	FM	
Smart, J.	270	Pte.	13.10.14	MT	
Smith, A.	267394	Pte.	4.10.17	TCM	
Smith, A.	3264	Pte.	25.4.15	YPR	
Smith, A.C.	28229	Pte.	14.10.17	DZ	27352 Hussars
Smith, E.	2722	Pte.	11.5.17	CM	
Smith, E.F.	16491	Pte.	12.10.16	TH	
Smith, F.W.	29376	Pte.	30.8.18	VEM	36393 Suffolk Regt.
Smith, G.	9505	Pte.	30.8.18	EP	M.M.
Smith, G.S.	10911	Pte.	23.10.16	TH	
Smith, H.	1869	Sgt.	11.5.15	YPR	
Smith, H.	27581	Pte.	12.10.16	TH	25010 S. Staffs. Regt.
Smith, H.	27808	Pte.	8.8.18	LM	24609 Shrops. L. I.
Smith, H.	3933	Pte.	25.4.15	YPR	
Smith, H.J.	16547	Pte.	3.5.17	AR	
Smith, H.	14435	Pte.	5.10.17	PO	
Smith, J.	17491	Pte.	3.5.17	AR	
Smith, J.T.	7189	Cpl.	30.5.15	BO	
Smith, J.W.	20305	Pte.	16.3.17	STH	
Smith, P.	158	Pte.	26.4.15	NI	
Smith, P.	398	Cpl.	5.2.15	LR	
Smith, P.	9639	Pte.	12.11.16	BW	
Smith, R.	985	Pte.	24.5.15	–	
Smith, T.	6909	Pte.	26.4.15	YPR	
Smith, T.	42490	Pte.	24.10.18	DE	
Smith, W.	4480	L/Cpl.	10.5.17	CM	
Smith, W.	7270	Pte.	25.4.15	YPR	

Smith, W.	9377	Pte.	9.7.15	YPR	
Smith, W.G.	203711	Pte.	14.10.18	–	
Smith, W.H.	1672	Pte.	25.4.15	OO	
Smitten, W.H.	9443	Pte.	9.5.15	YPR	
Snelling, O.	33085	Pte.	30.8.18	VEM	2284 Surrey Yeomanry
Snook, T.	25432	Pte.	12.10.17	TCM	
Soden, W.	10136	Pte.	9.5.15	YPR	
Soles, W.	9525	Pte.	25.4.15	YPR	
Solomon, C.J. WG	9262	Pte.	9.4.19	BW	
Solomon, W.I.	16016	Pte.	28.3.17	BO	
Soughan, F.	6841	Cpl.	26.8.14	LF	
South, S.	1718	Pte.	10.10.16	TH	
Southam, J.	28690	Pte.	31.3.18	CA	
Southam, W.	6734	Pte.	25.4.15	YPR	
Sparkes, E.	8987	L/Cpl.	10.5.15	WM	
Sparrow, F.	16190	Pte.	11.4.17	BS	
Spencer, A.	27617	Pte.	17.10.16	SM	16763 South Staffs. Regt.
Spencer, T.	136	L/Cpl.	4.11.14	LK	
Spiers, G.	4115	Cpl.	3.5.17	BS	
Spry, P.C.	9355	Pte.	12.11.18	BLH	
Squires, E.C.	9611	Sgt.	4.10.17	PO	
Stanley, A.	28297	Pte.	12.2.17	FI	27461 Hussars
Steadman, C.G.	2442	Pte.	27.10.14	SR	
Steadman, W.	8894	Pte.	25.4.15	YPR	
Steele, F.	9244	Pte.	30.8.18	VE	
Steels, W.	24798	Pte.	3.7.17	CM	1669 Hunts. Cycle Battalion
Stevens, J.A.	7093	Pte.	9.4.17	SN	
Stevenson, H.	1722	Pte.	5.7.15	–	
Stevenson, A.	9178	Pte.	25.4.15	YPR	
Stirk, F.	2606	Pte.	25.4.15	YPR	
St. Ledger, H.	8957 or 8951	Pte.	26.10.14	CB	
Stocks, G.	1063	L/Cpl.	1.7.16	TH	
Stockwell, P.E.	1608	Cpl.	25.6.16	AV	
Stokes, T.	35418	Pte.	16.4.18	LP	
Stone, F.H.	13711	A/Sgt.	8.3.19	–	8162 Worcester Regt.
Stopps, H.E.	24328	Pte.	30.8.18	VEM	
Storer, J.	6714	Pte.	24.5.15	YPR	
Stott, R.N.	29741	Pte.	20.7.18	–	40200 Durham Light Inf.
Stratford, W.	1853	Pte.	29.10.16	GR	
Stretch, H.	9084	Pte.	27.8.14	HN	

Stride, H.	3270	L/Cpl.	16.2.17	FI	
Stuart, A.	9293	A/Cpl.	30.11.17	WDM	
Sturt, N.H.	9621	Sgt.	25.4.15	YPR	
Stych, S.	1051	L/Cpl.	8.1.16	SU	
Styles, S.F. WG	944	Pte.	22.7.17	BW	
Such, H.	21864	Pte.	3.5.17	AR	
Sullivan, J.	3613	Pte.	11.5.15	YPR	
Summerfield, A.	3627	Pte.	6.7.15	BC	
Sutton, S.	2455	Pte.	24.6.16	BV	
Sutton, W.	50916	Pte.	31.8.18	VEM	54451 Cheshire Regiment
Swainston, W.E.	9486	Pte.	26.7.15	SU	
Swan, G.H.	20313	Pte.	3.5.17	CM	
Sweeney, D.W.	981	Pte.	26.8.14	LF	
Tapp, W.	8970	Pte.	25.4.15	YPR	
Targett, F.	2401	Pte.	8.9.14	LF	
Tarver, W.	10167	Pte.	26.7.15	SU	
Tate, T.T.	35424	Pte.	15.4.18	PL	
Taylor, A.	670	Pte.	14.10.14	PL	7834 Border Regiment
Taylor, C.	2091	Pte.	28.4.15	HZ	
Taylor, C.R.	1027	Pte.	8.8.18	–	
Taylor, E.	28298	Pte.	2.5.17	–	27433 Hussars
Taylor, G.E.	11418	Pte.	3.7.17	CM	
Taylor, H.	7951	L/Cpl.	3.5.17	AR	
Taylor, J.	9951	Pte.	13.10.14	MT	
Taylor, J.R.	16681	Pte.	12.8.16	ES	
Taylor, J.	7513	Pte.	25.4.15	SF	
Taylor, R.	6794	Pte.	10.12.14	PW	
Tayton, J.H.	267116	Sgt.	29.3.18	DN	
Teager, W.	6711	L/Cpl.	23.10.16	TH	
Tedds, J.	42233	Pte.	18.10.18	SA	
Templeton, R.	268558	Pte.	12.10.17	TCM	
Tennant, J.	27776	Pte.	11.1.17	–	24133 Shropshire L. I.
Testsall, H.	970	L/Cpl.	11.4.17	BS	
Thomas, J.	2064	Pte.	25.6.16	AV	
Thomas, T.	4573	L/Cpl.	9.2.15	BA	
Thomas, W.	1806	Pte.	26.4.15	YPR	
Thompson, /Thomas, W.	27610	Pte.	11.4.17	BS or –	5525 South Staffs. Regt.
Thompson, W.	9786	Pte.	23.10.16	TH	
Thorne, T.H.G.	35419	Pte.	15.4.18	PL	
Thornhill, G.	6607	Pte.	26.4.15	YPR	

Thornton, E.	6443	Pte.	25.6.16	AV	
Thornton, P.	9484	C/Sgt.	13.10.14	MT	D.C.M.
Thorneycroft, G.T.	6648	Pte.	23.10.14	PL	
Timmins, E.	28371	Pte.	3.5.17	AR	29909 Hussars
Timmins, W.J.H.	3750	L/Cpl.	12.10.16	TH	
Timms, W.G.	21405	Pte.	3.5.17	–	
Todd, E.	9148	A/Sgt.	2.5.15	–	
Tolley, W.	13270	Pte.	12.10.16	TH	
Tomlinson, H.	763	Pte.	25.4.15	–	
Toon, W.	9252	Pte.	25.4.15	YPR	
Tooth, B.	3938	Pte.	25.4.15	YPR	
Topping, G.	3226	Pte.	25.4.15	YPR	
Tovey, S.	9602	L/Cpl.	1.1.15	BO	
Tranter, H.	9760	Pte.	4.6.15	YPR	
Tranchard, H.	839	Pte.	11.5.15	YPR	
Trentham, T.H.	2915	L/Cpl.	12.10.16	TH	
Trentham, G.T.	3486	Pte.	8.6.15	–	
Truby, A.W.	19169	Pte.	23.10.16	TH	
Trumpess, A.	12463	Pte.	12.10.16	TH	54551 R.G.A.
Tuckey, C.E.	242325	Pte.	4.10.17	TCM	
Tunstall, W.	4565	L/Cpl.	27.7.17	DN	
Turner, A.F.L.	9064	Pte.	26.8.14	LF	
Turner, G.F.	11782	Pte.	23.10.16	TH	
Turvey, H.	2322	Cpl.	12.10.16	TH	
Twigger, A.	4423	Pte.	17.4.17	AR	
Twigger, J. WG	159	Pte.	9.8.16	BX	
Twocock, E.	34178	Pte.	25.4.15	DN	1447 Hussars
Twynham, H.R.	2007	Pte.	19.6.15	YPR	
Tyler, F.	9740	Pte.	3.5.17	AR	
Underhill, F.	3517	Pte.	1.7.16	TH	
Underwood, C.	9535	Pte.	9.7.15	YPR	
Underwood, S.J.	7408	Cpl.	11.4.17	AR	
Underwood, W.	9880	Pte.	18.3.15	PW	
Urquhart, C.	1180	L/Cpl.	26.4.15	YPR	
Urry, W.S.	18355	Pte.	4.10.17	TCM	23133 Somerset Light Inf.
Usher, T.M.	1998	Pte.	31.3.18	CA	
Vallance, R.	1785	Pte.	25.4.15	YPR	
Varley, T.	9851	Pte.	25.4.15	YPR	
Varney, J.	203698	Pte.	17.10.18	SA	
Vaughan, E.C.	2039	Pte.	25.6.16	AV	
Vickery, R.J.	20584	Pte.	12.10.16	TH	10831 Army Cyclist Corps

Vidion, C.	33183	Pte.	23.12.17	HV	23028 Lancers
Vincent, W.	9994	Pte.	16.5.15	WM	
Wade, W.H.	18458	Pte.	3.5.17	AR	24218 Somerset L .I.
Wakelin, C.	3290	L/Cpl.	26.7.17	CM	
Wakeman, F.	6458	Pte.	2.4.16	BI	
Waldron, F.	9530	Pte.	25.4.15	OO	
Walker, B.	9251	Pte.	19.6.15	YPR	
Walker, C.G.	27901	Pte.	11.4.17	AR	
Walker, H.W.	2352	Pte.	7.4.15	RT	
Walker, T.	4498	Pte.	3.6.15	YPR	
Walker, W.	118	Pte.	28.8.14	MC	
Wall, C.	9439	Pte.	13.10.14	MT	
Wall, H.J.	9296	Pte.	13.10.14	MT	
Wall, J.H.	18393	Cpl.	12.10.17	TCM	23472 S. L. I.
Wall, J.H.	21089	Pte.	15.4.18	PL	
Wallace, F.A.	1880	Pte.	18.10.16	GR	
Wallace, J.	28354	Pte.	11.4.17	AT	27223 Hussars
Wallen, A.	9701	Pte.	24.11.14	TA	
Walmsley, J.I.	22042	Pte.	12.10.17	–	3118 Liverpool Regt.
Ward, A.	24079	Pte.	15.4.18	PL	
Ward, C.	148	Pte.	25.4.15	YPR	
Ward, D.	9757	Pte.	27.10.15	HP	
Ward, S.	1455	Pte.	25.4.15	YPR	8726 Leicester Regt.
Waring, J.	9456	Pte.	27.7.16	YPR	
Waring, W.	2204	Pte.	26.8.14	FN	
Warr, J.	25708	Pte.	29.7.18	GN	029030 R.A.O.C.
Warren, V.H.	28719	Pte.	18.5.18	ET	
Warwick, G.F.	30468	Cpl.	5.10.17	TCM	77895 Royal Engineers
Washbourne, E.	10408	Pte.	13.10.16	GR	
Watkins, J.	458	Pte.	8.7.15	YPR	
Watkins, W.	8665	L/Cpl.	2.10.17	CF	
Watson, A.T.	4594	Cpl.	3.5.17	AR	
Watson, V. WG	909	L/Cpl.	21.5.21	BW	M.M.
Watson, W.H.	16122	Pte.	23.10.16	TV	1871 R.A.S.C.
Watts, A.	2210	Pte.	27.10.14	FN	
Watts, E.	18650	Pte.	3.5.17	AR	24524 Somerset L.I.
Watts, W.	9507	Pte.	9.5.15	YPR	
Watts, W.	15048	Pte.	11.4.17	AR	
Weale, C.	11664	L/Cpl.	12.10.16	TH	
Weaver, R.	1861	Pte.	25.4.15	YPR	
Webb, E.	3681	Pte.	7.11.15	SU	

Webb, G.	27019	Pte.	21.3.18	–	5491 Lincs. Regt.
Webb, R.	9666	Pte.	12.10.16	TH	
Webb, R.	27601	Pte.	23.10.16	TH	5546 South Staffs. Regt.
Webb, W.	6473	Sgt.	11.1.15	PW	5147 Suffolk Regt.
Wedge, E.	130	Sgt.	31.3.18	CA	
Weeks, F.E.	9367	Pte.	25.1.15	–	
Weeks, P.G.	305351	Sgt.	30.8.18	EP	
Welch, A.	17028	Pte.	31.8.18	VEM	
Welch, C.	10839	Pte.	3.5.17	AR	
Welch, J.	1798	Pte.	18.12.14	PL	
Welch, W.A.	19602	Pte.	3.5.17	BS	
Wells, F.W.	22382	Pte.	22.4.18	LP	
Wells, W.	9962	L/Cpl..	29.12.14	IP	
Westall, S.G.	456	Pte.	25.4.15	SF	
Weston, W.H.	9798	Pte.	26.8.14	LF	
Wharton, F.	9785	Pte.	26.4.15	YPR	
Wheatley, C.H.	24125	Pte.	5..9.18	CE	
Wheeler, E.	2241	Pte.	22.3.15	RT	
Wheeler, E.G.	3390	Pte.	25.4.15	YPR	
Wheller, E.	28305	Pte.	3.5.17	AR	27466 Hussars
Whelan, T.	7476	Sgt.	1.7.16	SS	M.M.
White, C.	30390	Pte.	29.7.18	MG	19754 Worcester Regt.
White, A.S.	41286	Pte.	5.8.18	T	
Whitehead, W. WG	1850	Pte.	18.11.20	BW	
Whitehouse, A.	7623	L/Cpl	3.11.14	PL	
Whitehouse, J.T.	9604	Pte.	11.7.15	–	
Whiting, R.	6901	L/Sgt.	23.10.16	TH	
Whiting, W.H.	22183	Pte.	12.5.17	AR	
Whitlock, W.	20626	Pte.	3.5.17	AR	8147 Army Cyclist Corps
Wicks, F.E. WG	9367	Pte.	25.1.15	PW	
Widdows, W.	1952	Pte.	3.1.16	BH	
Wild, G.	9298	Sgt.	19.9.14	VXB	
Wilde, J.	20976	Pte.	15.4.18	PL	
Wilde, J.W.	1215	Pte.	26.4.15	YPR	
Wiles, B.	2445	Pte.	11.10.16	TH	
Wilkins, H.M.	16531	Pte.	12.10.16	TH	
Wilkins, R.G.	16008	Pte.	12.10.16	CT	
Wilkins, W.	3515	Pte.	4.5.15	WM	
Wilkinson, F.	429	Pte.	25.4.15	YPR	
Wilkinson, L.	9830	Pte.	25.4.15	YPR	

Wilkshire, W.	498	Pte.	25.4.15	YPR	
Williams, A.E.	3	Pte.	13.10.14	MT	
Williams, B.J.	10721	Pte.	25.4.16	BI	
Williams, E.S.	29436	Pte.	31.8.18	VEM	61987 Cheshire Regt.
Williams, E.A.	1406	Pte.	26.4.15	YPR	
Williams, E.	3717	Pte.	26.7.15	SU	
Williams, F.	27583	Pte.	16.2.17	FI	24644 South Staffs. Regt.
Williams, H.	2428	Sgt.	21.6.17	LX	D.C.M., M.M.
Williams, J.	2223	Pte.	14.10.14	T	
Willis, C.H.	4456	Pte.	14.10.16	GR	
Willis, T.W.	20556	Pte.	12.10.16	TH	9877 Army Cyclist Corps
Willsdon, J.	28306	Pte.	11.4.17	BS	27358 Hussars
Wilson, A.	10823	Pte.	24.8.16	RW	
Wilson, R.	17967	Pte.	12.10.16	TV	
Wilson, E.	1731	Pte.	19.6.15	YPR	
Winkley, H.	9910	Pte.	26.8.14	LF	
Winter, T.E.	34201	Pte.	17.4.18	CC	1369 Welsh Horse
Withers, G.F.	2198	Pte.	13.10.18	BL	
Withey, W.	10437	Pte.	8.7.15	–	
Wood, J.	33117	Pte.	10.7.18	LV	7887 Dragoons
Wood, P.H. WG	4661	Pte.	22.11.16	LN	
Woodham, F.J.	38098	Cpl.	10.7.18	LV	S/24018 Glos. Regt.
Woodhurst, F.	925	Pte.	1.7.15	–	
Woodward, W.H.	16911	Pte.	29.11.15	CG	
Woolfson, S.	24700	Pte.	1.11.18	–	
Wooliscroft, W.H.	17765	Pte.	11.4.17	PJ	
Wooton, C.	1026	Pte.	15.4.18	PL	
Wooton, G.L.	39246	Pte.	11.5.18	MG	
Worrol, G.	2260	Pte.	25.4.15	YPR	
Wragg, A.	1237	Pte.	25.4.15	YPR	
Wright, T.T.	4500	Pte.	2.8.15	SU	
Wyatt, W.H.	307263	Pte.	4.10.17	TCM	2058 Manchester Regt.
Yapp, A.	3035	Pte.	8.2.15	LC	
Yates, F.	607	Pte.	10.12.14	PW	
Yates, T.	9747	Cpl.	25.4.15	YPR	
Yeatman, E.	268883	Pte.	12.10.17	TCM	
Yeomans, J.O.	11343	Pte.	23.10.16	TH	
Young, L.J.	17408	Pte.	3.7.17	LX	

N.B.: In compiling this data the writer has cross-checked wherever possible. However, because of the complexity of the exercise and differing research sources, there may be occasional errors.

APPENDIX VIII

1st Battalion Royal Warwickshire Regiment Honours/Decorations List 1914–1918 – Other Ranks

Name	Rank	No.	Honour/Decoration
Arris, F.	CSM	5580	D.C.M. Citation:"For great zeal and devotion to duty from the commencement of the campaign, especially in the trenches at St. Yves, Company Sergeant Major Ariss has set a splendid example to the men of his company."
Ashby, T.	Corp.	9067	M.M.
Ball, S.	Pte.	27483	M.M.
Barnes, W.	L/Cpl.	9728	D.C.M. Citation: "For gallant conduct on 18th September, 1914, at La Montagne Farm, when the post occupied by him was wrecked by a shell and his two comrades wounded, he remained attending on them with great gallantry under trying circumstances."
Beck, G.	RSM	6229	M.C., D.C.M. Citation: "For conspicuous gallantry and good work throughout the campaign. His fine conduct, example and devotion to duty have frequently been brought to notice."
Blatchford, W.F.	Pte.	40950	M.M.
Bragg, C.	Pte.	9596	M.M. Citation: "In recognition of gallant conduct and determination displayed in escaping or attempting to escape from captivity."
Bricknell, H.	Cpl.	266889	M.M.
Charman, A.	L/Sgt.	6856	D.C.M. Citation: "For conspicuous good service at a critical moment, whereby he was mainly responsible for averting the capture of many men."
Chivers, F.	L/Cpl.	203817	M.M.

Collins, J. T.	CSM	15108	D.C.M. Citation: "For conspicuous gallantry and devotion to duty during the period April to 11th November 1918. He has commanded a platoon in action on several occasions, when he showed fine courage, initiative, and power of leadership. He has always set a high example to all those under him."
Cooper, H.	Pte.	242513	M.M.
Cresswell, J. H.	Sgt.	1065	D.C.M. Citation: "For conspicuous gallantry. Sergeant Cresswell made the greatest possible use of his machine-gun. The parapet was twice blown in and rebuilt, and he continued with great coolness and bravery to serve his gun with good effect."
Crisp, A.E.	Sgt.	22138	M.M.
Darlow, E.	Pte.	2195	D.C.M. Citation: "For great gallantry on 13th October, (1914), in volunteering to go forward to a place where extreme danger was to be expected, and helping to bring in Major Christie who was dangerously wounded."
Dixon, S.	Pte.	33155	M.M.
Elson, O.F.	Pte.	28327	M.M.
England, R. T.	Sgt.	17988	D.C.M., M.M. D.C.M. Citation, "As platoon commander, on 24th October, 1918, during the attack near Verchain, he displayed marked courage and ability in leading and handling his command. During the advance, the line was held up by hostile fire from two machine gun posts. He rushed his Lewis guns round the flank and rushed the position, capturing two guns and their teams. Later on, when consolidating, he got three captured guns into position and engaged the enemy whilst his men were getting protection. Throughout the day he set a splendid example to his men."
Foxon, T.	Pte.	11364	M.M.
Gibson, J.A.F.	Pte.	6440	M.M.
Gibson, R.	Sgt.	503	M.M.
Green, L.	CSM	6243	D.C.M. Citation: "For great zeal and devotion to duty from the commencement of the campaign, especially in the trenches at St. Yves. Company Sergeant-Major Green has set a splendid example to the men of his company."

Greenfield, T. F.	Sgt.	8142	D.C.M. Citation: "For continuous good work during the period 25th February to 16th September, 1918. He has shown at all times great courage and devotion to duty. In numerous actions he has proved himself a valuable and capable NCO, often acting as Platoon Commander, when his example, ability and powers of leadership have been of the highest order. All his duties have been carried out in a most efficient manner."
Grimes, A.J.	Pte.	200520	M.M.
Guest, H.	L/Cpl.	1226	M.M. War Diary Addition: "This NCO did extremely good work carrying messages to and from Battalion HQ and the front line during the operations on 11th April, 1917 near Fampoux. All messages had to be carried through heavy artillery and machine gun fire in full view of the enemy. During the early part of the battale this NCO was blown up by a shell and badly shaken but continued to carry on all day. He showed great devotion to duty."
Henson, H.W.J.	CQMS	85	M.M.
Hackett, J.	Pte.	17340	M.M.
Hand, W.	Pte.	27038	M.M.
Harman, J.	Pte.	32458	D.C.M. Citation: "For conspicuous gallantry and devotion to duty. He took command of a Lewis gun team during the attack and used the gun with excellent effect against enemy machine guns until it was put out of action. He then led his men in a bombing attack on a machine gun which was holding up the advance, and killed all the team. He set a splendid example of determination and resource."
Harrod, P.	Sgt.	924	M.M.
Harvey, W.	Pte.	1656	D.C.M. Citation: "He has repeatedly shown gallantry and devotion to duty of a high order, and his work as a Lewis gunner has been of great value during the period 25th February to 16th September 1918. In a raid carried out by his battalion east of Riez du Vinage, on 30th June, when in charge of a Lewis gun, he was twice blown up, but on each occasion recovered himself and continued to fire his gun. He has set a fine example to all ranks."

Harwood, C.F.	L/Cpl.	6563	D.C.M. Citation: "For conspicuous gallantry and complete disregard for the enemy's fire at all times. He rendered the most valuable assistance in rallying the men when a retirement was necessary, and gave a splendid example of courage and devotion to duty."
Hazell, W.	Cpl.	9865	M.M. Citation: "For gallantry in a raid on German trenches 12.4.16 No. 9865 Private Hazell led Lt. Shute's group in the raid, withdrew after shots were fired, returned with Lt. Shute to throw eight bombs in a dug-out."
Hems, J.	Sgt.	942	M.M.
Hibbs, G.	Pte.	655	M.M.
Holden, C.	L/Sgt.	9055	D.C.M. Citation: "For conspicuous gallantry and devotion to duty. He succeeded in getting rations and ammunition to a detached post during an intense bombardment. He has previously done fine work and has set a fine example."
Holmes, B.	L/Cpl.	1664	D.C.M. Citation: "For conspicuous gallantry and devotion to duty. Acting as a company runner for over two years, he has been in the majority of the actions in which the battalion has taken part. He has always proved himself most reliable, and on many occasions has taken messages through very heavy fire, displaying singular devotion to duty."
James, W. J.	Pte.	2510	D.C.M. Citation: "For gallantry on 13th October, (1914). Volunteered to go forward to a place where the greatest danger was to be expected and helped to bring in Major Christie who was dangerously wounded."
Jilks, W.	Pte.	18165	M.M.
Jones, W. H.	Pte.	23775	M.M.
Jones, W.H.S.	Pte.	1610	M.M.
Lakin, S.	Pte.	18811	M.M.
Lambert, H.A.	Pte.	28334	M.M.
Lampett, E.	Pte.	6345	M.M. and bar
Lancett, W.	Pte.	27827	M.M.
Lilja, A.	Sgt.	7861	M.M.
Lyons, H.	Pte.	30161	M.M.

M.C. Gill, G.	Sgt.	34180	D.C.M. Citation: "For conspicuous gallantry and devotion to duty on 30th August, 1918. During the attack on St. Severins Farm ridge, when all his officers had become casualties, he took charge of his platoon and led them to their second objective."
Milner, W.	L/Cpl.	9623	D.C.M. Citation: "For conspicuous gallantry on 24th May 1915, near Wieltje, when he carried a machine gun over three-quarters of a mile of open ground, which was being heavily shelled, eventually getting his gun into the firing line. He showed the greatest bravery and coolness, and by his fine example gave great encouragement to the men in his command."
Montgomery, F.T.	Sgt.	9445	D.C.M. Citation: "For great courage and determination displayed while with a small party of men who had been cut off from our forces during a retirement. The party was in the area occupied by the Germans from August 26th to September 5th 1914 but succeeded in escaping."
Murrell, S.	Sgt.	1076	M.M.
Owen, W.	Pte.	658	M.M.
Pennington, E.	Pte.	23599	M.M.
Poste, J. H.	RQMS	7014	D.C.M. Citation: "For conspicuous gallantry and devotion to duty. During the past three years he has rendered consistent good service, and by his great devotion to duty has set a fine example to all under him."
Radford, J.	Pte.	39793	M.M.
Rogers, H.	Cpl.	265405	M.M. and bar
Roots, W.	L/Cpl.	1205	D.C.M. Citation: "For conspicuous gallantry in carrying messages under heavy fire, and later on, in rallying men at a very critical time. He has frequently been noted for his bravery and devotion to duty."
Rowley, C.	Pte.	9845	D.C.M. Citation: "At Meterin on 13th October, volunteered to go back for ammunition from the forward firing line to the support trench, a distance of about 300 yards, under heavy rifle fire. He succeeded in his mission, and later on took a message over the same piece of ground under the same conditions."
Salmons, W.	Cpl.	27918	M.M.
Sawyer, E.	Cpl.	23056	M.M.

Shepherd, F.	CSM	7436	M.M.
Smart, J.	L/Cpl.	1115	M.M.
Smith, G.	Pte.	9505	M.M.
Smith, J. W.	Cpl.	17311	M.M.
Tallis, W.	Pte.	201825	M.M.
Taylor, H.	A/Sgt.	9262	D.C.M., M.M. D.C.M. Citation: "During the operations in the neighbourhood of Verchain on 24th October, 1918, he showed conspicuous gallantry and ability. He was in command of a platoon which was meeting opposition from two hostile machine-gun posts. He quickly engaged the posts with fire from his Lewis guns, and, working round the flanks, captured and disposed of both of them. He assisted the platoon on his right by engaging a machine-gun that was holding them up. Later on, when digging in under hostile fire, he moved about amongst his men encouraging and stimulating them."
Tedder, G.	Cpl.	1158	M.M.
Thornton, P.	A/CSM	9484	D.C.M. Citation: "For gallant conduct in endeavouring whilst wounded and accompanied by only a few men, to capture the enemy's machine guns. In this attempt he failed owing to there being no support at hand at the moment."
Watson, V.	Cpl.	909	M.M.
Webb, J.	Sgt.	2244	D.C.M., M.M. D.C.M. Citation: "For conspicuous gallantry and devotion to duty in handling his platoon. While trying to establish posts in a wood, he was twice surrounded, and it was only his courage and skill that enabled the platoon to fight their way back. Later, during an attack, he again displayed the greatest courage and ability, penetrating far into the enemy's position, and when forced to withdraw, bringing back prisoners."
Whelan, T.	Sgt.	7476	M.M.

Whopples, C.	Pte.	12144	M.M. Citation: "For gallantry in bringing in wounded under heavy fire on 15th April, 1918. This Stretcher Bearer repeatedly crossed the pontoon over La Bassee Canal near Pacaut Wood when fire was heaviest and brought in wounded men. Later when the action had died down, and all through the night 15/16th he made journeys in search of the wounded, going into the wood and close up to the enemy line. Owing to his gallant and untiring work, only two of all our wounded were not recovered."
Williams, H.	L/Cpl.	465	M.M. and bar
Williams, H.	L/Sgt.	2428	D.C.M., M.M. D.C.M. Citation: "For conspicuous gallantry and devotion to duty. When exposed to heavy artillery and machine gun fire in full view of the enemy, he continued to dress the wounded, and carried them to a place of safety. He showed a total disregard for personal safety."

N.B.: In compiling this data the writer has cross-checked wherever possible. However, because of the complexity of the exercise and differing research sources, there may be occasional errors.

Notes

Prologue

1. For a complete history see Kingsford, *The Story of the Royal Warwickshire Regiment.*
2. ibid.
3. Bremner, *The 1st Battalion The Royal Warwickshire Regiment.*

Chapter 1

1. Clouting, *Tickled to Death to Go.*
2. Lloyd George, *War Memoirs of David Lloyd-George.*

Chapter 2

1. Simpson & Beckett (Eds.), *A Nation in Arms.*
2. ibid.
3. Haldane's 1913/14 unpublished Shorncliffe diaries (Imperial War Museum).
4. Bolwell, *With a Reservist in France.*
5. Haythornthwaite, *The World War One Source Book.*
6. Clouting, op. cit.
7. Clouting, op. cit.
8. Needham, *The First Three Months.*
9. Gould, "The 1st Royal Warwicks Go To War".

Chapter 3

1. Papers of Artillery Sergeant Albert George (Imperial War Museum).
4. Osburn, *Unwilling Passenger.*
5. George, op. cit..
6. Papers of Captain A.H. Habgood, R.A.M.C., 3rd Field Division Ambulance, 3rd Division (Imperial War Museum).
7. Elkington, Statement concerning St. Quentin – see Appendix II.
8. 1st Battalion Royal Warwickshire Regiment War Diary (PRO WO95/1484).

9. Clarke, "Through the German Lines".
10. Montgomery, *The Memoirs.*
11. Dalton, "A Subaltern's Diary".
12. Elkington, op. cit.
13. Dalton, op. cit.
14. Mainwaring, *A Statement* – see Appendix I.
15. Mainwaring, op. cit.
16. Tomes, "The Great War Battle Honours".
17. ibid.
18. ibid.
19. ibid.
20. Hart, "Narrative of Retreat from Mons: 1st Battalion Royal Warwickshire Regiment" (PRO CAB45/196).
21. ibid.
22. ibid.
23. ibid.

Chapter 4

1. Private Papers of General Sir H. Smith-Dorrien relating to the Battle of Le Cateau (Imperial War Museum).
2. Elkington, op. cit.
3. ibid.
4. Mainwaring, op. cit.
5. ibid.
6. Elkington, op. cit.
7. Mainwaring op. cit.
8. ibid.
9. Elkington, op.cit.
10. Mainwaring, op.cit.
11. Elkington, op.cit.
12. Bridges, *Alarms & Excursions.*
13. ibid.
14. Osburn, op. cit.
15. ibid.
16 Mainwaring, op. cit.
17. Osburn, op. cit.
18. Bridges, op.cit.
19. Osburn, op. cit.
20. Mainwaring, op. cit.
21. Hart, op. cit.
22. Clouting, op. cit.

23. Elkington, op. cit.
24. Scott, *Dishonoured.*
25. Elkington, op. cit.
26. Mainwaring, op. cit.

Chapter 5

1. Cooper, *Born to Fight.*
2. The *Times*, 6 September 1916.
3. McLeave, *The Damned Die Hard.*
4. ibid.
5. ibid.
6. ibid.
7. Porch, *The French Foreign Legion.*
8. The *Times*, 6 September 1916.
9. Rockwell, *American Fighters in the Foreign Legion 1914-1918.*
10. Rockwell, op. cit.
11. The *Times*, 19 September 1916.
12. *Newbury Weekly Times*, 29 June 1944.
13. *Newbury Weekly Times*, 23 May 1946.
14. *Sussex Express*, 17 October 1930.

Chapter 6

1. Tomes, op. cit.
2. ibid.
3. ibid.
4. Bairnsfather, *Bullets and Billets.*
5. ibid.
6. ibid.
7. *Rugby Advertiser,* 18 September 1915.
8. *Rugby Advertiser,* 18 September 1915.
9. 1st Battalion Royal Warwickshire Regiment War Diary (PRO WO95/1484).
10. Various issues of The *Wipers Times*, dates as indicated.
11. 1st Battalion Royal Warwickshire Regiment War Diary (PRO WO95/1484).
12. Williams, unpublished postgraduate thesis on 8th Battalion Royal Warwickshire Regiment
13. 1st Battalion Royal Warwickshire Regiment War Diary (PRO WO95/1484).

14. Ibid.
15. Ibid.
16. Donald Hankey's civilian occupation was as a journalist with the Spectator. A series of interesting articles from that journal and the *Westminster Gazette* were published as one volume in 1916, under the title *A Student in Arms*.
17. 1st Battalion Royal Warwickshire Regiment War Diary (PRO WO95/1484).

Chapter 7

1. *Illustrated War News*, 1917.
2. *The War Illustrated*, 1917.
3. 1st Battalion Royal Warwickshire Regiment War Diary (PRO WO95/1484).
4. *Nuneaton Observer*, 18 May 1917.
5. 1st Battalion Royal Warwickshire Regiment War Diary (PRO WO95/1484).
6. ibid.
7. ibid.
8. ibid.
9. Kingsford, op. cit.
10. 1st Battalion Royal Warwickshire Regiment War Diary (PRO WO95/1484).
11. Letter in the private collection of Lee Lindon.

Bibliography

Unpublished Sources

Imperial War Museum

1913 & 1914 Shorncliffe diaries of General Sir Aylmer Haldane.
Papers of Artillery Sergeant Albert George.
Papers of Captain A.H. Habgood, R.A.M.C., 3rd Division Field
  Ambulance.
Papers of General Sir Horace Smith-Dorrien relating to the Battle of Le
  Cateau.

Royal Warwickshire Regiment Museum, St. John's House, Warwick

1st Battalion Royal Warwickshire Regiment War Diary (see also Public
  Records Office, PRO WO95/1484).

Public Records Office

Hart, Captain H.C. "Narrative of Retreat from Mons; 1st Battalion Royal
  Warwickshire Regiment" (PRO CAB45/196).
Poole, Major A.J. (PRO WO/1477).
Snow, Major General T.D'O. (PRO CAB45/129).
4th Division General Staff War Diary (PRO WO95/1439).
10th Infantry Brigade Headquarters War Diary (PRO WO95/1477).
2nd Battalion Royal Dublin Fusiliers War Diary (PRO WO95/1482).
1st Battalion Royal Irish Fusiliers War Diary (PRO WO95/1481).
2nd Battalion Seaforth Highlanders War Diary (PRO WO95/1483).
4th Royal Irish Dragoon Guards War Diary (PRO WO95/1112).

Papers from Private Collections

Elkington, John F. 'Statement concerning events at St. Quentin on 27
  August 1917'.
Mainwaring, Arthur Edward. 'A Statement'.
Williams, Rob. Postgraduate thesis on 8th Battalion Royal Warwickshire
  Regiment (University of Birmingham, 1999).

Published Sources

Newspapers & Magazines

The Antelope – The Journal of the Royal Warwickshire Regiment, various dates.

Clarke, Capt. N.P. "Through the German Lines". *Blackwoods' Magazine,* June 1915.

Daily Telegraph, August 1914.

Dalton, Lieutenant C.E. "A Subaltern's Diary". *The Antelope,* Vol. XI No.2.

Gould, Robert "The 1st Warwicks Go To War". *Haywards Gazette,* April 1975.

Illustrated War News, Vol. I: August 1914–October 1914.

London Gazette, 30 October 1914 & 27 October 1916.

Newbury Weekly News, 29 June 1944 & 23 May 1946.

Nuneaton Observer, 18 May 1917.

Rugby Advertiser, 18 September 1915.

Sussex Express, 17 October 1930.

Times, 6 September 1916 & 19 September 1916.

Tomes, Colonel C.T. "The Great War Battle Honours". *The Antelope,* Vol. IX, No.2.

The War Illustrated, A Pictorial Record of the Conflict of the Nations, 1914.

Books

Bairnsfather, Bruce *Bullets & Billets.* New York: Garden City Press, 1916.

Bairnsfather, Bruce *Fragments From His Life.* London: Hodder & Stoughton, for *The Bystander,* c.1916.

Barthorp, Michael *The Old Contemptibles.* London: Osprey, 1989.

Beckett, Dr. I.F.W. *The Judgement of History: Sir Horace Smith-Dorrien, Lord French & 1914.* London: Tom Donovan: 1993.

Beckett, Ian & Keith Simpson *A Nation In Arms.* London: Tom Donovan: 1990.

Bolwell, F.A. *With a Reservist in France.* London: Routledge, n.d.

Bremner, Fred *The Royal Warwickshire Regiment.* Quetta: Fred Bremner, 1907.

Brereton, J.M. *History of 4th/7th Royal Dragoon Guards.* Catterick: Privately printed for the Regiment, 1982.

Brereton, J.M. *The British Soldier: A Social History from 1661–Present Day,* London: Bodley Head, 1986.

Bridges, Brig.-Gen. Sir Tom *Alarms & Excursions: Reminiscences of a Soldier.* London: Longmans Green, 1938.

Brown, Malcolm *The Imperial War Museum Book of the Western Front.* London: Sidgwick & Jackson, 1983.

Brown, Malcolm *The Imperial War Museum Book of the First World War.* London: Imperial War Museum, 1991.

Caffrey, Kate *Farewell, Leicester Square: The Old Contemptibles 12 August–19 November 1914.* London: Andre Deutsch, 1980.

Clouting, Ben *Tickled to Death to Go.* Staplehurst: Spellmount, 1996.

Cooper, Adolphe Richard *Born to Fight.* London: Blackwood, 1969.

Cooper, Adolphe Richard *March or Bust.* London: Blackwood, 1972.

Elkington, A.E.H. & G.M. *The Elkingtons of Bath.* Woodstock: 1959.

Finley, R. Mainwaring. *A Short History of the Mainwaring Family.* Research Publishing: 1976.

Gibb, Rev. Harold *Record of the 4th Irish Dragoon Guards in the Great War 1914–1918.* Canterbury: Privately printed, 1925.

Gilbert, Martin *First World War.* London: Weidenfield & Nicolson, 1985.

Hamilton, Nigel *Monty; The Making of a General 1887–1942.* London: Hamish Hamilton, 1981.

Houlihan, Michael *World War I – Trench Warfare.* London: Wardlock, 1974.

Haythornthwaite, Philip J. *The World War One Source Book.* London: Arms & Armour Press, 1992.

Kingsford, C.L. *The Story of the Royal Warwickshire Regiment.* London: Country Life, 1921.

Lawrence, James *Raj: The Making and Unmaking of British India.* London: Abacus, 1997.

Lloyd-George, David *The War Memoirs of David Lloyd-George.* London: Odham Press, 1938.

McLeave, Hugh *The Damned Die Hard.* New York: New York Saturday Evening Revue Press, 1973.

Mainwaring, Major A.E. *Crown and Company: The Historical Records of the 2nd Battalion Royal Dublin Fusiliers.* London: A.L. Humphreys, 1911.

Montgomery, Field Marshal The Viscount *The Memoirs.* London: Collins, 1958.

Morlae, Edward *A Soldier of the Legion.* Boston/New York: Houghton & Mifflin, 1916.

Needham, E.J. *The First Three Months: Impressions of an Infantry Subaltern.* Aldershot: Gale & Polden, 1936.

Osburn, Arthur *Unwilling Passenger.* London: Faber & Faber, 1932.

Owen, Edward *1914 – Glory Departing*. London: Buchan & Enright, 1986.

Parker, John *Inside the Foreign Legion*. London: Judy Piatkus, 1998.

Romer, Major C.F. & Major A.E. Mainwaring *The Second Battalion Royal Dublin Fusiliers in the South African War*. London: A.L. Humphreys, 1908.

Porch, Douglas *The French Foreign Legion: A Complete History*. London: Macmillan, 1991.

Prior, Robin & Trevor Wilson *Command on the Western Front*. Oxford: Blackwell, 1992.

Rockwell, Paul Ayres *American Fighters in the Foreign Legion 1914–1918*. Boston/New York: Houghton Mifflin, 1930.

Scott, Peter *Dishonoured: The "Colonels' Surrender" at St. Quentin, The Retreat from Mons, August 1914*. London: Tom Donovan: 1994.

Terraine, John *Mons, The Retreat to Victory*. London: Batsford, 1960.

Travers, Tim *The Killing Ground*. London: Allen & Unwin, 1989.

Warner, Marten & Muir *The New Groundwork of British History*. London: Blackie & Son, 1943.

Wilson, H.W. (Ed.) *The Great War: The Standard History of the All-Europe Conflict*. London: Amalgamated Press, 1914.

Winter, Jay & Blaine Bagget *1914–18. The Great War and the Shaping of the 20th Century*. London: BBC Books, 1996.

Winter, Dr. J.M. et al *World War I 1914–1918*. London: Chanceller Press, 1993.

Wylly, Colonel H.C. *Crown and Company: The Historical Records of the 2nd Battalion Royal Dublin Fusiliers. Vol. 2 1911–1922*. Aldershot: Gale & Polden, 1923.

Young, John Robert *The French Foreign Legion*. London: Guild Publishing, 1984.

Index

Notes

Only place-names directly connected with the 1st Battalion's 1914–18 war service have been indexed. For locations connected with the Royal Warwickshire Regiment before 1914 see pp.7–19. The following abbreviations have been used to signify members of particular units:

1RWR   1/Royal Warwickshires
2RDF   2/Royal Dublin Fusiliers
2RM1E   2e régiment de marche, 1er étranger (French Foreign Legion)
4DG   4th Dragoon Guards